*History of*
**COLQUITT
COUNTY**

# History of
# COLQUITT COUNTY

By W. A. COVINGTON

*1937*

CLEARFIELD

Originally published
Atlanta, Georgia, 1937

Reprinted for
Clearfield Company, Inc. by
Genealogical Publishing Co., Inc.
Baltimore, Maryland
1997

International Standard Book Number: 0-8063-4741-4

*Made in the United States of America*

*THIS HISTORY is dedicated to the children and descendants of the Colquitt pioneers, generally; and especially to Hon. John Harris Smithwick, a descendant of North Georgia pioneers, who married Miss Jessie Vereen, a child of a pioneer family of Colquitt County.*

—*By The Author*

*Moultrie, Ga.,
April 11, 1937.*

## Author's Note

IT SEEMS PROPER to say here that while this History has been written entirely by the County Historian, it could not have been written but for assistance coming from many sources, some of which will be now and here set forth:

First, assistance in the way of documents and oral legends has been rendered by I. McD. Turner, Isaac Turner, Spencer Norman, Hon. G. W. Newton, Jack Strickland, Lewis Perry, J. O. Gibson, A. Huber, W. E. Aycock, T. E. Lewis, S. M. DuPree, John A. Owens, N. N. Marchant, Harry Halpert, and others. Thanks are extended to the Moultrie Rotary Club and the Moultrie Kiwanis Club for initial action of a highly helpful character; to Judge Wm. E. Thomas and the October, 1935, Grand Jury, for energetic aid rendered at that term of Colquitt Superior court; to the Board of Commissioners of Roads and Revenues of Colquitt County; and to the Mayor and Aldermen of the City of Moultrie for indispensable financial assistance in the enterprise.

MRS. MATTIE OGLESBY COYLE's "History of Colquitt County" has been drawn on for essential facts, as has IRWIN MCINTYRE's "History of Thomas County."

Finally, much use has been made of the unwearied and cheerful courtesy of Miss Ruth Blair, until recently Georgia's State Historian and Director of the Department of Archives, in answering some fifty letters of inquiry as to pertinent facts of record in her department. This service has been invaluable.

The chapter containing biographical sketches has more than paid its own way, since nearly all such sketches have been paid for at prices that have left available a surplus which has contributed greatly to rendering the publication of the History possible. At all that, too, it will not escape attention that general and loving attention has been paid to the common run of the county's pioneers, which includes a complete copy of the U. S. Census of the county four years after its creation.

Finally, the assurance is cordially extended to the present generation of descendants of the pioneer men and women that the pioneers are good people to be kin to, and a source of proper pride on the part of the present and all succeeding generations.

W. A. COVINGTON,<br>
*County Historian.*

February 5, 1937.
Moultrie, Ga.,

## TABLE OF CONTENTS

| | PAGE |
|---|---|
| CHAPTER I | 1-3 |
| De Soto's Expedition | |
| CHAPTER II | 4-9 |
| The First Georgians | |
| CHAPTER III | 10-16 |
| General Jackson Causes Trouble—The Seminoles | |
| CHAPTER IV | 17-20 |
| Colquitt Land Titles | |
| CHAPTER V | 21-29 |
| Slavery and Secession | |
| CHAPTER VI | 30-38 |
| The Civil War | |
| CHAPTER VII | 39-45 |
| Reconstruction | |
| CHAPTER VIII | 46-52 |
| The County Site | |
| CHAPTER IX | 53-57 |
| First White Settlers | |
| CHAPTER X | 58-61 |
| The Pioneer Family | |
| CHAPTER XI | 62-66 |
| Diversions in the Pastoral Era | |
| CHAPTER XII | 67-69 |
| Education in the Pastoral Era | |
| CHAPTER XIII | 70-74 |
| Women in the Pastoral Era | |
| CHAPTER XIV | 75-80 |
| A Friendly Custom | |
| CHAPTER XV | 81-84 |
| Early Occupations | |
| CHAPTER XVI | 85-88 |
| A Notable Wedding | |
| CHAPTER XVII | 89-94 |
| Colquitt Courts | |
| CHAPTER XVIII | 95-101 |
| Colquitt's Early Bench and Bar | |
| CHAPTER XIX | 102-107 |
| The Moultrie Bar in the Nineties | |
| CHAPTER XX | 108-149 |
| The Census of 1860 | |
| CHAPTER XXI | 150-152 |
| Colquitt's Slaves in 1860 | |
| CHAPTER XXII | 153-157 |
| The Georgia-Northern Railway | |
| CHAPTER XXIII | 157-162 |
| Moultrie Speaks | |
| CHAPTER XXIV | 163-168 |
| Colquitt in 1898 | |
| CHAPTER XXV | 169-171 |
| Old Greenfield | |
| CHAPTER XXVI | 172-177 |
| Some Important Visitors to Colquitt County | |
| CHAPTER XXVII | 178-184 |
| Being More About the Women | |
| CHAPTER XXVIII | 185-189 |
| Christian Churches in Colquitt | |
| CHAPTER XXIX | 190-193 |
| The Moultrie Methodist Church | |

# TABLE OF CONTENTS

| | PAGE |
|---|---|
| CHAPTER XXX | 194-198 |
| Moultrie's Missionary Baptist Church | |
| CHAPTER XXXI | 199-204 |
| Moultrie Presbyterian Church | |
| CHAPTER XXXII | 205-209 |
| Colquitt's Educational Facilities | |
| CHAPTER XXXIII | 210-211 |
| Women's Clubs | |
| CHAPTER XXXIV | 212-215 |
| The Moultrie Banking Company | |
| CHAPTER XXXV | 216-218 |
| Moultrie National Bank | |
| CHAPTER XXXVI | 219-221 |
| Moultrie Cotton Mills | |
| CHAPTER XXXVII | 222-225 |
| The Moultrie Packing Company | |
| CHAPTER XXXVIII | 226-228 |
| Crime in Colquitt | |
| CHAPTER XXXIX | 229-231 |
| Colquitt Weather | |

## BIOGRAPHIES

| | PAGE | | PAGE |
|---|---|---|---|
| Barber, William Henry | 233 | Matthews, William Jefferson | 267 |
| Bivins, Frank Jarvis | 237 | Millsap, Zachary Thomas | 269 |
| Blasingame, Wesley Futrell | 238 | Moore, Lammie Lamar | 270 |
| Coleman, James William | 240 | Newton, George William | 272 |
| Covington, William Alonzo | 242 | Norman, Jeremiah Bryant, Sr. | 274 |
| DeLoache, Waldo | 244 | Norman, Jeremiah Bryant, Jr. | 276 |
| Folsom, Montgomery M. | 246 | Potts, Lindsey Monterville | 280 |
| Free, Richard Lewis | 250 | Rhoden, Emanuel William | 281 |
| Hires, Jacob Hunter | 252 | Rhodes, William Henry | 283 |
| Hunt, George B. | 254 | Shavers, George Alexander | 285 |
| Jenkins, Cliff | 255 | Suber, John | 286 |
| Johnson, Chas. H. | 256 | Tillman, William | 287 |
| King, W. W. | 256 | Tucker, W. R. | 290 |
| Ladson, John Elzie | 257 | Turnbull, Samuel P. | 291 |
| Lee, Matthew Lawrence | 260 | Vereen, William Coachman | 292 |
| Leverett, Paul DeWitt | 261 | Vereen, Eugene Michael | 298 |
| Lewis, Richard Jonathan | 262 | Vereen, William Jerome | 301 |
| McCall, William Frank | 264 | Vick, Aaron, Jr. | 303 |
| McClendon, Claude Early | 265 | Weeks, Family The | 305 |

## MISCELLANEOUS

| | | | |
|---|---|---|---|
| Colquitt County Board of Education | 308 | Final Word of Historian | 358 |
| Colquitt County— | | Heads of Families, Lowndes County, Georgia | 359 |
| Justices of the Inferior Courts | 319 | Heads of Families, 8th District, Thomas County—now Colquitt County | 363 |
| Ordinaries | 320 | | |
| Sheriffs | 320 | | |
| Surveyors | 322 | Professional Men of Colquitt County | 327 |
| Tax Collectors | 323 | | |
| Tax Receivers | 324 | Attorneys | 327 |
| Treasurers | 325 | Dentists | 327 |
| Mayors and Clerks of the City of Moultrie, 1893-1937 | 326 | Physicians | 327 |
| | | Justices of the Peace | 328-334 |
| Congressional Representation of Colquitt County | 312 | State Senators—Colquitt County | 315 |
| County School Commissioners | 311 | World War Veterans | 335-357 |

X

*Extract from the General Presentments of the Grand Jury of Colquitt County, October, 1935, Term*

"We hereby nominate Judge W. A. Covington as Historian of Colquitt County, and give him the right to secure the services of anyone to help in this undertaking; and urge the Board of County Commissioners of Colquitt County, to cooperate with him."

T. A. DEKLE, Foreman,
J. F. TRICE, Clerk.

J. H. Brady, J. T. Sharpe, A. H. Gregory, N. D. Norman, B. D. Gay, R. H. Perry, W. S. McMullen, C. C. Freeman, J. H. Burroughs, M. J. Sorrell, Henry Clark, W. F. Walters, J. H. Dooley, Byrd Powell, James D. Edmundson, John T. Barlow, Grand Jurors.

BRYANT LANIER, County Commissioner, elected January 1st, 1937

Board of Colquitt County Commissioners. Picture taken in May, 1936. *Left to right:* VAN T. CROSBY, JOHN F. SUBER, WILLIAM TILLMAN, Chairman, T. B. MOUNT, Clerk, MRS. JOHN T. COYLE, Assistant Welfare Worker, W. W. KING, CLIFF JENKINS.

# Walter T. Colquitt

Walter T. Colquitt, for whom Colquitt County was named, was born in Halifax County, Virginia, in 1799, and while still a child moved with his parents to Hancock County, Georgia. He studied at Princeton, read law at Milledgeville, Georgia, was called to the bar in 1820, and commenced the practice of law, at Sparta. He was a member of the Georgia State Senate, in 1835-37. He was in the National House of Representatives, in 1839 and in 1840, till the date of his resignation. In 1842-43, he was again in the National House of Representatives. From 1843 to his resignation in 1848, he was a Senator of the United States. Originally, he was a States-Rights Whig, he came to be a Van Buren Democrat. He opposed the Wilmot Proviso, limiting slavery. He was a local Methodist preacher.

Miller, in his "Bench and Bar of Georgia," says of Walter T. Colquitt:

"It made no difference how many speakers of note were assembled on the platform of a mass-meeting, whether Governors of States or members of Cabinets, he towered above them all. He had an eye that could look any man or any peril in the face. He imitated no model. He grasped the hand of a poor man as cordially and treated him with as much respect as if he had the richest in the land; and, if his attentions to either varied, it was only to show more kindness to the humble poor, to take care of his feelings, and avoid any appearance of neglect or slight. As a lawyer he stood not only above Georgia, but the whole South. In Criminal cases, he swept everything before him, and stirred the souls of jurors to their very depths."

We have heard it said that Walter Colquitt would sometimes procure an acquittal of a client charged with murder, in the morning; make a political speech, at the noon recess of court; and preach at revival services, at night.

This remarkable man died a few weeks before Colquitt County was created; and this perhaps is the reason our great County bears his name. He lies buried on the Jeter Lot, in Linwood cemetery, at Columbus; but his grave is unmarked; although his descendants are still social and financial leaders in Georgia.

## CHAPTER I

# De Soto's Expedition

THE FIRST WHITE PEOPLE ever in Georgia were members of De Soto's expedition.

Fernando De Soto, a companion of Pizarro in the conquest of Peru, obtained from the King of Spain, in 1537, permission to conquer Florida, which was claimed by Spain in virtue of the discoveries of Columbus. While this design was in agitation, one Cabeca DeVaca, returned to Spain from a voyage of discovery in the New World; and, for purposes of his own, spread abroad the report that Florida, in gold, silver, and gems, was the richest country yet discovered in the New World—richer than Mexico and Peru, for instance; all this resulting in the boosting of De Soto's enterprise. Nobles and gentlemen vied with each other for the privilege of being enrolled under De Soto's standard; and so he set sail for what is now known as Tampa Bay, with six hundred and twenty chosen young men and 200 horses—a band as gallant and well-appointed, as eager in purpose, and as audacious in hope as ever trod the shores of the Western Hemisphere.

For month after month, and year after year, this procession of priests and cavaliers, crossbowmen, arquebusiers, and Indian captives, laden with baggage, still wandered on, through wild and boundless wastes, lured hither and thither by the *ignis fatuus* of the hopes of discovering gold.

De Soto and his people passed through at least the southern part of Georgia, forty-five years before Sir Walter Raleigh sailed the western seas; sixty-five years before Captain John Smith's adventures at Jamestown; seventy-eight years before the Mayflower landed at Plymouth Rock; and one hundred and ninety-two years before Oglethorpe settled at Savannah.

There were four members of the De Soto expedition who kept diaries, as follows: Ranjel, nephew and secretary of De Soto; Bedenia, the treasurer of the expedition; "The Inca"; and "a certain gentleman of Elvas." These diaries are the first authentic written documents which undertake to give information regarding human life in south Georgia, and the Gulf section. Geographic features are described, mounds and rivers are noted, and villages are described by their Indian names.

Notwithstanding these diaries, there is considerable discussion as to the situs of the route of the expedition in Georgia. It is known definitely that the expedition went north for some hundreds of miles—possibly to a point near the present site of Augusta; and then crossed Georgia to the northwest, and proceeding in that direction, finally reached the Mississippi, probably near what is now Memphis; then, proceeding two or three hundred miles northwest of this point, before they practically abandoned their search for gold, and turned southeast, striking the Mississippi again near the mouth of the Red River. Here De Soto died, his cruel, haughty spirit broken by disappointments and disease; and the remnant of his followers, wrapping his corpse in gunny-sacking, dropped it, under cover of night into the middle of the mighty stream, to remain there till the "sea, as well as the Great River, shall give up their dead."

Some three hundred survivors of the expedition constructed a rude raft, or boat, and a month or two later, drifted down to a Spanish settlement.

According to Jones' History of Georgia, De Soto spent the winter of 1539-1540 at Anhayca, near the present City of Tallahassee, where Spanish armor and other relics have been exhumed.

On Wednesday, March 3, 1540, De Soto launched his land expedition by marching north from Anhayca, and on the 4th day of the march, crossed the "Ochlockny" River, near Hadley's Ferry, in Grady County, formerly Thomas County, having passed between Lake Iammonia and Lake Jackson. On March 21st, he had reached a point which Jones fixed as being in Irwin County, having gone northward on the right side of the Ochlochnee River.

Since the Ochlochnee runs from north to south, practically through the center of what is now Colquitt County, it is a fair conclusion that De Soto and his mailed and plumed warriors passed through the county three hundred and ninety-six years ago. Since people, whether Indians or white explorers, always traveled along watercourses in those early days; and since the Ochlochnee River was always full at the beginning of Spring, it is practically

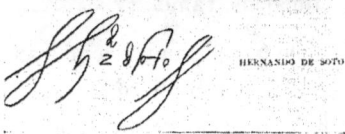

HERNANDO DE SOTO

certain that De Soto's expedition passed near Moultrie, along the Ochlochnee, near or across the farm of Joe N. Horne, sweeping upward along the course of the stream, always as close to the run of the stream as possible.

## CHAPTER II
## The First Georgians

THE DIARIES AND CHRONICLES of the De Soto expedition all speak of fairly constant contacts with the Indians. At that time, Georgia seems to have been occupied largely by the Creeks and the Cherokees. The northern part of the State then, and for two hundred years afterwards, constituted a part of an extensive Cherokee Empire; while the Creeks, during this period of time, occupied the southern portion of the State. The Seminoles, a smaller tribe, resided for the most part in northern Florida. By the beginning of the American Revolution, the Cherokees, by their contacts with the American colonists, had made considerable strides in civilization; but having sided with the British in that struggle, they were penalized by the loss of over half of their territory. Their holdings in what is now the State of Georgia, however, remained the same.

The Creeks and Seminoles had made less advances in what were called civilized ways. In 1763, England acquired the whole of Florida by treaty with Spain; but re-ceded it to Spain at the Treaty of Paris, in 1783. During the succeeding thirty-five years, clashes were frequent between the pioneer settlers of Georgia and Alabama and the Creeks and Seminoles, whose holdings in Georgia and Alabama had not been extinguished by treaty or otherwise. This friction was especially troublesome along the Chattahoochee River. While the land hunger of the whites, and the greed of the white purveyors of intoxicants, who always and everywhere were found on the ragged edge of the frontiers of America, explained some of these clashes; the fact is, that the main cause is to be found in the fact that there was a constant stream of runaway Negro slaves from the plantations of Georgia, Alabama and South Carolina into the territory occupied by these Indian tribes. Arriving into such territory, these fugitives were sheltered by the Indians, who frequently intermarried with them. In this respect, the policy of the Creeks and Seminoles differed from that of the Cherokees to the north, who reduced such fugitives, as a rule, to slavery to themselves.

The attitude of the Creeks and Seminoles toward runaway slaves led to forays by the white owners to recover their slaves; and along with this, there arose a system of just plain hunting among the Indians, by unprincipled whites, for any Negroes they could lay their hands on, and driving off the catch "regardless of right or title." As the whites had all the means of publicity, and practically all political power; and as human nature was what it was, and what it is, the struggle could have only one ending—namely, the practical destruction of the rights of the Indians. But from the first, the ordinary rules of civilized warfare went into the discard, and atrocities on both sides were justly complained of. The Federal Government was called on by Georgia and Alabama to help out against the Creeks, whose holdings in land and pasturage lay on both sides of the Chattahoochee River; and in response to these demands, General Andrew Jackson, in 1812, was sent into the troubled territory, commissioned to discipline the troublesome Indians. His campaign seems to have been considerably like that of Mussolini in Ethiopia. There was a lot written and published about the scalping parties of the Creeks; but not so much about the Jackson methods. We, however, can remember hearing our grandmother tell of one of her uncle's campaigns as a member of Jackson's army of relief in Alabama, in which they got out of rations, and came near starving to death; but just then they set fire to an Indian stockade of logs, which was full of Indians of all kinds, and which had a cellar, filled with sweet potatoes. Her uncle said the potatoes were well roasted and thoroughly soaked with the Indian grease, furnishing very toothsome eating indeed. We could be disposed to think our grandmother's uncle was drawing on his imagination in this recital, after the fashion of veterans of wars since the world began, were it not for the fact that after we were grown up, we saw the story about the potatoes, roasted in Indian grease, in print in some of the annals of those times. It was at the end of his campaign against the Creeks that Jackson was ordered to New Orleans, which led him into imperishable renown on one January 8, 1815, in a battle with Sir Edward Packenham, a brother-in-law of the Duke of Wellington.

In 1818, the raids of slave-owners from Georgia and the Carolinas into the Seminole country in the Spanish territory of Florida, for the purpose of recapturing their runaway slaves were increasing, and as there were the counter-raids of the Seminoles, particularly along the Georgia bank of the Chattahoochee River, as far north as Columbus; pressure was again brought on Washington by the white settlers of southern Georgia to furnish protection, and General Jackson was again authorized to organize a band of militia. As Florida at that time belonged to Spain, a friendly power, the General seems to have had orders to push the Indians back to the Florida boundary line; but not to invade Florida. This was in the year 1817.

As Jackson pushed down the Chattahoochee, the gardens and patches of the Indians filled with growing corn and beans showed that they were not on the war-path; but he pressed right on into Florida across the international boundary line, and brought up at Saint Marks, on the Gulf Coast. When he got there, the Spanish garrison put up no defense, being surprised and outnumbered; and "Billy Bow-legs," the Seminole Chief, was gone with his followers, he having been apprised of Jackson's coming. So Jackson pushed out of Saint Marks to the southeast, a distance of a hundred and forty-three miles, where he expected to capture "Billy Bow-legs" and his force; but again the "birds had flown," with the exception of two aged Indian chiefs. Jackson promptly hanged them, although there is no record that either of them was guilty of violating any law.

By the time the General got back to Saint Marks, he was very angry and tired; so he arrested Alexander Arbuthnot, a Scotch trader, aged seventy-one, and Robert Ambrister, an English trader, aged thirty, "because he believed they had sold supplies to the Indians"; and sent them to a drumhead court-martial, on the instant and on the spot. The court-martial, composed of petty officers, named by Jackson, proceeded to investigate the charges; and, although the evidence failed to show that Ambrister was guilty, and affirmatively showed that Arbuthnot was innocent, the finding as to Arbuthnot was guilty with recommendation of death by hanging. Jackson reviewed this finding, and wrote "approved" under it on the paper; and so Arbuthnot was hanged next day. The court-martial also found Ambrister guilty and recommended a penalty of death by shooting; but, an hour afterwards, reconvened, and recommended a penalty of fifty lashes on the naked back, and confinement in jail for a term of twelve months. The General wrote "disapproved" under the second recommendation, and the word "approved" under their first sentence.

Not much is known of the history and characteristics of Alexander Arbuthnot. The Scotch are not famed for much talking. But Romance has embalmed the memory of Robert Ambrister. Before he was out of his early twenties he had, as a member of the British Royal Marines, seen practically every land under the sun. As a member of Wellington's "Guards," he had lain all of that momentous day at Waterloo prone on the ground, under the pounding of the military genius who had well-nigh conquered the world. The next year, he had assisted to guard Napoleon at St. Helena. Finally, on a visit to his brother, the Governor of the Bahamas, he heard of Florida; and came to Saint Marks—and to Jackson's Firing Squad.

The men went to their deaths the day after their trial, Jackson having ridden away early in the morning, leaving a detachment of troops to carry out the sentences. Ambrister spent his last night with his guards, who were fascinated by the flow of his brilliant conversation, so that neither he nor any of them slept. A sweetheart was waiting for him in London.

There is nothing to record as to the history of Arbuthnot, nor as to how he spent his last hours; but it seems certain that, like his companion in misfortune,

"He nothing common did nor mean,
On that memorable scene."

Both comported themselves with the dignity of members of the great races to which they belonged, and to which so many of us are proud to belong.

Some prominence seemed due these unfortunate men, on account of a great wrong done them both by a representative of our country—a wrong which would appear to have been condoned by their own country, owing to the fact that Britain and the United States had just closed a foolish war; and consequently, there was the less disposition to precipitate another war between the countries.

Then, too, Ambrister at least was young and adventurous. He spent more than a year at Saint Marks before his arrest.

He sold hunters' supplies to the Seminoles, and took their wares in return. Doubtless he joined them in their fishing and hunting trips. And, since what is now Colquitt County was less than a hundred miles from Saint Marks, it is altogether likely that Ambrister accompanied the Indians on some hunting and fishing trips to this section, perhaps camping with them along the Ochlochnee, the Warrior, the Big Indian, and the Ocapilco. Anyhow, we are pleased to imagine that he did; and if Arbuthnot came along sometimes, that is alright too.

CHAPTER III

## General Jackson Causes Trouble---The Seminoles

GENERAL JACKSON closed his campaign against the Seminoles, in 1818, with net results already stated, as follows: Two old Indian Chiefs hanged out of hand; two British subjects killed after farcical trials; the bundling up and shipping to Pensacola of the Spanish garrison at Saint Marks. Also, the United States had acquired a splendid opportunity to go into a war with England, which haughty State had in the preceding century plunged into a war with half of Europe about the loss of an ear by one of her subjects, named "Jenkins." However, she had just emerged from the Napoleonic struggle, which had shaken her to her foundations, and included an incidental conflict with the United States, and this doubtless influenced her to finally back away from her angry demands made on the Government of the United States. Nor was this trouble all. Spain at that time was a very much stronger power than the United States. At the commencement of negotiations with Spain concerning the violation of her territory, and the shipping of her troops about in the Gulf as if they were African slaves, the war clouds hovered ominously, and in sight of those that hovered in the direction of England; and so President Monroe and his cabinet had many anxious hours; and the report gained circulation, twenty years afterwards, that at one of these cabinet meetings, John C. Calhoun, Secretary of War, suggested that Spain be placated and England appeased by hanging General Jackson. This was, of course, in executive session; and when Jackson heard of it for the first time, the people had put him in the presidential chair. This was owing to a popularity which had grown up around him on account of his victory over the British, at New Orleans, three years before the Seminole War. The remark of Calhoun greatly excited the General; who, however much he was in favor of hangings generally, was decidedly opposed to them when it involved his own neck.

ANDREW JACKSON

Finally, Spain took the sensible view that it was impracticable for two nations, speaking different languages, whose capitals were so far removed as were Madrid and Washington from the frictions arising along an international boundary line, to attempt to maintain peace; and so they suggested bluntly the sale of the Floridas, both east and west, to the United States for the sum of $5,000,000 which being accepted, they pulled down their flags, and went home.

In the meantime, white settlers at once commenced to come into the Jackson Cession, rendering the Seminole question more acute than it had ever been. In 1804, on the Georgia side of the Chattahoochee River, a boy child was born to a daughter of a Creek chief, by a white trader named Powell. The child was named "Osceola" by its mother, who took him when he was four years old across the Jackson Cession into Florida, and joined the Seminoles who adopted her and the child. When he grew up, he became the chief of that tribe. Of course, Spain, in ceding Florida to the United States, stipulated for the safe-guarding of the lives and property of her nationals; but this did not include the Seminoles, whose condition was thus rendered more precarious. In the meantime, pressure was increased by the Gulf States, and by Washington, on the Seminole leaders to consent to the removal of their people beyond the Mississippi River. The young chief Osceola set his face like flint against removal; and notified General Thompson, Indian Commissioner for the Florida territory, that he would himself kill any Seminole leader undertaking to bind his people by a treaty of removal. One Seminole chief did sign such a treaty, whereupon Osceola kept his word and killed him. About that time, the wife of Osceola, who was the daughter of a runaway Negro slave, was seized and carried away to Georgia by a white man who claimed to be the owner of the runaway mother of his wife; and when Osceola went to Thompson with his grievance, that functionary threw him in irons for four days. Shortly after he was released, he raided Thompson, accompanied by a few men, and killed him with his own hands. Soon after this, he duplicated the "Custer Massacre" by ambushing Colonel Dade, and killing every one of his force of six hundred men. This incident is referred to in Florida history as the "Dade Massacre."

Presently, the Washington Government had three generals, Scott, Wiley and Gaines warring with Osceola for a year. They finally turned the war over to General Thos. S. Jessup, who invited Osceola into his tent under a flag of truce, under the ostensible purpose of arranging terms of peace, and then ordered him arrested, and sent to Saint Augustine. Escaping from this, he was captured and confined at Fort Moultrie in Charleston harbor, where he died in 1838, of a broken heart. This conduct on the part of General Jessup has been generally denounced by historians as perfidious, which, in fact, it is; but Martin Van Buren, alter ego of President Jackson, was at the head of the Nation; and there can be no doubt that Osceola's continued imprisonment was directed from Washington.

GENERAL JACKSON CAUSES TROUBLE   13

However, this treatment is on the whole not quite as bad as that accorded to the ten-year-old child of King Philip by the New England Puritans in the preceding century. This child narrowly escaped hanging; but, upon second thought, the Puritans shipped him along with a few other Indians to the West Indies and sold him into slavery. His father's crime was exactly the crime of Osceola, an armed defense of the lands which had been occupied by his progenitors from time immemorial. Both Osceola and Philip, considering the smallness of their resources, rank in history as military chieftains of the first order. The United States expended $60,000,000 in this second war with the Seminoles, and some 1500 lives.

During the progress of this war, a company of cadets from the United States War College at West Point was stationed at Fort Meade, in Florida. This company contained a young lieutenant who wrote frequent letters home. In one of these letters, he says he "thinks, this so-called war against a helpless people is not very creditable to us." Again, he writes,

"Our company made a surprise attack on the Seminoles yesterday; and captured thirty prisoners, mostly women and children. One little girl, shot through the cheek, made scarcely a murmur. Another—a woman—shot through and through with a buckshot; conducted herself with all the fortitude of a veteran soldier."

In other letters, he expresses his disgust at finding his first duties as a soldier confined to cutting and slashing with swords among roasting-ears and pumpkins; never foreseeing that as the years should run by, he would attain some fame in that kind of warfare himself. The name of this lieutenant was William Tecumseh Sherman.

As late as 1856, the birth year of Colquitt County, Captain Casey, Indian agent for Florida, published in the Thomasville newspaper a reward for live Indians, as follows:

For each warrior, 250-500 dollars.
For each woman, 150-200 dollars.
For boys over ten years old, 100 to 200 dollars.

These, when captured and delivered would be shipped to Indian Territory. As late as 1860, a carload of these captured people passed through Thomasville en route to Indian Territory. There remain in the Everglades of Florida, near Miami, today, some three hundred and fifty of this indomitable people, occupying a reservation in their ancient fastnesses, where they live in pretty much the same primitive manner their ancestors did a hundred years ago in Colquitt County.

In the second Seminole War, numerous raids were made by the Seminoles into the white settlements in Early County, Georgia, and perhaps into Decatur County. We have talked to aged residents of these counties, who remembered such raids. Remembered, too some of the women who were scalped on such raids, wearing ever afterwards, caps to conceal such disfigurement. We have, however,

Osceola

never heard of such raids into what is now known as Colquitt County. In White's *Collections of Georgia* appears a rather lengthy account of a "great battle" fought in what is now east Colquitt, and in western Cook County, between a band of Creek Indians and two or three companies of militia, led by Col. Michael Young, of Thomasville, with Captains Newman, Tucker and Sharp, all of Thomas County, and Captain Pike, of Lowndes County. There were about a hundred and twenty

## GENERAL JACKSON CAUSES TROUBLE

of the militia, and about a hundred and fifty of the Indians. The valiant Col. Young first sighted the Indians in the fork of Little River and Warrior Creek, and raised the alarm. The Indians got across the river and entered a swamp about four miles down. The "battle" lasted a matter of a day and night. The militia lost two killed and eight wounded—none of them mortally. The Indians escaped, leaving twenty-two dead and two Negroes. Nine squaws and nine children were captured. It is easy to see that this was in no sense a hostile raid; but simply a trek by some Alabama Creeks across the Jackson Cession, in an effort to reach the Seminoles in Florida. The battles happened in July, 1836.

It is only just to say that the methods of the Indians in making war were not different from the methods employed by the whites against them all the way from Quebec to Argentina. Scalping itself was introduced into the Western Hemisphere by colonists from Europe. Alexander H. Stephens in his "History of the United States," speaking of all North American Indians, and especially of those who inhabited Georgia at any time, says, "The Indians were a simple, kindly and child-like race"; and he says that there seems to be no record of any Quaker ever killed by an Indian. He further says that the fact that General Oglethorpe marched entirely across the State of Georgia to a conference of Creek and Seminole chieftains, accompanied by only three armed men, which conference was held on the Chattahoochee River, near Columbus, remained at this conference till his business was transacted, surrounded by fifteen thousand braves, who knew that the Spaniards had a reward for his head, delivered either in Pensacola or Saint Marks, and then returned in perfect safety to Savannah, is a very wonderful tribute to their character and good faith. In this connection,

Mr. Stephens quotes Osceola as saying, after he was captured, "The whites had the newspapers, and therefore, everything they did was right, and everything we did was wrong."

Grave of Osceola, Outside Fort Moultrie, Charleston, S. C.

## CHAPTER IV
## Colquitt Land Titles

AFTER GENERAL JACKSON fought the unofficial ex-parte war against the Spaniards and Indians, he had the Creeks and Seminole Indians cede to the State of Georgia, by the Treaty of 1818, an area about seventy-five miles wide from north to south, lying immediately north of the Florida territory, and extending east and west from the Chattahoochee River to the Okefenokee Swamp. This he did for the purpose of creating a barrier against either permanent or temporary combinations of the Creeks and the Seminoles, and for no other purpose, he having no idea that the area so ceded had any value for any other purpose to the State of Georgia, or to the nation as a whole.

Two or three years later, when it was sought in the legislature of Georgia to create three counties, Early, Irwin and Appling, from the territory thus "wished on" the State of Georgia, certain gentlemen in the legislature are said to have opposed the expenditure of funds for building roads in this territory, because "they were opposed to spending the State's money in the effort to develop a section which God Almighty had gone off and left half finished."

On an old map, of the date of 1818, no town is shown in the vicinity of what is now known as Colquitt County, except Micosoukie, Florida, and the words "pine barrens" are written over the area now known as southwest Georgia.

Finally, the Jackson Cession was made into three counties —Early, Irwin and Appling. Next, Decatur County was created in 1823 from Early and Irwin counties. Hon. Martin Hardin was its first representative in the Georgia House of Representatives. In 1825, the Hon. Thomas J. Johnson, who lived six miles south of what is now known as Thomasville on the Tallahassee Road, became representative of Decatur County, and immediately introduced a bill, creating two counties: Thomas and Lowndes. The bill provided that the 17th and 18th Districts, and all of the 19th and 23rd Districts, lying east of the "Oaklockny" River, all in Decatur County, and the 13th and 14th Districts of Irwin County constitute the new County of Thomas; and that the 8th, 9th, 10th, 11th, 12th, 15th and 16th Districts of Irwin County constitute the new County of Lowndes.

The next year, 1826, the legislature changed the 8th District of Irwin County from Lowndes to Thomas County; and it remained a part of Thomas till it became a part of Colquitt County, at the creation of Colquitt County, in 1856. Hence it is, that the description in many a land deed in Colquitt County reads "land lot No. ...., in the 8th land district of originally Irwin, then Thomas, and now Colquitt County, Georgia."

The following bill was introduced in the Georgia House of Representatives, at the session of the General Assembly of 1856, by the Hon. J. C. Browning, representative from Thomas County:

"An Act To Lay Out and Organize a New County, From the Counties of Thomas and Lowndes, and For Other Purposes.

"1. *Section I.* Be it enacted by authority of the General Assembly of Georgia that from and after the passage of this Act, a new county shall be laid out and organized, from the counties of Thomas and Lowndes, including the 8th Dist. of originally Irwin, now Thomas County, and all that portion of the 9th Dist., of originally Irwin, now Lowndes, lying west of Little River, to where the river crosses the dividing line between Lots of Land Nos. 443 and 444, in the 9th Dist., thence south to the Dist. line between the 9th and 12th Districts.

"2. *Section II.* And be it further enacted, That the new county described in the preceding section of this Act shall be known by the name of Colquitt County, and shall be attached to the Southern Judicial District, and to the First Congressional District, and Second Brigade, and Sixth Division, Georgia Militia.

"3. *Section III.* And be it further enacted, That the persons included within the said new county legally entitled to vote shall on the first Monday in March next elect five Justices of the Inferior Court, a Clerk of the Superior and Inferior Court each, a Sheriff and Coroner, a Tax-Collector and Receiver of Tax Returns, a County Surveyor, and an Ordinary for said county, and that the election of said county officers shall be held at the house of Elijah English, now in the County of Thomas, and superintended as now prescribed by law, and such persons as shall be elected shall be commissioned by the Governor as now prescribed by law.

"4. *Section IV.* And be it further enacted, That the Justices of the Inferior Court, after they shall have been commissioned, shall proceed to lay off said county into militia districts, and advertise for the election of the requisite number of Justices of the Peace in such districts, which shall likewise be commissioned by the Governor.

"5. *Section V.* And be it further enacted, That the Justices of the Inferior Court of said county, after they shall have been commissioned, shall have power and authority to select and locate a site for the public buildings in said county; and the Justices, or a majority of them, are hereby authorized to purchase a tract of land for the location of the county site, to lay off town lots, and sell them at public outcry, for the benefit of said county, or to make such other arrangements of contracts concerning the county site and location and erection of public buildings.

"6. *Section VI.* That all officers now in commission who shall be included in the limits of said county shall hold their commissions, and exercise the duties thereof, until the several officers for the new county are elected and commissioned.

"7. *Section VII.* That all the cases now pending in either of the counties of Thomas and Lowndes, and the papers connected therewith between persons residing within the limits of said county of Colquitt shall be transferred to said county for trial, and everything done which shall be necessary for trial, and any defect that may happen shall be amended instanter.

"8. *Section VIII*. And be it further enacted, That the Superior Courts for said county shall be held on the Mondays before the first Monday in June and December of each and every year, and the Inferior Courts on the first Monday in January and July.

"9. *Section IX*. And be it further enacted, That the county taxes paid by the persons within the limits of the said new county the present year, shall be refunded and paid to the Inferior Court of said new county, to aid them in erecting public buildings.

"10. *Section X*. And be it further enacted, That all laws and parts of laws in conflict with the provisions of this Act are hereby repealed."

Approved February 25, 1856.

This Act was approved by David J. Bailey, President of the Georgia State Senate, and by the Hon. William H. Stiles, Speaker of the Georgia House of Representatives, and by the Hon. Herschel V. Johnson, Governor of the State of Georgia. More than eighty years have passed since then. Victoria was Queen of Great Britain; Napoleon III was Emperor of the French; and Franklin Pierce was President of the United States.

The English Home

## CHAPTER V

## Slavery and Secession

THE COLONY OF GEORGIA organizing itself as such, in 1732, passed two prohibition laws. First, they forever prohibited the making and selling of intoxicating liquors; and, second, they forever prohibited human slavery. This was more than a century after a New England ship had brought a cargo of Negroes to Jamestown, Va., this being the first cargo of Negro slaves ever brought to America. These prohibitions, however, were repealed at the behest of the "Money Power" of that time; and, by the end of the Revolution, African slavery was fairly general throughout the Colonies.

However, by the end of the Eighteenth Century, there was perceptible a growing feeling against slavery. The sect of Quakers started organized opposition to it, and maintained it consistently to the end. Washington freed all his slaves under the terms of his will, explaining his failure to do this sooner. Jefferson gave entire freedom to all his slaves, long before he died, in 1826, saying, on one occasion, "When I contemplate slavery, I tremble for the fate of my country, knowing that God is a just God, and that His justice will not always sleep." Under the influence of such generous impulses, slavery in America seemed doomed; and there is no doubt it would have completely perished in all the states in another generation, but for the invention of the cotton gin, by Eli Whitney, in 1820. This placed the Southern States in possession of a monopoly in the production of the leading material for clothing in the world; this rendered big plantations necessary; and Negro slavery was peculiarly adapted to this. In fact, it was impracticable to maintain slavery on small farms.

Court records now in the Thomas County courthouse, show that for the purpose of valuation in the administration of estates, Negro slaves, about 1826, were appraised at around $450 for adults; while other records, in 1855, show the same character of slaves appraised at about $1800 each.

In 1857, when there were 928 poll tax payers in Thomas County, slaves were returned for taxation at $3,773,634.00; while the value of all real estate was $2,438,800.47.

The census of 1860 shows that in Thomas County there were, in that year, 4488 white people, and 5985 slaves, and thirteen free Negroes. Brooks County had that year 3272 whites, and 3282 slaves, and two free persons of color. Leon County, Florida, had 3194 whites, and 9089 slaves, and sixty free Negroes. Jefferson County, Florida, had 3498 whites, and 6374 slaves, and forty-three free Negroes.

The 1860 census of Colquitt County, Georgia, showed 1152 whites, and only 110 slaves, divided among twenty-seven slave-holders. And this, perhaps, because agriculture had not become an industry in Colquitt County at that time. There were not a half dozen hundred-acre clearings in the county. But this is not the only reason for the scarcity of slaves. There is not wanting evidence that the overwhelming majority of Colquitt's citizens pitied the condition of these wretched people, and feared results, remembering the history of the Chosen People in Egypt. This writer recalls a vivid description by a son of one of the pioneers of Colquitt County who died here nearly twenty years ago. He was a boy in the 1850's, and he told me of living near a slave plantation; and of constantly hearing in the early nights the cries of slaves under the strokes of the lash of the whipping boss—"sometimes," as he expressed it, "his whip would cry for half an hour," and at every stroke of the whip, following it so closely as to seem a part of it was the cry of the sufferer to the Lord. "And," said the aged man, "Judge, He heered 'em."

By the time the census of 1860 was taken, the "irrepressible conflict" had come into sight. The question of Negro slavery had thrust itself to the front, over the protests of a great race of statesmen. Compromisers like Clay, Benton and Webster cried "Peace, Peace!", as the clouds gathered, portending the storm. The Whigs in their Boston Convention, in 1848, ignored the slavery question in their platform; and under leadership of Abraham Lincoln and Alexander H. Stephens placed in nomination for President, General Zachary Taylor, who had never voted, and who was the owner of twenty slaves. Taylor was elected, but the Whig party died that year. The Democrats won with Franklin Pierce, in 1852, and again with James Buchanan, in 1856—Colquitt's birth year. Then, in 1860, the Democratic party itself was destroyed on the rock of slavery, at the Charleston Convention. Afterward, three sets of electors were put out by the three divisions, thus making it possible for the Republicans to elect Lincoln and Hamlin. The three divisions of the Democratic party put out sets of electors, as follows: The fire-eaters, as the extreme defenders of slavery were called, nominated Breckenridge and Lane at the head of electors as follows:

| | |
|---|---|
| C. S. McDonald | H. Buchannon |
| H. R. Jackson | L. Tumlin |
| Peter Cone | H. Strickland |
| W. M. Slaughter | W. A. Lofton |
| O. C. Gibson | W. M. McIntosh |

The regulars, at the Charleston Convention nominated Stephen A. Douglas for President and Herschel V. Johnson of Georgia, for Vice-President, heading a set of electors, as follows:

A. H. Stephens          H. Warner
A. C. Wright            J. W. Harris
J. L. Seward            J. P. Simmons
B. Y. Martin            J. S. Hook
Nathan Bass             J. Cumming

That element of the party disposed to compromise and professing to be deaf to the rumblings of the approaching storm, put in nomination Bell and Everett over a set of electors as follows:

Wm. Low                 W. F. Wright
Ben H. Hill             J. R. Parrot
S. B. Spencer           J. E. Dupree
M. Douglas              L. Lamar
L. T. Doyal

The Republicans put out no ticket in Georgia.

As has been said, the Breckenridge and Lane ticket was put out by the extreme Southern Rights wing of the party. The Douglas and Johnson ticket represented the views of Douglas on the slavery question, namely—that each territory and new state should be allowed to decide for itself whether or not it would have slavery; and the Bell and Everett ticket had the shortest platform ever put out by a political group in America, namely: "The Union, The Constitution, and The Laws."

It was Colquitt's first presidential election. One hundred and eighty-three votes were polled in all. The Breckenridge and Lane electors receiving 115 each. The Bell and Everett electors got 67 each, while the Douglas and Johnson electors got only 1 each, a remarkable circumstance considering the fact that the second name on this ticket was Governor Herschel Johnson, one of the most distinguished sons of Georgia. Jeremiah Bryant Norman, Sr., managed for the Bell and Everett ticket, while Henry Gay led the fight for the fire-eaters, Breckenridge and Lane. One wonders who cast the solitary ballot for Douglas and Johnson.

This election was held throughout the Union on November 6, 1860, and the Breckenridge and Lane ticket carried Georgia, easily triumphing over Douglas and Johnson, although the fight for it in the State was led by Alexander Stephens and Governor Johnson. Neither ticket received a majority of the votes cast in Georgia, and the Republicans did not put out a ticket in this State. Joseph E. Brown, who at that time was Governor of Georgia, although sprung from a "poor white family," like Lincoln, had already allied himself with the slave-holding aristocracy, and so on the 20th of November, he wrote the General Assembly, which was in session, saying that considering the fact that it was a certainty that the "Black Republican" ticket had been elected, he suggested that the election be not carried into the legislature for the purpose of determining Georgia's electors. On the very day of the election he had written to the legislature expressing his opinion that the Republican ticket would win; and that if it should be shown that such was the case, he recommended that Georgia secede from the Union.

As soon as the result of the election was generally known, South Carolina did secede from the Union, being swiftly followed by Alabama, Florida, Mississippi, Louisiana and Texas.

In the meantime, Governor Brown had seized the United States Arsenals at Augusta and Savannah, and was hurrying the State of Georgia along toward secession. Finally, the matter was submitted to a referendum in which delegates were selected to meet at Milledgeville, then the capital, on January 16, 1861, for the purpose of considering "the state of the Union." It was a red hot election, in which the advocates of secession were led by brothers, Howell Cobb and Thomas R. R. Cobb, Robert Toombs and Governor Brown; while the conservatives, or opponents of secession were led by A. H. Stephens, Benj. H. Hill and Herschel V. Johnson.

In this referendum, Colquitt seemed to change position, since she presented practically a solid front for the Union. Only three votes were cast for secession, as follows: John D. Dalton, Allen Creed and Darling Creed, the last two being brothers, and all three being natives of South Carolina. Colquitt's delegates, elected to the Convention at this referendum were Henry Crawford Tucker and John G. Coleman. Of course, we have heard of Elder Tucker before, and are to hear of him again. However, it was the only political commission that he ever held. The other delegate, Coleman, baffles us. The census of 1860 shows that he was a resident of Colquitt County at that time, having been born in South Carolina, and thirty-eight years old—that he had a wife and three children, and that he was one of the two wealthiest citizens in the county. Records at the State house at Atlanta show that within three weeks of the close of the Secession Convention, he was elected a judge of the Inferior Court of Colquitt County, for a term of four years. At this point he drops out of sight. No one remembers him here after these seventy years, and the courthouse records having been destroyed, in 1881, are out of the equation. He seems to have "sunk without trace," in the confusion incident to the Confederate War.

At the October, 1898, term of Colquitt Superior Court, this writer called on the Hon. Aug. H. Hansell, at that time presiding judge of the Superior Courts of the Southern Circuit, at his room in the old Fish Hotel. He was accompanied there by Hon. Matt. J. Pearsall, a very brilliant young lawyer at the Moultrie Bar. Among many reminiscences with which Judge Hansell favored us, was one concerning an experience he had as a member of the Secession Convention, where he headed the delegation from Thomas County; the Judge was invited to attend a conference held on either the first or second night of the convention, at the room of United States Senator Robert Toombs. When he got there, after supper, he found Alexander H. Stephens and others. A few moments after the company was assembled, Senator Toombs took the chair and said, "Gentlemen, I wanted to confer with you as to how I should answer a letter which I have today received from the Governor of South Carolina, asking what, in my opinion, would be the reaction of this convention, should he fire on Fort Sumter." This, of course, provoked difference of opinion; and Mr. Stephens deftly staved off a vote. Presently Senator Toombs excused himself from the room for a short time, and on his return, said, "Gentlemen, I have just received a telegram from the Governor of South Carolina, urging that I wire him what I think would be the reaction of the delegates here, in case he should fire on Fort Sumter."

At this, Mr. Stephens procured an adjournment; and as he and Delegate Hansell walked away, Mr. Stephens asked Delegate Hansell to join him in a plate of oysters in a restaurant nearby; and, when they were seated, Delegate Hansell said, "Mr. Stephens, don't you think that if Senator Toombs had exhibited and read his letter and telegram to us tonight, it would have produced a stronger effect?"

To which Mr. Stephens answered, "Ah, Hansell, you just don't know Bob. Now I know that he had not received any such letter, and that he had not received any such telegram, but he thinks he got them."

At the time this convention was deliberating, the Secession movement had reached a stalemate, the situation being as follows: South Carolina had seceded on December 20, 1860; and her action had been followed by Mississippi, three weeks afterward; Florida had gone out of the Union January 10, 1861; and Alabama had gone along on January 11, 1861.

Georgia's referendum had sent to the Milledgeville convention a majority against the Secession movement. The whole movement therefore stood to turn out a fiasco, unless Georgia should reverse her position; because Georgia was, as Horace Greeley expressed it, a short while before the date of the convention, "The Empire State of the South." The Georgia Secession Convention was one of the most important political gatherings that ever met in the history of man—a fact recognized fully by the leaders of both factions in Georgia.

Leading the Secession minority were Thos. R. R. Cobb, aristocratic Presbyterian elder, who lived his religion every day, and Governor Joe Brown, also a leading churchman of Georgia, whose parents were the poorest of the "poor-whites" of the mountains.

Fiery Cobb, really a great orator, was telling the delegates that Secession would cause no war—that the North would not fight—that he would agree to drink all the blood that would be shed as a consequence of Secession. Poor man: less than a year afterwards, he was to meet Benj. H. Hill, and tell him how much mental distress he was in as he saw the country standing on the threshold of a tremendous conflict, saying, "I am opposed to war on principle: it is against my religion; but, having led my State into this war, there is no honorable course open to me, except to go in and get killed." He resigned his position in the Confederate Congress; went in; and was shot to death, next year, on the heights of Fredericksburg.

His co-worker at the convention, and the one having equal responsibility for the convention's ultimate action,—Governor Joe Brown, in all probability had no definite opinions as to whether war would come or not. We are of the opinion from his record, that the only thing about it that Governor Joe Brown knew perfectly well was that regardless of

Cobb's fate, or the fate of any other, he did not expect to encourage himself in getting killed, then or later.

The anti-secessionists in caucus named Herschel V. Johnson to close the argument for their side. When all the others had spoken in the debate, rumor has it that some secessionist put through a motion to adjourn for lunch, just as Governor Johnson was on the point of taking the floor and making the speech which, the friends of the Union expected would do the business for the Secession movement, and that something happened to him, at lunch. Anyhow, there seems to be no doubt that when it came his turn to speak at the reassembling of the convention after lunch, his eagle refused to soar. It is said that when that great man arose to address the convention upon the momentous issue, he placed his feet somewhat apart; and looking vacantly around over the audience, said "I am standing on a rock." He then looked around some more—started off again, and said, "I am standing on a rock; and nobody can't move me." That's all. He was led to his seat. The test vote was taken without the expected speech; and the result showed 160 votes for Secession against 130 votes against it. Georgia went out; the Confederacy was organized; and 350,000 men lost their lives.

Thomas County's three delegates voted for the ordinance. We are under the impression, from the talk of Judge Hansell, hereinbefore referred to, that they must have reversed their instructions. Colquitt's two delegates, Elder Tucker and John G. Coleman, both voted for the ordinance.

## CHAPTER VI
## The Civil War

AS HAS BEEN SEEN, Colquitt's delegates to the Secession convention, along with many other delegates, ran counter to the instructions of their constituents, and voted to take Georgia out of the Union.

Hon. N. M. Marchant, octogenarian resident of west Colquitt, tells us that there was some considerable criticism of their action, when they reached home; but this could not have been intense, as the record shows that delegate Coleman was elected to a position on the Inferior Court bench of Colquitt County, within a few weeks after the action and adjournment of the convention. The truth would appear to be that war sentiment swept all the South like a prairie fire, during the first part of the year 1861, engulfing, for the time, all opposition. For instance, A. H. Stephens, one of the leaders against Secession, so long as it was short of an accomplished fact, went to Montgomery as a delegate from Georgia, to a convention of delegates from the seceded states, and accepted the office of vice-president of the new "Confederate States of America"; and soon afterwards, went to Savannah, where he made a speech to a mass meeting of the citizens of that town, known to subsequent history as the "Corner Stone Address," in which he proclaimed to the world that the corner stone of the projected new government was the perpetual enslavement of the Negro race; and that this action placed the Lord Almighty on the side of the Confederacy, guaranteeing that the new government would never fall. It was an amazing speech, coming as it did from the second highest officer in the Confederacy, since it flew right in the face of the most generous impulses of that age. John Bright,

THE CIVIL WAR 31

leader of the Liberals in the British Parliament, denounced the new government as, "That unholy combination against human liberty." The Pope simply announced that he would pray for peace. The Czar of Russia, who had freed the serfs in his own country a few years before, quietly sent the Russian fleet into New York harbor, conveying assurance to Lincoln that it was at his service if needed.

Anyhow, by the time Fort Sumter was fired on, April 9, 1861, things were getting around to a fighting complexion; and when Lincoln, as a result of the bombardment of Sumter, called on the states remaining in the Union for three hundred thousand volunteer soldiers to coerce the Confederacy, a company was organized in Colquitt County to resist the coercion of a State, in its right to secede. This company was called "Company H," of the 50th Regiment, C. S. A. A copy of the roster of this company, as it was organized, is inserted here.

MUSTER ROLL OF COMPANY "H," 50TH GEORGIA REGIMENT, C. S. A.

J. J. Johnson, 1st Lieutenant    Jake Alger, Orderly Sergeant
John Tucker, 2nd Lieutenant    Jerry Wells, Captain
E. Tillman, 3rd Lieutenant

*Privates:*

| | | |
|---|---|---|
| Wilson Alger | Louis Bloodworth | Jake Kinard |
| Jackson Alred | John Bower | John Law |
| Vance Alger | Simon Connell | Marion Lee |
| John Alderman | Jake Croft | Wright Murphy |
| Thos. Alligood | James Castleberry | Solomon Mercer |
| Andy Alligood | Jake Creed | John Mercer |
| Jack Allred | Walt Hancock | James McMullen |
| Irain Allred | Harrison Hancock | J. J. Norman |
| Allen Allred | James Hood | J. S. Norman |
| Burrell Baker | Allen Hart | Malley NeSmith |

32       HISTORY OF COLQUITT COUNTY

W. W. Baker        Hardin Hancock       Joe Norwood
W. Bryant          Simon Hant           John Owens
Calvin Bryant      James Hardwick       Paul Creed
Thos. Baker        John Henly           Isaac Carlton
David Culpepper    Jack Hancock         Mitchell Tillman
John Crosby        Henry Hancock        Elbert Tillman
Miles Dukes        William Hall         Jordan Tillman
Wyatt Dukes        Jesse Hollingsworth  John Tillman
William Denmon     Wash Hollingsworth   Thomas Tillman
Elisha Davis       James Horne          John A. Tillman
Elijah Field       Willis Price         Harrison Tillman
N. Flowers         James Redd           Lot Townsend
J. Ganey           James Robertson      James Thompson
Hiram Gay          Thomas Roland        Richard Tucker
Matthew Gay        Robert Royles        Henry Varnadoe
Jack Green         Charles Royles       P. O. Wing
Moses Guyton       Joe Simpson          James Weeks
David Giles        George Suber         Pink Weeks

Mr. I. McD. Turner, good citizen of Moultrie now and for the past fifty years, was in Moultrie as a child, on the day the company was organized; and remembers the men volunteers, marching two abreast, making a procession of something like fifty couples, by where he was standing with his mother. He also remembers, after seventy-four years, the wailing of the women, whose men were being enrolled.

The following are reported to us as having been killed in action, or as having died in camps, as a result of wounds or disease: Burrell Baker, James Castleberry, James Hardwick, Miles Dukes, Willis Price, A. Alligood.

The name Malley NeSmith will be noted on this roster. Hon. J. B. Norman, Jr., once related to us a circumstance connected with his death, as follows:

Malachi NeSmith was a young married man when he went away with "Company H." He left a wife and two baby boys, living near the home of J. B. Norman, Sr., at what is now Norman Park, in Colquitt County. In the Seven Days' Battle, near Richmond, he was wounded desperately, and a letter so saying was received by his wife. Mail was brought to that vicinity at that time by Star Route once a week, from Thomasville; and Mr. Norman, Sr., habitually brought the mail. At any rate, on the day it was expected that another letter would be received, the anxious wife came with her babies to the residence of Norman, to await the coming of the mail. Finally Mr. Norman drove up, got out of the buggy, and proceeded leisurely to take out his horse. The two anxious women pressed out into the lot. "Did you get news?" they asked.

"Yes," said the man of few words.

"Well, is it good or bad?" they asked impatiently.

"Ah," said he, tactfully, "it's about like we were afraid it would be."

Then the ineffaceable recollection of the boy's mother, seeking to comfort the widow.

By the way, Mrs. NeSmith remained a widow until her death, after she had reared her two boys to maturity—no better men ever having been in the county—"Malley" Ne-Smith and "Matthy" NeSmith.

After "Company H" had gone away to "foe-fenced camps and bloody battle-fields," other war-like impulses beat in the bosoms of some of Colquitt's sons, witness the following letter, on file in the Georgia Department of Archives.

"Colquitt County, Georgia.
August 13th/61
"Hon. Joseph E. Brown,
Milledgeville, Georgia.
Dear Sir.

"I have been Instructed to Inform you that a portion of the citizens of this county assembled today for the purpose of organizing a Malitia or Battalion Master- and there being no lawful officers to order the same I was directed by them to request your Excellency to appoint or lawfully authorize legal officers to order the same. I was also authorized to recommend to your notice James Brown, Esq- of this county for the office of Battalion Collonel and James R. Alger Esqr for Major.

"Please put us in a way to prepare ourselves for the Exegencies of the times.

"Hoping Your Early attention
am yours
Verry respectfylly,
Jeremiah Hancock."

The prominence of the Tillmans in "Company H" will not have escaped attention of the reader, there being eight of them, if we count Third Lieutenant E. Tillman. Third Lieutenant E. comes into the picture later; as is shown by a record on file in the Georgia Department of Archives, of which the following is a copy:

MUSTER ROLL OF CAPTAIN ELIJAH TILLMAN'S COMPANY

*Muster Roll of Captain* Elijah Tillman's *Company, in the ............ Regiment, commanded by Colonel ........................ called into the service of the Confederate States for local defense, under the provisions of the acts of Congress, on the requisition of the President, by Joseph E. Brown, Governor of Georgia, from the* fourth *day of* August, *1863, date of this muster, for the term of six months, unless sooner discharged, and to serve* in the South Western Quarter of the state & West of the Altamaha River.

| No. | NAME<br>PRESENT AND ABSENT<br>(Privates in Alphabetical Order) | RANK | VALUATION IN DOLLARS OF HORSES |
|---|---|---|---|
| 1 | Elijah Tillman | Captain | 500 |
| 2 | John Selph | 1st Lieutenant | 500 |
| 3 | Linton Carlton | 2nd Lieutenant | |
| 4 | John Tucker | Ensign | |
| 5 | Flournoy Clark | 1st Sergeant | 400 |
| 6 | Seaborn Weeks | 2d Sergeant | 400 |

## THE CIVIL WAR 35

| | | | |
|---|---|---|---|
| 7 | Darlin Creed | 3d Sergeant | 500 |
| 8 | John Sloan | 4th Sergeant | 700 |
| 9 | Nathaniel Giles | 5th Sergeant | 500 |
| 10 | James E. Hancock | 1st Corporal | 300 |
| 11 | Abraham Gay | 2d Corporal | 500 |
| 12 | Elias Murray | 3d Corporal | 400 |
| 13 | Thomas Weeks | 4th Corporal | 400 |
| 14 | Jackson P. Bennet | | 125 |
| 15 | John S. Bloodworth | | |
| 16 | James W. Bloodworth | | |
| 17 | David Bland | | 300 |
| 18 | Ezekiel Crosby | | |
| 19 | Leroy H. Clark | | |
| 20 | David A. Giles | | |
| 21 | Mack L. Gay | | 500 |
| 22 | Jacob J. Giles | | 250 |
| 23 | Spencer Graves | | |
| 24 | Eveander Gunn | | |
| 25 | Wiley N. Holland | | |
| 26 | Abel P. Hutchison | | |
| 27 | James W. Hires | | 500 |
| 28 | Oliver Hays | | |
| 29 | Thomas F. Hampton | | |
| 30 | John Johnson | | 100 |
| 31 | William E. Johnson | | |
| 32 | James Mercer | | 400 |
| 33 | Reason J. Marlow | | |
| 34 | William H. McCall | | |
| 35 | Richard J. Mauldin | | |
| 36 | William Matthis | | |
| 37 | Moses C. Norman | | 500 |
| 38 | John T. Norman | | 600 |
| 39 | Richard J. Norman | | 400 |
| 40 | Thomas Norwood | | 250 |
| 41 | John N. Philips | | 500 |

42  George W. Tucker ..............................................
43  Matthew Tucker ..............................................
44  Benjamin Weeks ..............................................
45  Joshua Warren ..............................................
46  Stewart S. May ..............................................  500
   All present.

### Remarks On This Muster Roll:

The two Bloodworths have no horses and the Captain thinks they are unable to buy horses.

All others have horses or can purchase them.

---

Note: This muster roll was certified August 27, 1863, at Moultrie, Ga., by Elijah Tillman, Captain; appraised August 27, 1863, at Moultrie, Ga., by Daniel Thomas, Willis Bedinfield, and John Turner; certified August 27, 1863, at Moultrie, Ga., by N. T. MacIntosh, Lieutenant Colonel, 69th Regiment, Georgia Militia, mustering officer.

Original muster roll on file in Georgia Department of Archives. The part italicized is printed on original.

It will be noticed that Moses C. Norman, John T. Norman, and Richard J. Norman appear on the muster roll of Captain Tillman's Company. Also, that the names of J. J. Norman and J. S. Norman appear in the muster roll of "Company H." All these five men were sons of James M. Norman, the Colquitt pioneer. J. B. Norman, Sr., another brother, already referred to, held during the war the position of superintendent of the

J. J. Giles, 94 years old in August, 1936. Sole Survivor of Colquitt's contribution to the Confederate Armies.

distribution of the necessities of the families of the volunteers. But the mother of these men was Ruth Tillman, an aunt of Captain Elijah Tillman, and a near relative of all the Tillmans whose names appear as privates in "Company H." So, in a way, Colquitt County's Tillmans, who were a branch of South Carolina's fighting Tillmans, sent thirteen representatives into the armies of the Confederacy.

As has already been noted, Colquitt had very few slaves, at any time, and none of her citizens looked on slavery as indispensable to their welfare personally. While the county was a part of Lowndes and Thomas, the citizens of Colquitt territory, living remote from the county sites of these original counties, had practically nothing to do with politics, local, state, or national; and, when the Secession War came on, there was no great feeling among her citizens among themselves, or, for that matter, against any outsiders. In all, some fifteen or twenty of the men enlisted or conscripted in the armies of the Confederacy, lost their lives; but not a life was lost in guerrilla or partisan fighting.

Only two Union soldiers ever put foot on the soil of Colquitt; and these were prisoners of war escaped from the great war prison, at Andersonville, in Sumter County. Toward the end of 1864, these two unfortunate youths, making their way southward, stopped at the residence of J. B. Norman, Sr., near the present site of Norman Park, and asked for "something to eat." That good man and his wife entertained them over-night; and on the morrow, Mr. Norman gave them a little stake and let them proceed. It was done like him, even if the war hadn't been about over anyhow.

There has been much criticism of the South about the suffering of the prisoners at the prison at Andersonville in 1864. This was the year Sherman went through Georgia, when he himself said that he destroyed food and feedstuffs to the value of $100,000,000, three-fourths of which, he says, was

38     HISTORY OF COLQUITT COUNTY

sheer waste. This caused a scarcity, which undoubtedly reacted on the unfortunate prisoners at Andersonville.

We close this chapter with a snapshot of the John K. McNeil Camp, Confederate Veterans Association. This picture was taken on April 26, 1936, on the occasion of Memorial Day. All members from Colquitt County are in the picture except the venerable J. J. Giles, whose picture also appears separately—he being unable, from the infirmities of age, to appear for the group. He was, as will be noticed, one of Captain Elijah Tillman's Company, as per muster roll above referred to. The ages of these men are marked under the picture. Mr. Giles will be ninety-four in the month of October of the present year, and is the only surviving member of Colquitt's contributions to the armies of the Confederacy. The other veterans went into the war from other counties, and now reside here. Giles died February 18, 1937.

Left to right: J. A. OWEN, 92 years old, JOE OWEN, 88 years old, S. J. J. BRUCE 102 years old, J. H. BRIDGERS, 89 years old.

## CHAPTER VII

# Reconstruction

THE CIVIL WAR ended with the surrender of Lee, on April 9, 1865, and the surrender of Johnston, on May 30, 1865. President Johnson appointed James Johnson, of Columbus, Provisional Governor of the State. Governor Johnson called a convention of delegates for the purpose of abolishing slavery, as a thing preliminary to the restoration of Georgia's representation in the United States Congress. The Constitutional Convention met in November, 1865, abolished slavery; repealed the ordinance as Secession, and went home. Flournoy Clark and B. E. Watkins represented Colquitt in this convention.

Flournoy Clark was a Methodist preacher, progenitor of a family long prominent in Colquitt County at the time, and still prominent. He was the father of Rev. George Clark, prominent Baptist minister, and of R. G. Clark, for many years clerk of the Superior Courts of Colquitt County, and one-time representative of Colquitt in the General Assembly of Georgia. Dr. Baker E. Watkins was by profession a physician, and like Flournoy Clark, was a Methodist preacher. He was a native of Kentucky, who moved first to Alabama, and afterward to Terrell County, Georgia. He moved to "Old Greenfield," in Colquitt, in 1863, where he practiced his profession of medicine. He was the first resident doctor in Colquitt County and rode the three-path roads for many years in relief of the suffering.

C. J. Jenkins was elected Governor of Georgia, under the provisions of the Constitution of 1865, on November 15th of that year. In the meantime, much confusion had arisen in Georgia, and "carpet-baggers," a term applied to political adventurers from the North, appeared in the Fall of 1866. Congress passed the "Reconstruction Act," in March, 1867; and Georgia was again taken over by the United States Government, and placed under the control of Gen. John Pope. In December, 1867, Gen. Pope called another Constitutional Convention, for the purpose of acting on the Reconstruction Act of Congress, which provided civil rights for the Negroes resident in the State. There were 169 whites and 37 Negro delegates. The great majority of the white delegates belonged to the "poor-whites" of the State, as the non-slave-holding class had long been called, and at the time of the assembling of the Constitutional Convention of 1867, these white delegates were generally known as "Scalawags," a term of reproach applied to them because they had gone over to the reconstructionists. The convention ratified the Fourteenth Amendment to the Federal Constitution, which provides equal civil rights for Negroes, and all and any other classes of citizens. Immediately afterwards, Congress passed the Fifteenth Amendment to the National Constitution, providing equal political rights to Negroes, and forbidding any state paying out of its funds any past indebtedness incurred in support of rebellion or insurrection. The convention also ratified this amendment.

Colquitt's delegate to this convention was Rev. Melton C. Smith, who moved to Thomas County after the close of the Civil War from up near Atlanta—near McDonough to be more accurate. He was a Methodist preacher too; and the father of Col. Joe Smith, a member of the Colquitt County Bar for many years.

Willis W. Watkins was elected representative of Colquitt County in the Georgia House of Representatives, in the sessions of 1865-1866-1867. He was rated as a Republican, or "Reconstructionist." In fact, he was such, died such, and gloried in it while he lived, although he was a son of

Preacher-Doctor B. E. Watkins, the Democrat. Also, he was an ex-Confederate soldier; but then so was Gen. James Longstreet, Lee's "Right Arm," who went along with the Republicans or Scallawags of the time. Also, War Governor Joseph Emerson Brown joined the popular side, went as a delegate to the Republican Convention at Chicago, helped nominate Grant, and made a fiery speech in favor of the civil and political rights of the Negroes. In 1871-2-3, Isaac Carlton, another Republican, represented Colquitt in the legislature.

The 7th Senatorial District of Georgia, consisting at that time of Colquitt, Thomas and Brooks counties, was represented in the Georgia State Senate by Benning B. Moore, during the years 1865-6-7. In the years 1868-9-70, this District was represented by Rev. Melton C. Smith. In the years 1871-2-3, William L. Clark was State Senator. All these men were Republicans, and possibly Moore and Clark were Negroes. The Reconstructionists sent to the House of Representatives at Washington as Representative of the 2nd District of Georgia, which included Colquitt, Major Richard Whitely, of Decatur, during the years 1872-3-4-5. He was a Confederate soldier, and maintained an office at Bainbridge as a member of the partnership of "Donaldson and Whitely," Attorneys.

There is no occasion here for a discussion of Reconstruction as a general State question. This phase of it is sufficiently discussed by saying that now, at least, it appears that the giving of political rights to Negroes indiscriminately at that time, was a blunder in the science of government. In fact, Charles Francis Adams has said it was "the greatest blunder ever made in government by the Anglo-Saxon race, which has a genius for government, superior to that of ancient Rome." At the time it was done, however, Charles Sumner, a great senator, and a sincere patriot, said, "I recognize fully the incapacity of the Negro in practical government, but I shall adhere to the policy of political equality in spite of this incapacity, for the reason that I cannot see how in a democracy, the Negro can secure his civil rights unless he retains his political rights."

Nevertheless, notwithstanding the pressure from Washington, the Negro was steadily forced out of the political picture in Georgia, and in the South. From a representation of something like forty in the General Assembly of Georgia, in 1869-70, his numbers steadily decreased, until the Democrats captured the State in 1874-6. In the latter year, there were still sixteen Negroes left in the Georgia legislature. They constituted the balance of power in an exceedingly close race for the United States senatorship between Thomas M. Norwood, the incumbent, and Benj. H. Hill. After a long deadlock, during which they voted for Dawson H. Walker, a white Republican lawyer from Dalton, they finally swung to Hill, under the expert manipulation of Henry Grady and George N. Lester, Judge of the Superior Courts of the Blue Ridge Circuit, at the time. At no time since that time have they had any considerable representation in the Georgia legislature, and the last one came from Liberty County, more than twenty years ago.

In both state and national elections, in 1876, tremendous efforts were put out to recapture control of the southern states by the party of the old aristocracy. As has been said hereinbefore, a part at least of the old southern leadership—men like Longstreet and Joseph E. Brown, sat in the councils of the Republicans. There is no doubt but that in the elections of 1876 "no holds were barred." On the night before the presidential election of that year, schoolhouse meetings were held from North Carolina to Texas. A majority of these meetings were opened with prayer.

When the election was over, it was found that an unprecedented situation existed. It was the nearest thing to an outright tie in a national election that the history of the country furnishes; but the equities of the situation pointed to the election of Tilden, the Democratic candidate.

In the interval, between the date of the election and the fourth of March, 1877, the date of the inauguration of the new President, John B. Gordon and Wade Hampton approached the Hayes management and proposed to let Hayes get the presidency, provided that he would agree to withdraw from the South all detachments of Federal troops, all of which had been stationed there for more than ten years. The proposition was accepted. Hayes was made President, and the last Federal soldier was withdrawn from the South, during the first year of his administration. We believe that Wm. E. Smith, Congressman from the Second District of Georgia, was the only member of the Georgia delegation in that Congress who opposed the Gordon-Hampton deal.

Of course, when the Federal troops were removed from the South, down went the whole political fabric erected by the Reconstructionists. The victorious Democrats called another Constitutional Convention, which met in 1877, for the purpose of consolidating their 1876 gains. It was dominated entirely by General Robert Toombs, presided over by Governor Jenkins, and submitted to the electorate our present Georgia Constitution. Colquitt's representative in this convention was Henry Gay, the veteran Democrat.

In the meantime, let us see what was happening to our local Reconstructionists, before and during the year 1876.

In the year 1876, the opposition to the sway of the Reconstructionists arose in Mitchell County, on one bloody day, still referred to as the "Day of the Camilla Riots," on which a Negro or two were killed, several more crippled up, and the local Republican leader, a young Yankee, late from the North, escaped death only by putting out the Grand Hailing Sign of Distress of a well-known secret order. Right then, he removed to an adjoining county, and, henceforth eschewing politics, he spent a lifetime as a useful and valued citizen. Down in Thomas County, at the State general elections, Confederate Colonel Robt. G. Mitchell mounted his horse, rode down to the polling-place, pistol in hand, and single-handed dispersed the Negro voters, to return no more.

Willis W. Watkins, ex-Confederate soldier, who was a Republican and rejoiced in it, was a candidate for State Senator, in 1876, but was defeated by James McDonald—largely by the aristocracy of Brooks County. In fact his advertised Quitman meeting was broken up with eggs—"in due and ancient form."

In Colquitt, Republican Jim Murphy was defeated for the legislature by J. B. Norman, Jr., in a close race in which trouble was kept down by the cool counsels of both candidates.

Dan. Luke, resourceful leader of the Reconstructionists in Thomas County, has been dead more than a generation, and is buried in the Thomasville Cemetery. Willis Watkins died about 1898, and is buried in the same cemetery as Luke. Jim Murphy, who kept down a bloody riot at the elections in Colquitt County, in 1876, as he was being defeated by J. B. Norman, Jr., in his race for the legislature, lived quietly afterwards on his ancestral farm, near the Ochlochnee, in south Colquitt, where he died in good financial circumstances, in 1912. He is buried in the family graveyard, within a few steps of the house erected by his father, Henry Murphy, more than a hundred years ago. So much for the local aspects of what is still styled by politicians who consider themselves in danger, as "the Terrible Era of Reconstruction."

The Reconstructionists must be credited with giving the State an excellent judiciary, and with having placed the public school system in our fundamental law, where, of course, it will remain forever.

A thing, too, that has some of the elements of pathos in it, is this: The legislatures of 1866-7-8-9 appropriated $200.00 a year to pay the educational expenses of "crippled and indigent soldiers," at the University of Georgia, at Emory College, and perhaps at Mercer University. In the years during which this was done, some 350 or 400 such Confederate soldiers received aid. To say the least, this was a long way ahead of the "New Deal," smacks strongly of socialism, and antedates by several years any pension system in the State of Georgia. Not so bad for the ex-slaves and the "Scalawags."

## CHAPTER VIII
## The County Site

IN 1851, A POST OFFICE was established at the cross-roads near the center of what is now Moultrie, and named "Ocklockney." Of course, this was in Thomas County at the time, and when Colquitt was created, "Ocklockney" then became a post office in Colquitt County, and so remained until 1857, when the name was changed to Moultrie, a name which the post office and the town has retained until now, and of course will to the end of time. Doubtless the idea of change originated with Darling Creed, native of South Carolina.

The county site came near being located right on the east bank of the Ochlochnee River, and both sides of the Moultrie and Camilla road. In fact, the justices of the Inferior Court were on the point of buying fifty acres at that point, comprising at least a portion of the present property of the Moultrie Cotton Mills, from a Mrs. Bryan, when A. C. Butts, of Bibb County, Georgia, who owned property in the vicinity, made a deed of gift to a tract of fifty acres to the justices of the Inferior Court, for the location of its public buildings, and for sale for the benefit of the county. This was in 1859. The gift was accepted, and the new town was made the county site by the justices of the Inferior Court.

William Moultrie was born in the State of South Carolina in 1731. He was a captain in the South Carolina militia before the Revolution, his commission being dated in 1761. In 1775 he was a member of the South Carolina "Provincial Congress"; and in the same year, was made a colonel in the South Carolina militia.

In 1776, he erected a fort of palmetto logs and sand, on Sullivan's Island in Charleston harbor. This he did against the advice of his superiors, who told him it would never stand up against a bombardment. "Well, if they knock it down, we'll roll up behind the wreck; and still prevent them from landing troops," said Moultrie.

It did stand up against a bombardment of three days by the fleet of Admiral Sir Peter Parker. When a cannon ball would strike it, the soft logs and sand would absorb it, and there was no knocking down of the walls. We read all about it in a copy of "The Southern Reader," which bore all the marks of great age, when we were a boy. It sounded good to us—an American backwoodsman, ignorant of military tactics, whipping the hound out of a member of the British peerage, sporting so high-sounding a name as "Admiral Sir Peter Parker."

Seriously, our own personal opinion is that the name of Colquitt's county site was an inspiration.

The general post office directory shows a Moultrie in Ohio, and another in Florida. Which is good; but we think that Major-General William Moultrie's namesake in Georgia will, next after his construction of a fort of palmetto logs, be his best claim on immortality. There is "something in a name," after all. "Give a dog a bad name, and kill him," runs the adage; and, if this be true, then it is equally true that it works no injury to dogs or towns to name them well.

The Continental Congress formally thanked Colonel Moultrie for his palmetto log fort. He was a Major-General at the end of the Revolution; and was twice elected Governor of South Carolina. He died in 1805.

In 1873, Jane Fowler, an unmarried half-sister of Robt. Bearden, came to Moultrie to live with the Beardens, but did not remain long, for the reason, as rumor has it, that she and Aunt Sally Bearden did not get along in perfect concord. So a man named Billy Holt hired Miss Fowler to go out and stay at his home which was afterwards known as the "Joe Norman place" on the Moultrie and Sumner public road, and stay with his wife, it being necessary for him to be much absent from home to attend his extensive holdings of cattle and sheep.

Mr. Holt was accustomed, when he came to Moultrie, to ride a spirited horse, which he would put into a brisk gallop as he came into the town from the north. One morning, Miss Fowler put a sidesaddle on this horse, and rode it into Moultrie. As she came down the hill north of the present site of the present A. B. and C. Depot, she lost control of the horse, which ran away and dashed down West Broad or Main Street till it came to the courthouse square. There was no fence around the square, and so the horse ran into the west side of the square and into a chinaberry tree which stood near the present site of the Confederate monument, where it whirled suddenly, and throwing Miss Fowler around the tree-trunk, killed her instantly.

Robert Bearden was Moultrie's first merchant. As best we can learn, he came to Moultrie with his wife, "Aunt Sally," from Thomasville, about 1856, the birth year of the county. Of course, this was before there was any Moultrie, but the story goes that this couple drove up from Thomasville in a one-horse wagon; and that a Mr. Sheffield, a merchant of Thomasville, staked them with a small stock of goods—perhaps was a partner in the enterprise himself at first. John Sheffield of Americus, staked the Beardens for many years. The census of 1860 shows that both the Beardens were born in South Carolina.

So the Beardens put up a storeroom on the present site of the Moultrie Banking Company, which fronted south, being at the intersection of North Broad Street and West Broad Street—now at the northeast intersection of Central Avenue and Main Street. To the north of this storeroom were some rooms, which furnished a bar, and a big dining room. Still further north were other rooms containing beds for rent. Aunt Sally was a famous cook, and her praises have rung down the grooves of time, as they were sounded by her customers, until this good hour. Since the Beardens' establishment was really an inn, and sold drinks; and since in those days, the men frequently took "appetizers" just before sitting down to a meal, it is just possible that this circumstance influenced their appreciation of Aunt Sally's cookery.

However, we are not disposed to discount her art or its praises, as they come down to us from the remote past. In truth, our mouth waters at mention of the "chicken cooked with red rice and seasoned with butter and a little pepper and salt; green field peas with raw onions and green peppers, served with corn bread. Also served with coffee or both kinds of milk. Dessert: sweet potato custard."

The Beardens having bought out the interest of partner Sheffield, commenced life work on their own and became

"Two souls with but a single thought,
Two hearts that beat as one."

For more than thirty years, Aunt Sally, in addition to her culinary and household duties, could handle a customer in the store or inn, as well as her husband. Neither had any foolish extravagances—like helping the poor, giving to the church, or contributing to the missionary fund.

As the nearest trading points were at least thirty miles away, the Beardens had a monopoly, and so put on the traffic "all that it would bear." Far from discouraging credit, Bearden extended it freely, since it gave him a chance to charge exorbitant prices with a better face. His only diversion was fishing and hunting, in which Job Turner and John Tucker were his boon companions; but when he had accumulated a big account against each of these men, he didn't

## HISTORY OF COLQUITT COUNTY

hesitate a moment to sue his claims to judgment and levy his executions. And this was his invariable custom; notwithstanding the fact that he put prices on his wares the highest of which we have any account. Shoes of the coarsest grade at $6 per pair; coffee at 50c per pound, raw; meal at 50c per peck; and flour at $18 per barrel; and whiskey at $2 per gallon, although it could easily be made for 25c a gallon then, as well as now. The only contribution that the Beardens made to the welfare or progress of the human race, during their sojourn in Moultrie was Aunt Sally's cooking.

Along about 1892, the Beardens sold their stock of goods to Millsap and McPhaul; deeded away their property to the highest bidder for cash; and, taking the $150,000 that they had accumulated during their stay in Colquitt, they moved back to Thomasville, where Bearden soon died. Immediately a perfect swarm of elderly gentlemen, widowers and bachelors, began to fly around Aunt Sally, every one of them swearing to his undying love for her, based on her personal charms alone; but that bereft lady was adamant to their impetuous appeals till old Jack Alford, from up Poulan, appeared on the scene; and such was the witchery and potency of his "line" that in no time he had scattered his rivals, and took the memorable trip over the broom, a-holding Aunt Sally's hand. In about two years more, Aunt Sally lay down and died, leaving lover-Jack with nothing in the world to console himself for his bereavement except the little old $150,000 which he, under the Florida inheritance laws, took in its entirety, there being no inheritance tax foolishness in those halcyon days. Lover-Jack, too, has passed on, they tell us, having lost in some wild-cat scheme a considerable portion of the $150,000, and we have not thought it worth while to try to trace the remainder.

Moultrie's second merchant was William B. Dukes, already seen as an advertiser in Moultrie's first effort at advertising her resources in a big way. Mr. Dukes was a native of Thomas County, and by 1891, had built up a big general trade at Chastain, down on the Ochlochnee, on the Thomas County line. This was easy, since Chastain was not so far from Thomasville, which was its shipping point. Also, it catered to a big section of Colquitt. It is a fact that Mr. Duke's sales force at Chastain sold as much as $1500 in cash on Saturdays. His salesmen were Henry and Aaron Murphy, Jo. J. and George Battle, and a Mr. Munroe.

When the railroad came to Moultrie in 1893, Mr. Dukes moved his family and merchandise to Moultrie, bringing along his entire set-up of salesmen. He made money from the jump. In 1898, his residence on what is now First Street, S. E., was the most pretentious house in town. It is there yet, opposite the First Methodist Church, and a little south—a two-story frame building. In it lived Mr. Dukes and his family in 1898, and there he continued to live with his family until 1907. During this time, Mrs. Dukes kept boarders in this house. Some of whom will come into this history a little further on.

It will occasion surprise, we think, when we inform the present resident in Moultrie that in June, 1898, there were less than ten trees in Moultrie, four of which were in the street between the present Methodist Church and the front of the Dukes' residence. First Street came to a full stop a little further south, and Mr. Dukes, being a lover of trees and flowers, refused to allow his four pine trees to be removed from the street in front for a long time. On the corner where at present is situated the Methodist Church was a two-story frame building called the "Piney Woods Hotel"—a name possibly derived from the proximity of Mr. Dukes' four pine trees. North of the Methodist Church, and on the sidewalk opposite, being on the north side of Fourth Avenue, stands one of the oldest trees in Moultrie. It is sixty-two years old, a fact which is known from a story that Mr. A. B. Hall, a resident in Moultrie during the past sixty-two years, tells us of his having gone with his mother to this small oak for the purpose of getting some inside bark to be used for some indigestion ailment to which teething children were subject. Another rumor is that a tea made from such bark was a sure cure for digestive troubles sustained by a teething child that had never seen its father.

## CHAPTER IX
## First White Settlers

WE HAVE SEEN that the counties of Lowndes and Thomas were created in 1825 from portions of Decatur and Irwin counties; that the 8th Land District of originally Irwin was finally made a part of Thomas County; and that the 9th Land District of Irwin became a part of Lowndes.

We have also seen that the County of Colquitt, created February 25, 1856, was given the whole of the said 8th Land District of originally Irwin, then Thomas County, along with "all that portion of originally Irwin, then Lowndes County, lying west of Little River to where the river crosses the dividing line between lots of land Nos. 443 and 444, both in the 9th District, thence south to the district line between the 9th and the 12th Districts."

It is extremely difficult to obtain accurate statistics as to the first settlers of this territory comprising the present territory of Colquitt, all of which is included in the cession of land exacted from the Creek and Seminole Indians, in period covered by the years 1814 to 1818, inclusive, which cession, as we have seen was made to the State of Georgia. However, a list of the heads of families in Lowndes County, taken from the U. S. Census of 1830 (see Appendix) contains several names of citizens of that part of Lowndes County that was, twenty-six years later, incorporated into the new County of Colquitt. Some are recognizable as such. For instance the name of Randall Folsom is there; and a matter of three years ago, a Randall Folsom, at the age of ninety, passed away in that portion of Colquitt that was taken from Lowndes by the Colquitt Act of 1856.

Also, in this list of the heads of Lowndes families, made in 1830, appears the name of James M. Norman. We know that the name of this pioneer appears as a Justice of the Peace, in the Lowndes part of Colquitt's territory, as early as 1849. This indicates that he may have resided in the Colquitt part of Lowndes as early as 1830; or it could indicate that, in 1830, he lived in some other part of Lowndes, and, by 1849, had moved to the Colquitt part of Lowndes. In fact, there is a tradition around Nashville, Ga., that Jas. M. Norman moved from Liberty County, Ga., to a farm near Nashville, before 1830, lived there for some time, and then crossed over Little River into the part of Lowndes that came into Colquitt. It is to be remembered that the whole of Berrien County was a part of Lowndes in 1830, and for some years afterwards. All this may be said of Thomas Selph, another name on this 1830 list, as well as of the three listed Tillmans—John, Jeremiah and Joshua.

Finally, there appears in the 1830 list the name of "Henry Tucker," and we think it is entirely likely that this is the same as Colquitt's pioneer, Elder Henry Crawford Tucker, shown by his gravestone, now standing in the graveyard of Bridge Creek Primitive Baptist Church, eight miles west of Moultrie, and on the banks of Bridge Creek, to have been twenty-five years old, when the census of 1830 was taken.

In the Appendix to this book will be found a list of all the heads of families in Thomas County, as they existed in 1840, the list being separated into militia districts, existing at that date. Reference to this shows that Hilery Murphy (Hillary) and David Murphy, headed families in the Thomasville district, in 1840. These men pioneered from North Carolina to Thomas County, between 1830 and 1840, according to family tradition preserved by their descendants now residing in Colquitt County. These two men settled on the line separating the Thomasville district of Thomas County from the 8th

## FIRST WHITE SETTLERS

District of the same county, both finally getting over into the 8th, where they continued to reside until the 8th District was incorporated into Colquitt County. The list of heads of families in the 8th District of Thomas County (Colquitt County, since 1856) will have special interest for the student of Colquitt County's history. In addition to the Gregorys, the Hancocks, the Laniers, the Sloans, the Vicks, the Halls and the Stricklands, all of which names are now known or easily remembered by the average citizen of Colquitt, notice will be had of Henry Murphy, the great-great-uncle of the brothers Henry and Aaron Murphy, at present prominent citizens of Moultrie. We also note that the Henry Tucker appearing in the list of heads of families in Lowndes County in 1830, is listed in 1840 among the heads of families of the 8th Land District of Thomas County, as Henry C. Tucker. Doubtless both are aliases of Elder Henry Crawford Tucker, the Colquitt County patriarch.

In studying the lists of heads of families set out in the 8th Land District of Colquitt County division, we find that James M. Norman has moved, since 1830, from the 9th Land District of Lowndes to the 8th Land District of Thomas. There is no doubt about this, family tradition assures us. It is the same James Mitchell Norman, who lived from about 1845 to 1854 on land lot ...... in the 8th Land District of Colquitt, with his wife, Ruth Tillman Norman, the pair becoming the founders of the county's most noted family.

In the list of heads of families of Thomas County in 1840 will be noticed the name of Artaxerxes B. Norman, a full brother of James M. Norman, both having sprung from North Carolina stock and migrated to Georgia about 1820. It is thought that when the parents of this baby named him after the Persian king, he became the only person in the world called "Artaxerxes." This man had a son named David, whose tombstone is in the Sardis Primitive Baptist Cemetery, who had sons as follows, all of whom have lived in Colquitt: Philip, Moses Xerxes and Virgil, the last two of whom are still alive. A copy of "Plutarch's Lives" must have been lying around two or three generations of this branch of the Norman tribe.

HENRY CRAWFORD TUCKER

Photographs of the Colquitt Pioneers are not easy to obtain. Here is a chance find we picked up of Elder H. Crawford Tucker, born in 1803. He spent most of his life in the Colquitt territory. Married three times, the Elder was. The census-taker in 1860 found him and one of his wives with thirteen children. Probably the second wife.

## CHAPTER X
## The Pioneer Family

SPEAKING OF PRETTY GIRLS and sparking, the girls of the pioneer period were not only easy to look at, according to all accounts, and judging by such daguerreotypes as we have seen; but there was nothing to prevent Nature having her way in the business certain to arise, when youth meets youth. Marriage was both natural and easy. Land was cheap, sometimes selling as low as 25c per acre, and cheap land is essential to the organization of families.

It is a tradition in Colquitt that, when "Uncle Bryant Norman" appeared in the legislature as representative of Colquitt County, and was asked by some one what was the population of Colquitt, he answered, "mostly, beef and taters." The story is perhaps an invention of John Tucker, Norman's fellow citizen, at the time; but, if he did make that reply, he was not far wrong, at that. For cheap lands mean plenty of good solid foodstuffs; and Malthus is our authority for the assurance that a high birth-rate is dependent on a plentiful supply of "good rations." And it is easily demonstrated that a combination of good fat beef and baked yellow yams is about as perfect a food as has ever been in the world. Anyhow, the young folks of the pastoral era married, and were set up for making a living by their parents on a moderate sized piece of land with the necessary household equipment, and the babies came along as fast as the law allowed.

As illustrating this claim, reference is here made to Elder Henry Crawford Tucker, who had already settled in this section in 1830, and who died in the county about 1881. The Elder was married to three wives, who bore him thirty-two children, all of whom he brought to adulthood, and all of whom except one married and reared large families in Colquitt County. The exception was a girl of seventeen, who died from burns received when she fell into a kettle of boiling syrup and figs, which she was tending in the yard at her father's residence. The Elder himself was killed by a runaway horse, when he was still "going good" at eighty-one.

In 1898 Hiram Hancock, a grand-son, by the way, of Elder Tucker, married Emma Strickland, a grand-daughter of James M. Norman, another pioneer of Colquitt. This couple did not have a dime, but they bought some cheap land "on a credit," and went to work. Hiram "muscled out" the payments and got a deed to the land, which, by that time, was worth two or three times the original purchase price. In the meantime, his wife was doing her own work and having a girl baby every two years, and less time. She had eleven of them, one at a time, and died in child-bed with twin boys. The father himself is now dead; but every one of the thirteen children is alive and well, and a self-supporting citizen of Colquitt County.

Berry Hancock, a brother of Hiram, married Ella Strickland, a sister of Emma, and they had, in all, fourteen children, raising ten of them. Jim Strickland, their brother, has seventeen children living, by his two wives. J. R. Edmondson married Florence Strickland, sister to Emma and Ella, and this couple lives in Colquitt County with their eleven children. The parents of all these Stricklands had ten children themselves. Dan Strickland, their uncle, raised seventeen children by his two wives. Steven and Elijah Strickland, cousins of Emma, et al., have eleven children each, by one wife.

Instances of such large families in Colquitt, now and in the past, could be extended till it would make a good-size book. All this seems the more remarkable, when it is considered that, for the most part of the pastoral era, not a soul in the county had ever heard of a screened door or window, a germ, or a vitamin. Since seeing is believing, we close this chapter with a copy of a photograph taken at a family reunion on the occasion of a birthday of Hon. John Tucker. All in this group are descendants of Mr. Tucker, and his wife, Susan, except some elderly people, sitting at his right on the front row. It is put in because it is a good "Beef an' Tater" exhibit.

Hon. John Tucker and his descendants

John Tucker is the man with the big hat, sitting near the center. The woman standing back of him is Susan Jane Tucker.

## CHAPTER XI

## Diversions in the Pastoral Era

IT IS DOUBTFUL if there was a white settler in the territory that is now Colquitt County, before 1820; and it is not known who was the first. In the panel of the first grand jury ever impaneled in Thomas County appears the name of Michael Horne. This was in 1826, the year after Thomas was created. A few years later, a man of this name was living in what is now Colquitt—that is, he was living in the 8th Land District of Thomas County.

Investigation of the Thomas County records does not develop that citizens of the 8th Land District ever held public office in Thomas, willed property, or served on grand juries, although it was a part of the county from 1825 to the creation of Colquitt in 1856—a period of thirty-one years. The same thing may be said of that portion of the 9th Land District of Lowndes County that was incorporated with the 8th Land District of Thomas to make the County of Colquitt.

This condition was due to the fact that the sections that were joined in making Colquitt were remote from the county sites; were without a single foot of railroad; were not in the neighborhood of navigable streams; and had no adequate system of public or private schools; and no system of public roads, except the crude three-path roads of the period. And all these conditions continued after Colquitt was created, and till 1893. It is believed confidently that no such backward conditions existed in any county in Georgia from 1820 to 1893. In addition to these conditions, mail facilities were wretched. One mail delivery per week from such points as Thomasville and Albany; and during half of that time, there was not over one post office in the county.

## DIVERSIONS IN THE PASTORAL ERA

All this resulted in a curious thing: there was an actual falling off in literacy and culture. For illustration, the original settlers could, as a rule, read and write, having come from sections that maintained schools of some sort, but as a rule, their children could not read and write. These were followed by a third generation, alike illiterate. In preparation of this history, investigation has frequently confirmed this.

Emerson said somewhere that tragedy may lie largely in the eye of the beholder; so it is in order to take stock of some of the assets of life as it was spent in Colquitt County during the seventy years of the pastoral era.

To begin with, it was a hunter's and fisherman's paradise. Flocks of red deer could everywhere be seen, feeding on the wire-grass, cane-shoots and wild oats. "The saddles," as the hind and fore-quarters of venison were called, made good eating, either as fresh meat or as smoked; and the gravy was past all praise. Wild turkeys swarmed over wood and swamp in thousands; besides a wealth of squirrels, rabbits and partridges. A Mr. Jeff Holder, with his wife, a Miss Sheffield, married and set up housekeeping in Early County in the early 1830's. They put up a log house, and made their first crop on deer meat. For bread, they strung up and dried out the "white meat" of wild turkey-breasts, after which they cut it up and beat it into a kind of flour, and kneaded it for bread. After gathering their first crop of corn, they changed to corn bread and hog meat. So the bride told this writer when she was ninety-five. A Mr. D. A. Mashburn, who lived for many years on the old Moultrie-Doerun Road, told this writer, on the day before his death, about the red deer that swarmed in the vicinity of Moultrie, even as late as 1880. "We children doted on the gravy," he said. A pack of dogs were running a deer to the east of Moultrie, in 1881. In a panic, it ran westward squarely across the courthouse square. Seeing crowds on the west side, it whirled and dashed away to the south. As Miles Monk, Sr., was standing to be married, in a Colquitt County yard, in the middle 1860's, a young fawn ran out of the surrounding woods, and stopped between his legs. So goes the tradition, and the accounts of surviving witnesses.

The wild turkey, as is well known to every hunter, is the shyest of all American birds. The pioneer in Colquitt caught them in pens built of sapling logs. After these pens were erected, a ditch or trench was dug from some point outside the pen, extending under one of the sides. Corn or other grain was strewed at the bottom of the trench, all the way under the side; and when the leader of a flock of these birds got to "gobbling up" this bait, he would pass right under the side of the pen to be followed by all the others, as fast as they could enter. Then with heads directed at the open spaces between the poles above the ground they would run around until they were taken out by the trapper. Too, many a fat gobbler has fallen a victim of the gunner huntsman, who had a way of blowing a kind of whistle on a bone, in excellent imitation of the love call of the turkey gobbler to his mate. One living citizen of Colquitt has assured the writer that he has seen his father, David Murphy, former sheriff of this county, shoot more than one wild turkey from his porch, four miles from Moultrie, as late as the 1870's.

The streams of Colquitt County were choked with fish for many years. The older settlers now say that the astonishing thing about it was the number of fish found in the little branches and pools. David Murphy caught them in the Ochlochnee a few miles south of Moultrie, fifty years ago, by the wash-tub full. So aver his sons, Henry Murphy and Aaron Murphy, both well-known citizens of Moultrie, today. Their mother, so they assert, when she decided she wanted fish to eat, simply stepped down to the Ochlochnee from

## DIVERSIONS IN THE PASTORAL ERA 65

their nearby residence, and caught a "mess," with pole and line. Other streams like Little River on the east, and creeks like Bridge Creek, the Warrior, Big Indian, Little Indian and the Ocapilco, were jammed full of fish. This condition furnished an easily obtained and toothsome food; and also much diversion, when an entire family, either in a separate group or in groups of other families, fished and picnicked, cooking the catch by the side of the streams by frying the fish in plenty of hot grease, with an occasional rasher of the smoked bacon of the period thrown in; and all served with black coffee and corn pone. It is here confidently asserted that a world which furnishes such experiences is not an altogether bad place in which to do a little sojourning.

Here is a list of varieties of what the poet would call "the finny tribe" that swam the streams of Colquitt, in the days of old: trout, blue bream, red-breast perch, jack, red-horse sucker, blue cat, channel cat, red-finned pike, warmouth perch. Every one of the above varieties made eating fit for Lucullus's banquets, given to kings; but the red-finned pike, according to judgment of veteran fishermen, seems to have had it on all the others, having no bones except the backbone. However, the warmouth perch was perhaps the most popular fish, being plentiful that way, and sometimes so large as to make "more than a meal" for a single person.

And all these different kinds of fish are fairly plentiful in Colquitt streams, even at this late date; and there is no doubt that the stock could be so conserved that they would always be sufficient in numbers to make it possible to go fishing with hook and line, and come in with "a good mess of fish" for an ordinary family. Something should be done to protect our fish and wild life. Liming and other poisoning of our fish streams and lakes, which is now violative of our State law, should be swiftly and sharply punished. Moreover, it might be a good thing to condemn or purchase whatever swamp lands are available for fishing and hunting preserves, and place it under the care of wardens; so as to preserve for posterity a part, at least, of the hunting and fishing privileges of by-gone days.

## CHAPTER XII

# Education in the Pastoral Era

THERE WERE NO SCHOOLS in Colquitt County before the Civil War. At least, we have been able to hear of none. This, for the reason that there was no free school system in Georgia, anywhere, and the only schools at all were subscription schools, entirely dependent, for the teacher's salary, on tuition fees, paid by the parents and guardians of the pupils. Of course, there were none of these in Colquitt County, due to the scattered nature of the population. For these reasons, the children that came into existence during the pastoral era, very generally grew up illiterates, as did their children also, and sometimes, their grandchildren.

The first school we have been able to get an account of was a three-months term of a subscription school, taught by a Mr. Breeton, in 1866. It ran for three months and was held in a single room log residence, standing a little less than four miles north of Moultrie, on the west side of the old Moultrie and Albany public dirt road. Mr. I. McD. Turner, a present resident of Moultrie, has told us all about this school. He was one of the "scholars"; and, in company with his sister, Mary Lizzie, he "footed it" from the residence of his grandfather, Amos Turner, which stood on the present site of the Moultrie Carnegie Library. Two of the girl children of Peter O. Wing came and went with the Turner children. "Cam" Carlton, a daughter of Hardy Carlton, who lived in the Elijah English house, something like a mile on the Moultrie side of the schoolhouse, was a pupil, being about ten years old. Also, Nancy Tucker was there, being about eighteen years old, and the daughter of George Tucker, and a granddaughter of Elder Crawford Tucker, the patriarch, the prettiest girl in the school, Mr. Turner confidently avers, after seventy years. Of course, "'Twas ever thus, from childhood's hour"—a ten-year-old boy like Mr. Turner always gets interested in a grown "gal," his "hopeless fancy feigning kisses on lips that are for others." Two years later, Miss Nancy married John T. Register. We have seen her when she was a grandmother; and so make no doubt that the boy, I. McD., was a good picker. John T. Register was himself a handsome man; and their children were a good-looking lot.

O. N. Gregory's children came from a point north of the schoolhouse near what is now known as Schley, three or four miles away. The sister, Lizzie Turner, was to grow up and marry John Crosby.

Daniel Highsmith sent one or two pupils, and with them came Henry and Hiram Gay, all from the neighborhood of "New Elm," now so called.

Teacher Breeton whipped 'em when they did not "know their lessons," as Mr. Turner stands ready to vouch, having taken at least one in the palm of his hand.

There was only one room, and the boys and the girls occupied straight benches without backs on opposite sides of the room. At such times as "recess," or at the dinner hour, they played in separate playgrounds. No co-ed foolishness was tolerated by Master Breeton. None that could be avoided, certainly.

The favorite game among the boys was "deer-and-dog," one that is still played; but one that was closer to life at Master Breeton's school. There were plenty of gall-berry thickets in which a deer could conceal himself, when the pack of dogs would be unleashed; and the hunters would urge them on till the deer was "jumped." This was followed by the biggest kind of a race. If the deer was caught, the game

## EDUCATION IN THE PASTORAL ERA

was ended, after a little rough handling. It was over, too, if and when the deer was "shot." The guns were hollow joints of elder, or sections of reeds. The bullets were various berries, such as dogwood, forced out of the gun by compressed air.

Well, all this has been a long time ago. Gone, and about forgotten is Mr. Breeton; and gone, and in process of being forgotten, most of his scholars.

Eleven years later, Hon. G. W. Newton, with us now, went to a school kept by Judge A. D. Patterson, over near Norman Park. Mr. Newton was about ten years old. A bench full of little country boys spied a nice green lizard "lifting and listening," on a log of the schoolhouse, and got to laughing, which, teacher Patterson seeing, punished by making the boys stand in a row in the middle of the schoolroom—each standing on one foot. All the boys grinned a little, except Billy, who cried.

At that, and at everything else, G. W. N. relates that Patterson was a "good teacher," and that the scholars increased their stock of learning considerably—learned more, he thinks, than the children do nowadays, when there is so much to divert their minds from their studies. Mr. Patterson's school term was either two or three months, and it was one of the first free schools in the county. The first task in writing was to draw "free-handedly," a straight line. Norman Junior College stands on the site of Master Patterson's school, and there are three or four modern consolidated schools surrounding this spot.

## CHAPTER XIII
## Women in the Pastoral Era

FROM WHAT HAS BEEN SAID about the work of the pioneers in southwest Georgia, and especially in the Colquitt territory, conclusion will be arrived at without trouble that the struggle for the necessities of life drove very few of the men to the lunatic asylums, or the grave. In fact, the matter reads like the section was a lazy man's paradise. There was always present the greatest abundance of wild game and fish. The patchy crops and gardens added to the milk and butter and the beef and mutton taken out of their herds, settled the business of sustenance for themselves and their families, leaving nothing for them to do except to keep up with their hunting and fishing.

A little otherwise as to the housewives. There was plenty of work for them. Theirs was the task of bearing, nursing and feeding the children; and, in addition, they cooked the food for the entire family, including the hired help, if any. Finally, they made much of the clothing for the family with their own hands out of cloth which they wove with yarn which they spun. We are informed by Mrs. M. M. Marchant, who still survives the old days with her husband, that her mother, Mrs. John Nelson Phillips, the wife of a pioneer in northwest Colquitt, did all these things; and, in addition, manufactured a nice supply of table and bed linen. And this was the rule in the homes of that early period.

Cooking was done in skillets and pots, set on log fires in the fireplaces, or in crannies in the jambs. Sometimes, the cooking vessels were placed on beds of coals on the hearths, and at other times, suspended over revolving cranes over the wood fires. A place on the hot hearth rock was frequently

## WOMEN IN THE PASTORAL ERA    71

swept free of ashes, and a dough made from corn meal, seasoned with a little salt, was placed on it and cooked, being turned over once in the process. Very frequently, such "johnnycakes" were spread on hot metal plates and stood in front of the fire with the dough exposed to the fire as near at right angles as possible. Sweet potatoes were baked in convenient vessels over such fires and in numerous cases they were roasted in the hot ashes which would accumulate in the ash-pan under the fire, during the course of the day. Both these, and the "johnnycakes" made pretty good eating, when used in connection with homemade butter and either buttermilk or sweet milk. Not long ago, the grave of a woman who died at near eighty years of age was pointed out to us by an aged citizen of Colquitt, who summed up her fitness to live by saying, "She, for fifty years that I knew her, cooked the best corn bread in the world."

Lucifer matches were expensive in those days, coming in thirties, incased in round wooden boxes, the length of the match, which, with the contents, cost ten cents. So very generally, fire was "kept" in the fireplaces by covering up the burning chunks and faggot ends in ashes at bedtime.

During the first fifty years after the Jackson cession, the use of gourds was general, as receptacles for water, lard, tallow, syrup, sugar, milk and other articles. Hence the excellent note that sounds out of that era as a part of the ballads, exulting in "meat in the smokehouse, and sugar in the gourd." Gourds were grown that would hold as much as two gallons, and which being broad-based, would stand firmly alone on the base in the middle of the flowering end, which was exactly opposite to the straight handle. This handle, attached to a considerable portion of the body of the gourd, was cut out and used as a covering for the vessel part of the gourd.

Much smaller gourds, called "simlin gourds," and holding about a pint, were used for pepper, salt and other spices, as well as for individual portions of coffee or milk at the eating table, their long straight handles having been removed. By leaving the handle, and cutting out a good opening at the side of one of these "simlins," a splendid substitute for a dipper was obtained. In fact, there are plenty of us "old-timers" who are firmly convinced that drinking water is more satisfying when ladled out of a cedar bucket with a "simlin" than in any other way. And one of Georgia's later governors, Hon. Joseph M. Brown, kept such a gourd for use in the reception room of the executive offices, during the whole of his administration. The truth would appear to be that the poet who immortalized the "Old Oaken Bucket" that in his childhood "hung in the well," should have written at least a verse or two as a tribute to the "simlin dipper" that hung on a nail on the wall by the side of the cedar bucket.

We have already said that the housewife was the original textile manufacturer in this section, and this is how. Cotton was carded on a pair of hand cards, flakes of the raw cotton being first placed between the two cards, and by pulling the two cards against each other, the cotton became evenly distributed on the face of the bottom card. Then, by bringing the empty card over the face of the bottom card, the entire spread of cotton was rolled off deftly. A bundle of such "rolls" was then placed near a spinning wheel, which was manipulated by one hand, while the roll was drawn out by the other, the result being a thread, some five or six feet long, which was wound back on the spindle by the simple process of putting the drive wheel into reverse. Another roll would then be attached to the end of the length of yarn, and, in its turn, would be converted into yarn; and so on indefinitely.

A part of such spun yarn would be stretched in looms, worked by the feet of the weaver, operating treadles, this yarn being called the "warp," while a coarser yarn was carried at right angles to the warp in shuttles, by hand, this coarser yarn being called the "woof" or "filling." After about a generation from 1820, cotton factories were erected in the hill sections of Georgia and the Carolinas, and these turned out yarns for warp, of uniform sizes, which were sold at retail in the country stores of Colquitt County, and in fact, all over the State. This yarn came in "bunches" of four pounds each, and cost the housewife a dollar. In the meantime, the "filling" continued to be largely carded out and spun at home. All the above, of course, applies to cotton cloth. The housewife also made woolen "jeans" and linseys, cloths in which woolen yarn was woven into cotton warp. No hand cards could change the raw wool into rolls; and so "wool-carders" were erected at various points in the rural South, which were driven by water power; and the rolls so produced were carried to the farm houses, and spun into filling like the cotton rolls, to be used in making winter clothing. At least two sets of wool cards were operated in Colquitt County—one before the Civil War, near the old "Brick Church," eight miles southwest of Moultrie; and the other on the Ochlochnee River, three or four miles above Moultrie, at a point where is now located the swimming pool and pleasure resort of the Swift and Company Moultrie plant. Others there were in Berrien, Cook and Worth counties; but the two mentioned as being in Colquitt County constituted the beginning of the textile industry in this section. Also, at the "Brick Church," there was erected before the Civil War, by Joel Graves, a factory for making buckets and tubs from sycamore boards. "The bucket shop," it was called locally. While on the subject of cloth making, it ought to be said that for the most part, colors in the household in the early days were derived from certain weeds and shrubs, such as sumac. A nice brown for jeans was obtained from a dye derived from black walnut hulls. The average mother of those days carefully trained her girls in the domestic arts, doing this, in most cases, so that she could avail herself of her daughter's assistance in raising the younger children.

And, by the way, it is in such domestic duties and scenes that romance flourishes. Guided by an instinctive notion that this is true, the girl of that period did not hesitate to exhibit to her young man friend the products of her skillful hands, including a brave display of quilts and counterpanes, along with entire meals of victuals prepared by her exclusively. And it is here asserted with entire confidence that a pretty girl never appears to better advantage to men than when she is engaged in the discharge of such domestic duties. Maud Muller, as every one knows, came near landing her "judge" as it was; and to us it seems a certainty that she would have gotten him for life, had he chanced on her in the kitchen, with her sleeves rolled up, and flour on her elbows.

## CHAPTER XIV
## A Friendly Custom

For some sixty years after the opening of the Jackson cession to white settlement, and the organization of this territory into counties and militia districts, there were contests or fights between individuals at the Justice Courts and other gatherings; and naturally this resulted in the evolution of "champion fighters," for such subdivisions. Just "fist and skull" fights, with no holds barred. The truth is that, as Judge Longstreet has told us in his "Georgia Scenes," this custom was state-wide.

In a few years after the close of the Civil War, John Sloan, who lived on the present site of the Country Club, in southwest Moultrie, was considered Colquitt County's champion fisticuffer; and as such, had been invested with "The Belt." Finally, there moved to east Colquitt, from some point in Alabama, a man named Ab Nolan, who had been something of a fighter, where he came from. One Saturday, Nolan had come to Moultrie and bought some groceries. Additionally, it is just possible that he was slightly "lit up." He was about to go home, when someone called his attention to Sloan, and his record as a fighter. Ab decided on immediate action: and so he drove over to Sloan's house, called him out and told him that he had heard that he had "The Belt," and that he wanted to contest for it, then and there. Sloan instantly agreed; and they pulled off their coats, and went at it. Soon, Nolan had Sloan down, and was romping on him in great shape, when Mrs. Sloan came out of the house. Now, Mrs. Sloan's policy had always been never to suffer her man to be abused by anyone except herself; so she ran in the house, got the shotgun, and was in the act of drawing a bead on her husband's tormentor, when Nolan, seeing her, got up and ran off, leaving, not only "The Belt," but also his next week's groceries, and his coat.

Away back before the Civil War, when Uncle Dick Norman was sparking his pretty neighbor, Miss Fariba Tillman, he attended a dancing party one night, where his Dulcinea was in attendance.

Also, a champion fighter of the Tallokas District, in Brooks County, was there, with his second; and being one of the young folks present, he was in no time turning the corners with "Firby," which Uncle Dick coming in, saw, with a distinct sense of dissatisfaction; and so, when the set was danced out, he approached his rival, and asked him to step out doors with him for a minute. When they were on the outside, Uncle Dick explained, "I want you to fight me—you have danced with 'Firby,' and she is my girl."

"Alright," said the man, "I didn't know she was yours; but come on a little piece down the road. This is my second. Have you a second?"

Uncle Dick called his brother Joel; and so down the road they went, as friendly as anyone ever saw. When they got a proper distance, the man stopped, drew out a bottle, and said, "Gentlemen, suppose we take a little drink before the fight."

This little amenity having been properly attended to, the Tallokas man said to the seconds, "Now, gentlemen, it is understood that no holds are barred, and no weapons except fists and hands are to be used. If one of us should get the other one down, the top man is not to be pulled off, till the bottom man hollers. Is this agreed to by everybody?"

About this time, Uncle Dick, who had some considerable local reputation as a fighter, but who at that particular time

## A FRIENDLY CUSTOM

was getting more and more disposed to take a less war-like view of things in general, said, "Hold on there a minute. It's awful to think about a fellow being under there, when he might not be able to holler, and nobody know it; and so I think we had better take another little drink apiece, and drap this matter, and go back to the house."

Which was done without protest; they went back, and Uncle Dick danced the next set with "Firby"; and spent more than fifty years afterwards in her agreeable society.

The fights we have spoken of hereinbefore were in a way local social institutions. Differing from them slightly are the following:

Another famous fighter in Colquitt was Henry Gregory, who lived up towards Worth County, and who, so to speak, was born fighting. He was talked of as a fighter when we first came to Colquitt, although he had gone from Colquitt never to return. John M. Norman, oldest son of Uncle Joe Norman, used to regale us with the story of how "Griggory" went to Albany once, back in the eighties, and ran berserker. The first policeman that tackled him went down, which another seeing, ran up, and went down in his turn beneath "Griggory's" terrible fist; and it was not long before he had half of the force *hors du combat*. However, one man can't be expected to fight an entire police force—at least not out of the books—and so they finally reduced him, and put him in the calaboose.

Next morning he came before the recorder in due form, and John M. and some other Colquitt County friends were there to watch for an opening to help. John M. said the policemen, every one of them, seemed to have the warmest admiration for the fallen Samson from Colquitt. They spoke up and told the judge that he "fout fair" with his two fists alone, and that it was a fine fight." The judge gave him thirty days or $75. John said that "Griggory" was confused, and looked at the judge helplessly, and asked him if there wasn't a fine connected with the sentence; and how much, and that he seemed much relieved when the judge said, benevolently, "Yes—seventy-five."

Gregory lived about four miles from J. J. Norman, the father of John M. and Spencer Norman. Spencer told us that one night Gregory was at a dance at the residence of James Frazier, not far from the J. J. Norman residence; and that three good-sized men plotted together, while they were out in the yard, to beat him up; and that they sent a man into the dance room, who approached Gregory, and told him that the three men, naming them, wanted to see him in the yard. Gregory understood the meaning of the request perfectly; but he instantly said, "Alright—I'll come right now." Which he did, and the three commenced on him at once. So Henry squared himself and commenced knocking them down; and when they would get up, he followed the excellent procedure of knocking them down again; and when he had finally grounded two of them to stay, the third one ran up behind him and cut Henry several times in the back before he was knocked down. So Mrs. Frazier got him in the kitchen and washed the blood off him and then he walked home, which must have been four miles.

"The next day," says Spencer, "he came over to our house, and was telling Pa about it: 'You know, Mr. Norman,' he said, 'that was the worst fight I have ever had in my life. You see, three is really too many to fight at one time. When you are at work on one in front of you, another will slip up at your side, and maybe the third one will be doing something to your back. And so a man is kept busy a-whirlin' around.'"

Another man of tremendous strength in the nineties was Bob Register. His mother was Nancy Tucker, who was the daughter of George Tucker, and the granddaughter of Elder Crawford Tucker.

Jim Monk once regaled Mayo Kendall, Jack Strickland and this writer with an account of Bob Register's prowess:

"It was at a dance one night, at old man Bill Key's, and I was standing by Bitha Key, waiting for the music to commence, so as to dance the next set with her. Just then, Bob Register come in at the door. He was engaged to Bitha; and so when he saw us, he made for me. I backed off a little, and got ready for him; and in the meantime, the other boys commenced running in between us. Bob commenced knocking 'em down. He used both fists, and so made two piles of 'em. Finally, Bitha's Pa ran in, and Bob fetched him an uppercut, which sent him through the open door, going out at the top of the door." Just here, Jack Strickland took up the story, saying:

"Yes, I was out there in the yard with a crowd that was around a fire which had been built out there; and when old Bill dropped down out of the elements, it liked to a-scared us all to death; and old man Bryant, who was crippled in one leg, saw him drap down into the fire, he run around the end of the house into the clay-hole that they had made when they were digging up clay to daub a stick-and-dirt chimney. It hadn't been there long, and was full of water, and we had to pull him out, or he would uv drownded, maybe."

After this had had time to soak in, Jack said, reminiscently, "Bob Register was an awful man; and I have wished that he could have lived later, and got into the boxing business. I saw Sam Gay drive up to Pa's once, in a buggy, and Bob was in the yard. They seemed to have been at outs with each other just then, and so just as soon as Sam got out of the buggy, he went for Bob, and they went at it. I really never saw such fighting in all my life; it was like mules a-kickin'. Sam was much of a man himself, in them days; and so he kept goin' up inter Bob's face for it; and finally he got it, and went down. But it was pretty while it lasted. I doubt if any of the younger generation will ever see anything like it. They have quit makin' 'em like Bob and Sam, long ago."

## CHAPTER XV

## Early Occupations

From 1820 to 1890, the raising of cattle, sheep and hogs was the principal industry in the Colquitt territory. As a preliminary to success in this industry, it was necessary at first to exterminate the wolves with which this, as well as all other sections of the country, was infested. These wild dogs ran, hunted and fed in packs; pulling down even grown sheep, together with calves and pigs. The difference in wolves and ordinary dogs was found in their gregarious habits, and in the fact that the eyes of dogs are round, while the eyes of the wolf are elongated ovals. The first problem of the pioneer has always been to get rid of the wolves. For the most part, this was accomplished by constructing "wolf-pens," or "wolf-pits." And here is how: A big pit was dug, some ten feet in diameter, and some six feet deep. It was then covered by a camouflage of a light nature, above which, in the middle, arose a firmly planted stake, to which, at its top, was fastened firmly a good size chunk of raw meat. The wolves would lunge at the meat; and, of course, would fall into the pit, and be killed by the owner. Probably, not a county in the United States that did not, at its first settling have some of the pits. Colquitt had three or four, at least. Vagrant packs of wolves, however, made visits to Colquitt as late as the early eighties. About that time, strychnine was put out, along the Warrior Creek; and the wolves came no more.

The early settler in Colquitt was surrounded by nearly 900 square miles of wire grass and wild oats land. Practically none of this extensive area was under fence; but was what was called "commons," over which the cattle, hogs, and sheep "used" at will. Ownership was determined by marks and brands. The "marks" were notchings and croppings made in the ears of the animals; while the "brands" consisted of symbols or initials seared into the hides by impressions of red-hot irons. Each owner was required by law to register with the ordinary his individual mark or brand. And in this way these animals roamed the wilds. A little salt was put out for them by their owners, in the neighborhood of their homes.

As the young were dropped, in the spring, it was the custom for several adjacent live stock owners to take a few days off and drive all the animals within a given area together, and separate the mothers from the others. Then, the new calves would be turned loose, one at a time; and, as each calf would run unerringly to its mother, it would be seized, and put in its mother's mark.

Sheep were herded together in exactly the same way as the cattle, and the ownership of the lambs determined in the manner of the calves. At the same time the adult sheep would all be thrown down on the ground and their wool clipped off by experienced "shearers." Shearers were numerous who could take a pair of shears and clip off the entire covering of wool with one hand, while the animal was kept in position by the other hand. And so a lot of the older residents of Colquitt County understood fully what was meant when the newspapers advertised the fact that the father of the Dionne quintuplets is a professional "sheep shearer."

These Colquitt County herds of cattle went right along with very little feed. Mr. Wesley Weeks, a grandson of a pioneer of Colquitt, told us, the other day, that the rule as to feeding cattle was to approach one with a basket of corn shucks, and threaten it with a single shuck. If, in springing off, the cow fell, she was to have as feed the basket of shucks. If she did not fall, she got no feed at all. Seriously, if the winter was unusually hard, it was necessary to feed some, and it was done. Otherwise practically no feed was given. Of course, the cattle got rather thin, sometimes; but as long as they did not get "on the lift," they were allowed to make it over till the coming of a new crop of grass.

The upkeep of sheep cost just exactly nothing, in the old pioneer days, as sheep were not fed at all. This was due to the fact that a sheep could get along with what he could get on the commons. There were more things on the menu of a sheep which were accessible on the commons; and, too, sheep were not called on to eat for the purpose of keeping themselves warm.

The weight of the fleece of an ordinary sheep would run from two to three pounds; and the price for the entire fleece would average one dollar. This means that the owner of a thousand sheep had an assured income of one thousand dollars per annum. Practically every head of a family had some sheep; and we know of numerous flocks that ran from two hundred to one thousand. James T. Norman ("Sonny") was the owner of the rise of two thousand. As there was no danger of the wool crop deteriorating, this was a good business, and it brought in nice money.

Of course, too, there was nice money in cattle. Annually, there was a considerable percentage of the herd that was cut out for sale as beef cattle. These were herded together and driven to Columbus, or some other river or gulf port to be there sold to local dealers, and by them shipped alive to the West Indies. Hides were also things that found ready sale, as they have since the days of Abraham.

Of course, the average herd furnished plenty of milk and butter, during the spring and summer season; and, in the winter, some of the best milkers were kept up, and fed, in order to guarantee a supply of milk. Sometimes, the "busy housewife" made cheese and sent it to market, along with other commodities; but cheese and butter making was never anything except "the women's business," which at times brought in a little pin money.

Some of the pioneers butchered for home use as many as three to five beeves a week. It is to be understood in this connection that the range cows did not grow to be as big as those now butchered by the big packing houses, and which are fed on the farms of the northwest.

## CHAPTER XVI
# A Notable Wedding

THE COURTHOUSE of Colquitt County was destroyed by fire in 1881, with practically all the records kept therein. However, in a small black book in the present ordinary's office may be found a record showing that on the 14th day of October, 1873, Henry Gay, ordinary of Colquitt County, issued a marriage license to James T. Norman and Susan Jane Tucker. This license was returned into that office with a showing at the bottom that the ceremony was performed on the 23rd day of October, 1873.

Susan Jane Tucker was the oldest child of John Tucker, oldest son of Elder Crawford Tucker, already referred to in this book, and his wife Susan A. Stevenson. This same Susan A. S. Tucker was one of the notable women of Colquitt County, as demonstrated by the character of children that she turned into the body of the citizenship, numbering ten. We shall meet her further on in this book.

The father of the bride was a conspicuous leader in Colquitt, in 1873. He was the son of Elder Crawford Tucker, Colquitt County pioneer and patriarch. He was the owner of forty-three lots of Colquitt County land, each containing 490 acres, more or less; and his holdings of live stock were of greater value than his lands. He served as Colquitt's representative in the General Assembly of Georgia, at the sessions of 1873-4. He was accordingly the most important man in Colquitt County; and he was "feeling his oats."

James T. Norman, the bridegroom, known by his intimates as "Sonny," was the oldest son of Jeremiah Bryant Norman, who was one of the seven sons of James Mitchell Norman and Ruth Tillman Norman, who came to Colquitt County about the same time that Elder Tucker arrived. J. B. Norman, Sr., was himself the owner of much land and live stock; was politically inclined, and was going to represent Colquitt in the House of Representatives of Georgia more than once before his death.

For all these reasons, John Tucker decided to give Susan Jane a wedding that would set up an all-time record in Colquitt.

There were no such things as engraved invitations, innocent of initials, and spelling out each name in full; but messengers on horseback carried a most cordial invitation by word of mouth to every family in Colquitt to come to Susan Jane's wedding.

And, according to all accounts, they responded to the invitation, from Little River to the Mitchell County line, and from the Worth boundary straight south to Thomas. They came in families, the busy housewife bringing along her "numerous brood," and grandma with her snuff. Twelve hundred guests, according to the stories related to us in the present year, by Messrs. J. A. Owens, Dan J. Strickland, Henry Monk and Linton Hancock, all of whom are now octogenarians, and all of whom were guests.

And from these "Merrie gentlemen" comes a fairly unanimous account of whole carcasses, selected from the flocks and herds of John Tucker, barbecued to a turn, and served with all the "trimmin's." And every one of them, when the subject is mentioned, will immediately speak of coffee cooking in the yard in a 90-gallon syrup kettle, and chicken pilau a-simmering away in another kettle of the same capacity.

The opening rite of weddings, in those old days, was the "charge," a term applied to a procession of horseback riders made up of the unmarried men friends of the contracting parties. This procession rode two abreast, and was headed by the bridegroom, who was flanked on his right by his mounted "waiter," and on the left, by his "torchbearer." Such procession was accustomed to gallop about sundown in middle gear, down the road, straight by the home of the bride, and after getting a mile or so beyond it, they would stop, turn the procession around, and return to her home, in a walk, reaching which, they would stop, and friendly hands connected with the bride's establishment, would take charge of the mounts of the groom and his attendants, and tie them up, while all the other members of the procession would perform that office for themselves. In the meantime, the groom and his flankers, as their mounts were taken away, would go immediately into the yard, and pass through the front door into the "front room," where they would find the bride sitting, and sitting by her her own "waiter" and "torchbearer." There would be plenty of merry talking, of course. The groom and his attendants taking seats by the bride and hers, while torches were being lighted for the "torchbearers." The bride and the groom would then go out into the yard; the waiters would come next, and last would come the "torchbearers." Since there were no electric lights in those days, and since marriages were usually performed at "early candlelight," and since every one present on the whole premises wanted to see the ceremony, and "how the bride looked" on such occasions, the "torchbearers" were a necessary adjunct. We can find several surviving guests, including the ones already listed, who will say that "Sonny's charge had at least seventy-five young couples in it, and both horses and riders made a very brave show indeed."

After the wedding ceremony, the immense feast, prepared for this wedding by the Tuckers was served to the hundreds of guests, the hospitable suggestion made by the host being, "Eat till you bust."

As has been said, the ordinary lighting by tallow candles was quite insufficient for such great gatherings; and so a scaffold was generally erected in front of the house, and on it was spread a good covering of dirt, upon which a big pile of fat "lightwood" was kept blazing, this furnishing abundant light for the dance by the young folks, which invariably followed the close of the wedding rites. And the aforenamed surviving guests assure us that, in relays, the young folks fiddled and danced at Susan Jane's wedding all night long, and

> "When music arose, with its voluptuous swell,
>   Soft eyes looked love to eyes which spake again,
> And all went merry as a marriage bell."

This is written in August, 1936, and so it will soon have been sixty-three years since "Sonny" and Susan Jane got married. Some of our readers will want to know how their marriage turned out. And so, it is a pleasure to say that, by the united testimony of a whole country-side, this couple were ideally happy, every moment of their married life, till "Sonny's" death in 1896, leaving Susan Jane to carry on alone in the rearing of their eleven children. How well she succeeded will be shown in a separate chapter herein, entitled "Noted Colquitt County Women," and for the present, we close the account of the pastoral romance of "Sonny" and Susan Jane by expressing the hope that our unmarried readers may find as much happiness in their marriages as the hero and heroine of this story did in theirs.

CHAPTER XVII

## Colquitt Courts

WHEN COLQUITT COUNTY was created, in 1856, several Justice Courts had been functioning in that area, as follows: Districts Numbers 1151, 799 and 1020, all of which had been established while the area of Colquitt was still parts of Lowndes and Thomas counties. In these courts the Justices of the Peace issued criminal warrants, and held preliminary investigations based on such warrants. They also had jurisdiction to try civil claims not in excess of one hundred dollars. Too, they drew deeds, mortgages and other legal documents from such forms as were accessible. Also, they performed marriage rites; and, what was not the least of their doings, they gave free advice in many a local trouble among the citizenry. In appeals from their own verdicts they presided over juries of five; but were without authority to charge a jury.

On account of a fire that destroyed Colquitt County's courthouse with all records deposited therein, in 1881, little is known of the early Justice Courts. However, Spencer Norman, a grandson of James Mitchell Norman, pioneer settler in the Colquitt territory, has in his possession a small docket of the Justice Court for the 1151st District Justice Court, of Thomas County, which was presided over by him, the same showing some of the business of said court as far back as 1846. The oldest entry of this kind is that of a panel of "juroys," drawn by Judge Norman for the December, 1849, "tirm," of said court. A cut of this portion of the minutes is inserted here:

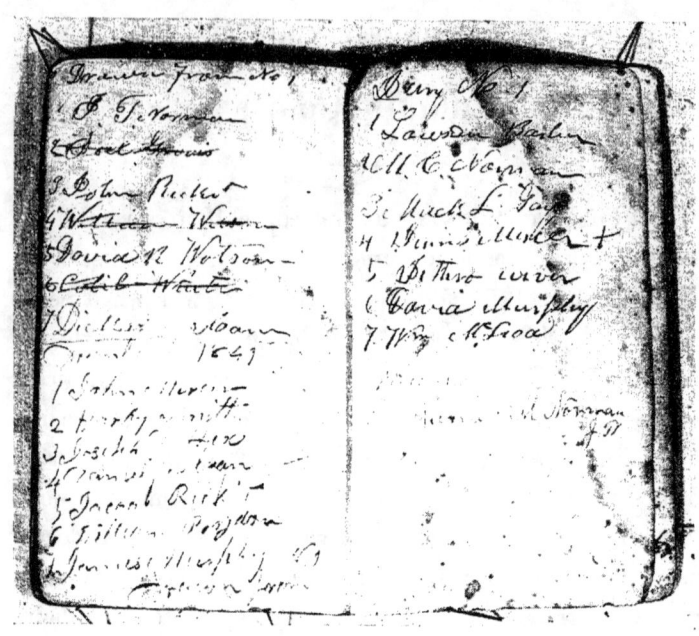

This, beyond doubt, is the oldest existing court record of Colquitt County. We also insert, along with it a record of the "juroys" drawn from Box No. 2, on February 9, 1850. This is done for the purpose of showing the copperplate nature of the handwriting, as well as the excellence of the ink in use by Judge Norman, as it appears after 86 years.

The first "sute" recorded in this docket is that of J. W. Jenkins versus Hardy Carlton, who fails to make any appearance, and so default judgment is taken against him, on April 26, 1862. At the same "tirm," Stewart S. May takes a legal shot at Geo. F. Herndon. Also, at this term, "Absolum Baker," a local capitalist, proceeds against David B. Bland, on a promissory note for $14.50, for which a judgment is taken by "default," "with interest and cost of sute," on January 23, 1863. At the March Term, 1863, Robert Bearden sues James Brown for $28.95, on a promissory note; and takes judgment by default at that term. Judge Norman died in 1864, and thus ended his judicial labors.

One of the extra judicial entries in this little book is a statement of a little account due by the judge himself to "Turner," as follows:

"to one Basin ..............$0.75;
2 sets spones .............. .75;
1 cork scrue .............. .50;
tobacco .............. 1.50;
linnin .............. .75."

In the months of September and October, of a year that is not recorded, Judge Norman gets up some hands, and takes a drove of beef steers, numbering thirty-one, on a long trek, as far north as Culloden and Zebulon, for the purpose of selling them along the way. The little docket contains an itemized statement of expenditures in the way of food and feed, which foots up as follows: "Travelling expence for hands, $24.50"; and "provision expence, $15.36." In "Pindertown," he spent 38c for "spirits"; and at "hockinvile," he spent 15c for the same commodity. He seems to have sold all his herd, at an average of about $10.00 each. An enterprising kind of a man for his day, this same James Mitchell Norman; and this quality has been much in evidence in many of his descendants. The court over which he presided— namely, the Justice Court in and for the 1151st District, G. M., for originally Thomas, and for the past eighty years Colquitt County, Georgia, still functions regularly, Judge John T. Coyle, presiding.

Site where first eight terms of Colquitt Superior Court were held.

The Browning Act, creating the county of Colquitt placed it in the Southern Judicial Circuit; and, by arrangement of the judges of the Inferior Court, the first term of this court was held at what was known at that time as the "Mims House," which was situated on the west side of the old Moultrie and Albany public dirt road, at a point about four miles north of Moultrie, on lot of land No. ........ in the 8th Land District of originally Irwin, then Thomas, and now Colquitt County. This building was originally constructed by George Tucker as a residence; and contemporaries still speak of it as the biggest "Double-Pen" log house ever seen by them. This type of "Colonial Architecture" is fully described in another chapter of this history; and for our present purposes it is sufficient to say that the two rooms were each some twenty-four feet square, and separated by an "entry" whose roof was a part of the roofing system of the two rooms, and whose floor was on an exact level with the flooring of the two rooms. The entry of this house was something like twelve feet in one of its dimensions; and, of course the other dimension was the same as the length of the sides of two rooms. There was therefore ample room for conducting an ordinary term of court.

We think that there is not in life, at the present time, a single participant of the first session of this court, which was held on first Monday in April, 1856. Mr. J. J. Giles, who at that time lived a matter of two miles to the north of the "Mims House," was a youth of fourteen years, or the rise; but, it is doubtful if he went to this term of the court. Hon. N. M. Marchant, now of active mind in the northwest part of the county, knows that his father-in-law, Hon. John Nelson Phillips, who had moved to Colquitt before it was a county, and who has been buried at Cool Springs graveyard, served at this first term of the Superior Court of Colquitt County as a grand juror. Since Colquitt's courthouse with its contents was destroyed by fire in 1881, much interesting historical records were destroyed. We know from records in the archives of Georgia preserved in Atlanta, that Judge

Peter E. Love, judge of the Superior Court of the Southern Circuit, presided at this term, and at the five next succeeding terms, till his resignation, in 1859; and that Honorable Edward Sheftall, solicitor-general of the Southern Circuit, performed the duties of solicitor-general, during the same terms.

Court House from 1881 to 1903

The above-mentioned Mr. Jacob J. Giles, who is still living with us, as he approaches his ninety-fourth year, made a joint contract with Mr. John Bryan to clear the present courthouse square of stumps and litter of various kinds, preparatory to building a permanent courthouse. Messrs. Bryan and Giles were hired by the judges of the Inferior Court to do this work, in the year 1859; and so they went out and cleared off the site, taking out the stumpage of the original long-leaf yellow pines, and burning them. The new courthouse was completed, after the resignation of Judge Love, and so Augustin H. Hansell, a young lawyer of Thomasville, Ga., who had succeeded him in the judgeship of the Southern Circuit, held the first term of the Superior Court in the new courthouse, in the fall of 1860. Hon. Erastus A. Smith, solicitor-general of the Southern Circuit, performed the duties of solicitor-general, at this term.

The "Mims House," used for a place for holding the first terms of Colquitt Superior Court was bought, soon after it ceased to be used for that purpose, by James Frazier, who used it as a residence, while he operated the farm on which George Tucker had originally built it. Frazier and his wife raised their children on this place. All traces of the original log double-pen are gone—no one knows how. However, considering the size of the logs, it is altogether likely that it was destroyed by fire. We present at the close of this chapter a cut of the building now standing on the site of the "Mims House."

The tree is an ancient magnolia planted by Mrs. George Tucker in her yard, nearly a hundred years ago. The photograph was taken in the blossoming season of 1936. The white patches in the foliage are made by the blooms.

Court House from 1903 until now

CHAPTER XVIII

# Colquitt's Early Bench and Bar

THE FOLLOWING is a list of the judges of the Superior Courts of the Southern Circuit in which Colquitt County was placed by the creating Act of 1856, and in which she has remained uninterruptedly until the present:

| | |
|---|---|
| Peter E. Love | 1856-1859 res. |
| Augustin H. Hansell | 1859-1868 |
| John R. Alexander | 1868-1873 |
| Augustin H. Hansell | 1873-1903 |
| Robert G. Mitchell | 1903-1910 res. |
| Joseph Hansell Merrill | 1910-1911 |
| William E. Thomas | 1911- |

The following is a list of the solicitors-general of the Southern Circuit, from February 25, 1856, when Colquitt County was created, and placed in the Southern Circuit, to the present:

| | |
|---|---|
| Edward T. Sheftall | 1856-1859 res. |
| Erastus A. Smith | 1859 |
| Samuel B. Spencer | 1859-1867 |
| William B. Bennet | 1867-1873 |
| Robert G. Mitchell | 1873-1884 res. |
| D. L. Gaulden | 1884-1885 |
| Daniel W. Rountree | 1885-1890 res. |
| John R. Slater | 1890-1892 died |
| Henry B. Peeples | 1892-1896 res. |
| J. L. Hall | 1896-1897 |
| William E. Thomas | 1897-1911 |
| John A. Wilkes | 1911-1917 |
| Fondren Mitchell | 1917-1918 died |
| Clifford E. Hay | 1918-1929 |

## HISTORY OF COLQUITT COUNTY

G. Clarence Spurlin ........................................1929-1934 died
George R. Lilly..............................................1934-

Colquitt County had only one resident lawyer prior to 1893; and the business of her Superior Courts was transacted by the judges and solicitors-general, assisted by attorneys from surrounding counties. These attorneys rode the Southern Circuit with the presiding judge and the solicitor-general, or such counties in it as furnished them business. For a long time, each county had two terms per year, arranged according to convenience and the necessities of the case.

There was not much business in Colquitt, anyhow, the population being sparse, and living so far apart that they did not irk each other in their contacts. When families lived anywhere from two miles to fifteen miles apart, there was not likely to arise trouble about gardens, chickens and children. Then, too, the necessities of life were too plentiful and too easily obtained for the citizens to give over much attention to property rights.

Some lawyers, however, did come to Colquitt's courts. Here is a partial list of them: The MacIntyres, father and son; R. G. Mitchell, and W. M. Hammond, all from Thomasville; Henry B. Peeples, and J. N. Talley, both from Nashville; W. B. Bennet, Dan Rountree and W. S. Humphreys, from Quitman; and I. A. Bush and C. O. Davis, from Camilla. All these came during the eighties, we know. All got some fees, of course; and all enjoyed practicing under such a judge as Augustin H. Hansell, and coming in contact with each other and with the Colquitt yeomanry. J. N. Talley, in his engaging classic "The Southern Circuit," has described with a poet's affectionate eye, the after-supper gatherings of these choice spirits, in front of Bob Bearden's Inn, which stood exactly where the Moultrie Banking Company's building now stands, at the northeast corner of Main Street and 1st Avenue, N. E. Among other things, Mr. Talley tells us how Judge

Henry Peeples, who had been a member of the Georgia House of Representatives, along with William H. Felton, of Bartow, and Simmons of Sumter, when these two had their celebrated clash over Felton's bill to take away juvenile criminals from the convict lessees—a clash which culminated in Dr. Felton's terrible castigation of Simmons, would, so long as he attended Colquitt Superior Courts, be called on at least once each term, to "take off" for the delectation of his associates, the doctor's devastating philippic. These meetings all happened before our time at Moultrie; but we were the guest of Judge Peeples at Nashville for a few hours in 1900; and he gave us "old Felton's speech against Simmons"; and he never had a more interested auditor; since, when we were only nine years old, we heard the doctor "work on" Judge George N. Lester, his antagonist in a fight over a seat in Congress from the 7th District of Georgia.

C. O. Davis, *sui-generis*, and altogether lovable, was the darling of the lawyers who attended these meetings; and was invariably called on to give an account of his "cause celebre," "The Cripple Niggers versus The Circus." John M. Norman, son of a pioneer, and grandson of two or three more, who had a nose for the humorous, and who made it a habit to sit in with the lawyers at their "after-suppers," at Bearden's, shall tell it for us and for posterity, as C. O. rendered it:

"Well, gentlemen, this here circus had showed at Thomasville, and left there on the rail-road for Albany and points North. They covered a flat-car with niggers, and hitched it to the rear of their train of cars. Over about Pelham, they took a curve too fast, and spilled niggers for a hundred and fifty or two hundred yards, and proceeded possibly without knowing of the accident. These hurt niggers comes up to my office next day, or sends word. I took their names and description of their injuries, and tore off after the show, over-taking it at Americus. I went to DuPont Guerry's office, a young lawyer there, and we fixed up a fist full of attachments, and I went on out to the show-ground and gave them to the Sheriff, and he levied on six Percheron hosses, three leopards, two tigers, and a geraffe. He just about had half of the animals levied on, when the show-man hunted me up, and asked me if I was ready to talk turkey. I told him I might, if he talked right; and in no time, I had settled all these claims with him for a total sum of three thousand dollars. I took the money to Guerry's office, showed it to him, and asked him how much he wanted. He says 'Oh, I don't know, C. O. —would five hundred dollars be too much?'

"I says, 'That's all right, DuPont. Here it is: count it.'

"Well, I took the balance and went back home, got the list of my clients, and sent for 'em. Next morning they were there bright and early, and I began to sort 'em around, according to how bad they was hurt. One nigger with an ear gone, I took as a startin' off basis, and put him down for twenty-five dollars, and then I commenced scalin' 'em up from that, but it was not long before I was out of money, and a whole gang of niggers not paid anything. Of course, you understand, I wasn't actually payin' out anything, but just sorta figgerin' out the situation, so's I'd know how to settle. When I saw I was goin' to run out of money, I says to myself, 'Pshaw! There just aint no nigger's ear worth $25.00'; so I reduced it to $20.00 and started again, with the same result. Well, gentlemen, no honest lawyer ever tried any harder to do the right thing than I did in working with this money, but I found that I could never do right between these people, and so I finally decided that I'd just keep it all myself."

At this point, Captain Hammond would slap the knee of the lawyer sitting most convenient to him, and say, "Gentlemen, that last part of his story is the exact truth!"

On the criminal docket of the Superior Court of Colquitt at the September Term, 1890, John A. Wilkes, a young lawyer who had just come to Moultrie from Nashville and got his first case: A citizen of Colquitt carried a friend around behind the courthouse, for the purpose of giving him a drink. He stopped directly under one of the windows of the grand jury room, squatted on the ground over his satchel to get out his bottle, and in so doing, brought into view a pistol, concealed in the satchel. At least, it was brought into view of two or three members of the grand jury, who happened to be looking out of the window at the time. "D. W. Rountree, solicitor-general," is marked for the State in this case on the docket, and "J. A. Wilkes" is marked for the defendant. Under the circumstances, it would seem to have been a pity for the case to have been pushed too vigorously; and this seems to have been the idea dominating the mind of General Rountree. Anyhow, the case seems never to have been tried.

Once, when Captain W. M. Hammond was speaking to the court and jury, in the defense of some case, and said, "Gentlemen, I think that even the State's evidence shows the innocence of the defendant," Uncle Dick Norman, who was on the jury, said right out loud, and with energy, "Yes, Captain Hammond,—and I think so too."

"The jury will keep quiet," said Judge Hansell, who was presiding.

At the Spring Term, 1893, of Colquitt Superior Court, the case of State versus Henry Gregory was sounded; and the defendant not answering to the call of his name, and the solicitor being about to forfeit the bond, or inquire why Henry had not been arrested, his brother arose and said: "There is no use bothering about this case any further: He is dead: I have a letter here that I'll read you. It is from Henry. He says, 'I am dead; that last spell of cramp colic I had was the worst one I ever had. It killed me.'" Captain W. M. Hammond, who was prosecuting the case, merely said, as he looked over his spectacles, "Is my friend sure of the veracity of the witness?"

John A. Wilkes introduced into his practice a lot of showmanship, for instance, he was representing a Negro schoolteacher whom Solicitor Dan Rountree had indicted for false swearing in connection with his school returns. Dan put a Justice of the Peace on the witness stand, who in response to questions, said: "Yes, that's his signature. Yes, that's my signature as a witness. Yes, he swore to it." John A. took him on cross-examination saying, "Judge, you say he signed this paper?"

"Yes."

"You say he swore to it?"

"Yes."

"Judge, at or before he fixed his signature to this here document, did you have him to place his hand on the Book of the Holy Evangelists of Almighty God, or elevate his right hand to the skies, and take the oath or affirmation that the law requires?"

"No, I didn't do that."

"Come down!" sang John A., and the Negro went out of court a free man.

Well, gone are all these unique spirits now—Judge W. B. Bennet, excellent lawyer and perfect gentleman, who raised four other excellent lawyers and perfect gentlemen, Joe Bennet, Stanley Bennet, Sam Bennet and Matt Bennet; Bill Humphreys, dangerous antagonist before a piney-woods jury; Dan Rountree, who left the Circuit, entered the practice in Atlanta, where he accumulated, it is said, a million dollars, and where he died three or four years ago; I. A. Bush, who was one of two or three lawyers in Georgia who knew all about ejectment law, who practiced law fifty years in a small town, generally taking his fees in land, which grew to be worth a million dollars; C. O. Davis, the friend of man; the Tom MacIntyres, father and son, who made a fortune in the practice at Thomasville; Henry Peeples, the unmatched host; W. M. Hammond, incomparable orator; Robert G. Mitchell, to whom fear was unknown, solicitor-general and judge of the Superior Court—all are gone to "that undiscovered land, from whose bourne no traveler returns."

AUGUST H. HANSELL

CHAPTER XIX

## The Moultrie Bar in the Nineties

As WE WRITE, we have before us a rather pretentious advertisement of Moultrie, gotten out in the year 1895, by Wade Hampton Cooper, the editor of the Moultrie Observer at that time. This advertisement was gotten out a matter of two years after the Georgia Northern Railroad came to Moultrie. Population of the town is claimed to be 1500; and everything booming. We shall have more to say of this ad later. For the present we are content to call attention to the fact that the ad shows that Moultrie had a bar in 1895. Here is the list: H. B. Lester, J. J. Walker, Joseph P. Smith, M. J. Pearsall, R. L. Shipp, J. L. Hall and D. F. Arthur.

There is no other record or account as to Col. Lester. One snap-shot at him on the wing, so to speak, and he is gone.

Our only authority for listing Mr. Arthur among the lawyers is that his name is marked as representing the defendant in the case of the State versus Ellis, on the Criminal Docket of Colquitt Superior Court, at the September Term, 1893. For many years after 1895, his time was devoted to abstracting the titles of Colquitt County lands. It is thought he died some years ago at some point in Florida.

Col. Joseph P. Smith came to this section from up about McDonough, soon after the War Between the States. He was the son of Rev. Melton Smith, and came with his father to this section. The father participated in local politics as a leader of the Reconstructionists. The son will be recalled by many as a member of the legal staff of the Georgia Northern Railway for many years. He was a man of well-furnished

THE MOULTRIE BAR IN THE NINETIES    103

mind, and well grounded in the principles of his profession. He has been dead now, some fifteen years.

J. L. Hall once represented Thomas County in the lower house of the General Assembly of Georgia. He was solicitor-general of the Southern Circuit, serving as such from about April, 1896, to April 1, 1897. Afterwards, he did a general practice in Colquitt, until his health failed him a few years later. He was a man of brilliant mind; and possessed of many of the qualities of leadership. He has been dead now a matter of twenty years. We are under the impression that J. J. Walker (Jack) was Colquitt's first native lawyer. He was a son of Frank Walker, who moved to the "Hempstead District" (Berlin, now), bought land and settled on it sometime about 1892. Frank Walker and his family graded high among their neighbors; and Jack had many friends among both the laiety and his brother members of the bar. Sometime about 1897, he removed to Ocilla, Georgia, where he died about 1915.

By June, 1898, when this writer came to the bar at Moultrie, the pastoral era was giving place to the industrial and farming era. This latter era will be written of in another chapter; and so at present, we are to write about the Moultrie bar as it existed at that time and later, under our knowledge.

Jack Walker, here in 1895, was gone, as was Col. Lester. W. A. Aaron, and one or two others who had come here after 1895, had also gone. The others, J. L. Hall and J. A. Wilkes, had formed a partnership for the practice of law; and on June 2, 1898, the date this writer came here, this firm was doing fairly well, being in charge of the campaign for all county offices which their faction was waging against the "Ins." But it is about the lawyers we should be writing.

Moultrie was by this time a good place for a young lawyer to locate. There was much activity in timbered land, the naval stores business was booming; and Moultrie's ten saloons turned out plenty of criminals. Also, there was plenty of ready cash to pay lawyers' fees, all of which combined to render this the Golden Age for the lawyers. During the four years following 1898, and until the county was made dry by the church people, the practitioner at criminal law was in clover.

And so the lawyers moved in; and practice in the "Big Court" boomed, as it did in the City Court, which was created in 1902, to relieve congested conditions in the Superior Court. Some of the old visiting practitioners died out, or ceased to visit their old haunts in Colquitt. In the first term of the Superior Court (October, 1898), the elder MacIntyre is remembered, as is John G. McCall, of Quitman; I. A. Bush, of Camilla, and Captain W. M. Hammond, of Thomasville.

The firm of Pearsall and Shipp has already been mentioned as being located at Moultrie in 1895. We now introduce the members of this firm: R. L. Shipp came to Moultrie, about 1893, from Americus, Georgia, where he had studied law in the office of Littlejohn and Thompson, Judge Littlejohn being his brother-in-law. From the first, he was always to be reckoned with among the practitioners at the Moultrie bar, as a formidable antagonist. He served Colquitt County very effectually as her representative in the General Assembly of Georgia, in 1901-2; and a few years later, he served a term as judge of the City Court of Moultrie. He removed to Miami in the boom days, and attained high rank as a lawyer. He died in 1934, and is buried in the Moultrie cemetery.

Matt J. Pearsall came to Moultrie about the same time Robt. L. Shipp came, having studied law with him at Americus. Before coming to Georgia, he read law in the office of the Hon. Marion Butler, United States Senator from North Carolina. Mr. Pearsall himself was a graduate of the University of North Carolina, and was well born, as to both his parents. He was killed in a railroad wreck near Moultrie, in 1902; but he did not pass away before he had reached a position of unquestioned leadership of the Moultrie bar; and there seemed to be no limit to his possible success, both as a lawyer and a politician, had he lived and remained in the State. His grave is at Morganton, North Carolina.

A new firm was organized, as a member of the Moultrie bar, about 1896—McKenzie and McKenzie, composed of H. C. McKenzie and J. D. McKenzie. They were cousins, and stood right at the top among the members of the Moultrie bar. J. D. McKenzie was elected judge of the City Court of Moultrie, where he rendered distinguished service till his death, which occurred long before he had reached the term set up by the Psalmist. He is buried here.

John A. Wilkes, who has already been mentioned, as practicing here in 1895, was here in 1898 in the active practice as a member of the firm of Hall and Wilkes. He was a very dangerous antagonist in a criminal case, being capable of devastating eloquence in crises. He knew how to pick a jury, and knew the Criminal Code of Georgia "by heart," a thing which, in itself, was frequently very inconvenient to his opponents. He commenced practice in the Southern Circuit as a member of the Nashville bar; when Dan Rountree was solicitor-general, whom more than once he brought to grief in the lists of the law. His special delight was in spectacular coups, in some of which he would put to flight both opposing counsel and the presiding judge—all this to the intense delight of the populace, who would come out of the courthouse, saying to each other, "Old John A. jist knows more damned law than judge and solicitor-general put together." He realized the ambition of his troubled youth, and attained to Dan Rountree's job, which he held for four years, until his death, in both public and private life, he walked in a straight line, "from his youth up."

While after W. S. Humphreys moved to Moultrie, his nephew, James Humphreys came here, and entered into a partnership with him. He survived W. S. Humphreys several years while he maintained his place among the leaders of the local bar. He knew all that his uncle did about the reactions of the wire grass jurors, and his uncle knew all there was to know; and he was even more resourceful in his tactics on the battlefield. "Little Jim," as we affectionately called him, died some years ago, leaving an excellent and popular wife, who has raised and turned into the local bar two members, both of whom are demonstrating already that they are "chips off the old block." "Little Jim" is buried in the Moultrie cemetery.

N. Marion Reynolds came to Moultrie, a-lawyering, about 1900, and did well; but decided to leave and go to Augusta, Georgia, where also he has done well in the profession of law.

Finally, there came along about the time that Reynolds came, T. W. Maddox, from "somers" over in southeast Georgia. From first to last, he has prospered, and has held creditably to himself and to the county, the solicitorship of the old City Court and the position of representative of Colquitt County in the lower house of the General Assembly of Georgia.

NOTE. After completing the above Chapter we came into possession of the Census of 1860. It shows that the first house entered by the Census Enumerator was that of "James M. Savage, whose occupation was put down as "Lawyer." Mr. Savage was 31, and a native of New York. His wife was "Caroline C. Savage," was the same age, but born in Georgia. They had a boy baby, named "Marion W." Mr. Savage had a double-pen residence, situated in the northeast corner of the block immediately south of the Courthouse Square, now called the "Watson Drugstore Corner." At least, this corner was known for many years as "The Savage House."

## CHAPTER XX
# The Census of 1860

COLQUITT'S FIRST CENSUS was taken in 1860, when she was four years old. It was taken by Peter O. Wing, "Asst. Marshal Census." Mr. Wing "censused" himself, as third man from the last head of family, as will be found by inspection of this census.

Mr. Wing was forty-three years old, as he was informed in taking the census; was by profession "Ordinary of Colquitt"; was the husband of Elizabeth A. Wing; and they had one child, named Sarah L. Wing. Mr. Wing was forty-three years old, as has been stated, and his wife was twenty-two. He was a native of Maine, and his wife was a native of Georgia, and one of the Alderman family, down about Tallokas. We have photostatic copies of Mr. Wing's census work, which shows him to have been a well-educated man, and he wrote a very legible hand. We know aliunde that he was by profession a shoemaker—one who could and did make excellent shoes. He was still a citizen of Moultrie in 1865, where his wife operated an excellent boarding house on the present site of Daniel's drug store. Mr. Wing is buried at Tallokas, having died at Moultrie in 1871. His wife took her two children and removed to her father's, at the death of Mr. Wing. All are now dead.

A review of Mr. Wing's census shows that the citizens of Colquitt had landed property worth $158,452 in 1860, while their personal holdings footed up $251,880. Such inspection will further show that the white population consisted of 615 males and 581 females.

The wealthiest man in Colquitt County, in 1860, was Charles H. Johnson, who is set down as the owner of real estate worth $4,500, and personalty worth $15,435. From sources outside the census, we know that Charles H. Johnson, in his early boyhood, like many English youths have done, and like many others will do, ran away from home, and became a seaman. He worked at his trade until about 1840, when he quit, leaving his ship at Saint Marks, Florida, and going north with his holdings in cash. He finally settled down near what is now Berlin, in Colquitt County, bought lands, erected one of the oldest houses in the county, part of which still stands, having the appearance of a fort. He then married a wife and raised a couple of children, a girl and a boy. After the Civil War, he was one of the three or four citizens in Colquitt from whom the average citizen might borrow a little cash. There were at that time, of course, no banks in the county. Mr. Lewis Perry, who married a granddaughter of pioneer Johnson, now lives on a portion of the original Johnson farm.

This census shows that John G. Coleman ran within two or three hundred dollars of Mr. Johnson's financial primacy in that year. As has been seen, Coleman was by birth a citizen of South Carolina, and that in 1861, he was a member of the Secession Convention. He lived over across the Warrior in north Colquitt. He was elected a judge of the Inferior Court of Colquitt in a week or two after he came home from the Secession Convention, a position which he held for about twelve months, when he disappeared "without trace," so far as our searchings after him have developed.

In 1860, the Hancock family was the largest in Colquitt, numbering sixty-two, separated into ten families. The Normans numbered forty-one; the Murphys, twenty-eight; the Crofts, twenty-three; the Hollands counted up thirty-four; the Tuckers, thirty-four; the Tillmans, twenty-three, and the Weeks, eighteen; and the Bakers, twenty-three.

Hon. N. M. Marchant, who assisted in taking the census of 1880, tells us that that census showed the Normans leading the population of the county, with ninety-two souls, and the Murphys came second with fifty-five.

The 1860 census shows that there were ten "free Negroes" in Colquitt County, all of whom were named "Thompson," the ages running from less than a year to thirty-seven years. Apparently, Nancy Thompson, aged thirty-seven, was the mother of all the others. At such time, this character of population was not uncommon in the slave states, where it had certain civil rights, depending upon the local laws; but of course, no political rights.

Edy Smith, born in South Carolina, is shown to have been eighty-seven years old at the date of the census, and it may be necessary to say, was a female. Elizabeth Bustle, found at the house of Dan Bustle, was seventy-five. Both these women were natives of South Carolina. "Fariba Mercer" was found to reside with John Tillman, leader of a prominent family in Colquitt. "Fariba Mercer" was a woman. Nevertheless, she made no effort to hold back her age. At least, she admitted that she was ninety. She was the mother-in-law of the man whose home she occupied.

Census Marshal Wing found that the very oldest person in the county was living up on the Warrior, at the home of Lewis Harrel. She also was evidently a relative of her host; but there is no way to judge what the relationship was. Her name was "Sally Hawkins," and she was born in South Carolina, just ninety-six years before Mr. Wing called to see her —twelve years before the signing of the Declaration of Independence, never having heard of germs, vitamins, or screened doors.

The Holland family, referred to above, was separated into five subordinate families, the heads of every one of which

## THE CENSUS OF 1860

came from North Carolina. Eli Holland has "primitive Baptist" written as his "profession." He was an elder in that church; but he had managed to lay up, where "moth and rust doth corrupt, and thieves break through and steal" $3,500 worth of real estate, and $3,059 worth of personal property. A tidy sum this was in those days, and still is.

Wiley N. Holland was the head of one of the families of the Holland clan. He was thirty-seven years old in 1860, and his wife "Diadama" was twenty-five. One of their children was named "Civil America."

Jackson P. Bennet, forty-three, and his wife, Polly, were both born in South Carolina. Among their numerous children were "Arkansas," "Texanna" and "Virginia."

John Gregory, sixty-three, apparent widower and farmer, was a native of South Carolina, living out toward the southwest part of Colquitt County, in 1860, having removed there some thirty years before. He told Mr. Wing that he had lands worth $4,500, and personalty valued by him at $3,470. As residents in his house he numbered two or three of his own name, whose ages indicated that they might be children, and others, of a different name, who might have been relatives, or house and farm servants. Near the bottom of the list in this big house are two children, of the Gregory name. One of them is written down as aged ten, and a girl child. Mr. Wing wrote her name down as "Unknown Gregory." We think it is the most curious name in this census.

We believe that our readers, especially such as are natives of Colquitt County, and descendants of the original settlers, will derive great pleasure from studying Mr. Wing's census. We present it at this place in the book, in its entirety, as being copied from the photostatic copies.

112       HISTORY OF COLQUITT COUNTY

## Census of 1860—Colquitt County

|   | Name | Age | Occupation | Birth-place |
|---|---|---|---|---|
| 1. | James M. Savage | 31 | Lawyer | N. Y. |
|   | Caroline C. Savage | 31 |   | Ga. |
|   | Marion W. Savage | 9/12 |   | Ga. |
| 2. | Zilpha Sloan | 56 | Seamstress | S. C. |
|   | Jasper Sloan | 24 | Laborer | Ga. |
|   | Newton Sloan | 21 | Farm laborer | Ga. |
|   | Daniel Sloan | 20 | Farm laborer | Ga. |
|   | Polly Ann Sloan | 14 |   | Ga. |
|   | William Sloan | 10 |   | Ga. |
| 3. | Darlin Creed | 40 | Farmer | S. C. |
|   | Sarah Ann Creed | 33 |   | Fla. |
|   | Mary Ann A. A. Creed | 3 |   | Ga. |
|   | James A. Creed | 8/12 |   | Ga. |
|   | Jacob Creed | 35 |   | S. C. |
|   | Elizabeth Barton | 16 |   | S. C. |
|   | Isaiah Barton | 13 |   | Ga. |
|   | Thomas Barton | 9 |   | Ga. |
| 4. | James E. Hancock | 35 | Farmer | Ga. |
|   | Martha Hancock | 35 |   | N. C. |
|   | Georgia Ann Hancock | 8 |   | Ga. |
|   | Linton C. Hancock | 7 |   | Ga. |
|   | Mary C. Hancock | 5 |   | Ga. |
|   | Caroline M. Hancock | 4 |   | Ga. |
|   | Nancy E. Hancock | 2 |   | Ga. |
|   | Barzell Hancock | 3/12 |   | Ga. |
| 5. | Paul M. J. Creed | 25 | Farm laborer | S. C. |
|   | Sarah Creed | 23 |   | Ga. |
|   | Nancy A. E. Creed | 2 |   | Ga. |
|   | Susan C. Creed | 7/12 |   | Ga. |
| 6. | Bartley Stephenson | 36 | Farmer | N. C. |
|   | Susan A. J. Stephenson | 21 |   | Fla. |

## THE CENSUS OF 1860

|    | NAME | AGE | OCCUPATION | BIRTH-PLACE |
|----|------|-----|------------|-------------|
| 7. | Daniel Creed | 47 | Laborer | S. C. |
|    | Eliza Creed | 37 | | Ga. |
|    | Elender Creed | 7 | | Ga. |
| 8. | Hardin Hancock | 29 | Farmer | Ga. |
|    | Lydia Hancock | 20 | | Ga. |
|    | Ansel Hancock | 1 | | Ga. |
|    | Thos. W. McLendon | 22 | Farm laborer | Ga. |
| 9. | Martin W. Hancock | 22 | Farmer | Ga. |
|    | Elva Hancock | 22 | | Ga. |
| 10. | Nancy Vick | 33 | | Ga. |
|    | James Vick | 14 | | Ga. |
|    | Aaron Vick | 12 | | Ga. |
|    | Missouri Vick | 11 | | Ga. |
|    | Timothy Vick | 9 | | Ga. |
|    | John H. Vick | 8 | | Ga. |
|    | Ezekiel Vick | 5 | | Ga. |
| 11. | John Sloan, Jr. | 45 | Farmer | N. C. |
|    | Martha Sloan | 34 | | Ga. |
|    | Susan Sloan | 10 | | Ga. |
|    | Mary Sloan | 8 | | Ga. |
|    | Daniel Sloan | 7 | | Ga. |
|    | Nancy Sloan | 5 | | Ga. |
|    | Dixon Sloan | 4 | | Ga. |
|    | Jeremiah Sloan | 2 | | Ga. |
|    | John Sloan | 77 | | N. C. |
|    | Rachel Watson | 19 | Domestic | Ga. |
|    | Antoinette Townsend | 17 | Domestic | Ga. |
| 12. | Zepheniah Rich | 37 | Farm laborer | N. C. |
|    | Sarah Rich | 40 | | N. C. |
|    | John R. Rich | 14 | | Ga. |
|    | Jas. H. Rich | 12 | | Ga. |
|    | William P. Rich | 10 | | Ga. |

## HISTORY OF COLQUITT COUNTY

| | NAME | AGE | OCCUPATION | BIRTH-PLACE |
|---|---|---|---|---|
| | Eliza H. Rich | 7 | | Ga. |
| | Mary J. Rich | 7 | | Ga. |
| | Martha A. Rich | 2 | | Ga. |
| 13. | Jeremiah Hancock | 56 | Farmer | Ga. |
| | Ellen Hancock | 54 | | Ga. |
| | Nancy Hancock | 29 | | Ga. |
| | Susan Hancock | 23 | | Ga. |
| | Harrison Hancock | 19 | Farm laborer | Ga. |
| | Martha J. Hancock | 14 | | Ga. |
| | Eliz. Hancock | 18 | | Ga. |
| | Rachel A. Hancock | 12 | | Ga. |
| | John D. Hancock | 12 | | Ga. |
| | William Hancock | 20 | Farm laborer | Ga. |
| 14. | Geo. T. Suber | 35 | Farm laborer | S. C. |
| | Sarah E. Suber | 32 | | Ga. |
| | Felen G. Suber | 9 | | Ga. |
| | Sarah E. Suber | 6 | | Ga. |
| | James F. Suber | 3 | | Ga. |
| | Serena Suber | 1 | | Ga. |
| 15. | Hardin Hancock | 43 | Farmer | Ga. |
| | Eliz. Hancock | 45 | | Ga. |
| | Sarah Hancock | 21 | | Ga. |
| | Jane Hancock | 18 | | Ga. |
| | Georgia Ann Hancock | 15 | | Ga. |
| | Menita Hancock | 12 | | Ga. |
| | William J. Hancock | 8 | | Ga. |
| | General J. Hancock | 5 | | Ga. |
| | Martha E. Hancock | 2 | | Ga. |
| | Orilla Hancock | 6/12 | | Ga. |
| 16. | Steven Johnson | 71 | Blind | N. C. |
| | Delilah Johnson | 59 | | N. C. |
| | Neri Johnson | 23 | Farmer | N. C. |
| | Lebana Johnson | 20 | Farm laborer | N. C. |

## THE CENSUS OF 1860

| | Name | Age | Occupation | Birth-place |
|---|---|---|---|---|
| 17. | James R. Alger | 25 | Farmer | Ga. |
| | Nancy J. Alger | 22 | | Ga. |
| | Emerson L. Alger | 3 | | Ga. |
| 18. | William J. Smith | 34 | Farmer | Ga. |
| | Sarah Ann Smith | 30 | | Ga. |
| | William Smith | 7 | | Ga. |
| | Caroline Smith | 5 | | Ga. |
| | John Smith | 2 | | Ga. |
| 19. | Hardy Smith | 27 | Farm laborer | Ga. |
| | Sarah J. Smith | 15 | | Ga. |
| 20. | Steven Smith | 67 | Farmer | Ga. |
| | Winney Smith | 58 | | Ga. |
| | Melinda Dunner | 32 | Seamstress | Ga. |
| | Georgia Ann Dunner | 10 | | Ga. |
| 21. | Jas. Woodcock | 35 | Farm laborer | Ga. |
| | Alla M. Woodcock | 31 | | Ga. |
| | Edward Woodcock | 12 | | Ga. |
| | Alla M. Woodcock | 10 | | Ga. |
| | Steven Woodcock | 8 | | Ga. |
| | Winnie Woodcock | 6 | | Ga. |
| | America Woodcock | 3 | | Ga. |
| | James Woodcock | 10/12 | | Ga. |
| 22. | Wilson L. Alger | 26 | Farmer | Ga. |
| | Mary Alger | 25 | | Ga. |
| | Joseph Hutto Alger | 6 | | Ga. |
| 23. | Thos. P. Scarber | 38 | Farmer | Ga. |
| | Martha E. Scarber | 30 | | N. C. |
| | Charles G. Scarber | 6 | | Ga. |
| | Mary J. Scarber | 3 | | Ga. |
| | Sarah E. Scarber | 1 | | Ga. |

|  | Name | Age | Occupation | Birth-place |
|---|---|---|---|---|
| 24. | Daniel Bustle | 43 | Farmer | Ga. |
|  | Margaret Bustle | 36 |  | N. C. |
|  | Mary Ann Bustle | 10 |  | Ga. |
|  | Eliz. Ann Bustle | 10 |  | Ga. |
|  | Dorinds Bustle | 9 |  | Ga. |
|  | Margaret Bustle | 4 |  | Ga. |
|  | Larinia Bustle | 1 |  | Ga. |
|  | Eliz. Bustle | 75 |  | S. C. |
| 25. | John N. Philips | 30 | Farmer | Ga. |
|  | Amelia Philips | 26 |  | Ga. |
|  | William Philips | 10 |  | Ga. |
|  | Gillis Philips | 8 |  | Ga. |
|  | Mary J. Philips | 6 |  | Ga. |
|  | Lewis Philips | 4 |  | Ga. |
|  | Disa Philips | 2 |  | Ga. |
|  | Jackson Philips | 1 |  | Ga. |
|  | Edie Smith | 87 |  | S. C. |
|  | Patience Smith | 48 | Domestic | Ga. |
| 26. | Isaac Alger | 55 | Farmer | Ga. |
|  | Jane R. Alger | 48 |  | Ga. |
|  | Napoleon Alger | 16 | Farm laborer | Ga. |
|  | Benj. F. Alger | 14 |  | Ga. |
|  | Arabella Alger | 9 |  | Ga. |
|  | Mary J. Alger | 7 |  | Ga. |
|  | Marg. Alger | 4 |  | Ga. |
|  | Edward W. Creed | 24 | Farm laborer | S. C. |
| 27. | Eli R. Clark | 40 | Farmer | Ga. |
|  | Eliza Clark | 36 |  | Ga. |
|  | Lydia Clark | 17 |  | Ga. |
|  | Eli Clark | 16 |  | Ga. |
|  | Henry Clark | 14 |  | Ga. |
|  | Samuel Clark | 12 |  | Ga. |
|  | Mary E. Clark | 11 |  | Ga. |

## THE CENSUS OF 1860

| | Name | Age | Occupation | Birth-place |
|---|---|---|---|---|
| | Moses W. Clark | 9 | | Ga. |
| | Rebecca F. Clark | 7 | | Ga. |
| | James L. Clark | 5 | | Ga. |
| | Marg. E. Clark | 2 | | Ga. |
| | Susan Clark | 1/12 | | Ga. |
| 28. | Eli Holland | 68 | Prim. Baptist | N. C. |
| | Edith Holland | 63 | | N. C. |
| | Maria Holland | 13 | | N. C. |
| | Joseph P. Holland | 9 | | Ga. |
| 29. | Ezekiel Crawford | 45 | Farm laborer | Ga. |
| | Martha A. Crawford | 28 | | N. C. |
| | Jane Crawford | 22 | | Ga. |
| | John L. Crawford | 21 | Farm laborer | Ga. |
| | William B. Crawford | 16 | Farm laborer | Ga. |
| | Henry Crawford | 13 | | Ga. |
| | Benj. Crawford | 9 | | Ga. |
| | Leonard Crawford | 7 | | Ga. |
| | Louisa Crawford | 5 | | Ga. |
| | Florida Crawford | 8/12 | | Ga. |
| 30. | Wiley N. Holland | 37 | Farmer | N. C. |
| | Diadama O. Holland | 25 | | Ga. |
| | Benj. Holland | 7 | | Ga. |
| | Wiley N. Holland | 5 | | Ga. |
| | Civil A. R. Holland | 3 | | Ga. |
| | Eli Holland | 2/12 | | Ga. |
| 31. | Jackson P. Bennet | 43 | Miller | S. C. |
| | Polly A. Bennet | 42 | | S. C. |
| | Marg. A. Bennet | 18 | | S. C. |
| | Arkansas S. Bennet | 13 | | S. C. |
| | Alphine S. Bennet | 11 | | S. C. |
| | James M. Bennet | 9 | | S. C. |
| | Mary A. Bennet | 5 | | S. C. |

|     | Name | Age | Occupation | Birth-place |
|-----|------|-----|------------|-------------|
|     | Josiah Z. Bennet | 3 | | S. C. |
|     | Texanna Bennet | 1 | | S. C. |
|     | Virginia Bennet | 1 | | S. C. |
| 32. | John T. Holland | 39 | Farmer | N. C. |
|     | Maria Holland | 43 | | N. C. |
|     | Julius H. Holland | 6 | | Ga. |
|     | Edy Ann Holland | 4 | | N. C. |
|     | Eliz. A. Holland | 2 | | Ga. |
|     | Thos. E. Holland | 1 | | Ga. |
| 33. | Alvin Holland | 36 | Blacksmith | N. C. |
|     | Mary Holland | 30 | | Ala. |
|     | William P. Holland | 10 | | Ala. |
|     | Frances Holland | 8 | | Ala. |
|     | Ella Holland | 6 | | Ala. |
|     | George D. Holland | 4 | Idiot | Ala. |
|     | Bright Holland | 1 | | Ga. |
| 34. | Enas Holland | 70 | Blacksmith | N. C. |
|     | Susan Holland | 60 | | N. C. |
|     | Eson Holland | 40 | | N. C. |
|     | Eliz. Holland | 39 | | N. C. |
|     | Mary J. Holland | 18 | | N. C. |
|     | Enos Holland | 14 | | N. C. |
|     | Susan Holland | 11 | | N. C. |
|     | Alson G. Holland | 10 | | Ga. |
|     | Martha E. Holland | 8 | | Fla. |
|     | Eliz. Holland | 6 | | Ga. |
|     | Melinda H. Holland | 4 | | Ga. |
|     | Kitty L. Holland | 11/12 | | Ga. |
| 35. | John Gregory | 63 | Farmer | S. C. |
|     | Richard B. Gregory | 36 | Farmer | Ga. |
|     | Jemima Gregory | 34 | | Ga. |
|     | Samuel C. Gregory | 32 | Blacksmith | Ga. |

## THE CENSUS OF 1860

|     | Name | Age | Occupation | Birth-place |
|-----|------|-----|------------|-------------|
|     | William R. Edwards | 18 | Farm laborer | Ga. |
|     | Samuel Gregory | 17 | Farm laborer | Ga. |
|     | Eleanor Boatwright | 24 | Domestic | Ga. |
|     | Sarah A. Boatwright | 22 | Domestic | Ga. |
|     | John F. Boatwright | 17 | Farm laborer | Ga. |
|     | Unknown Gregory | 10 | (Female) | Ga. |
|     | Mary E. Gregory | 5 | | Ga. |
|     | Byson Boatwright | 4 | | Ga. |
| 36. | Merrit Johnson | 47 | Farmer | N. C. |
|     | Mary Johnson | 40 | | N. C. |
|     | Sarah A. Johnson | 16 | | N. C. |
|     | Wiley E. Johnson | 14 | | N. C. |
|     | Richard S. Johnson | 4 | | Ga. |
|     | James R. Johnson | 2 | | Ga. |
| 37. | Elijah Fields | 26 | Farmer | Ga. |
|     | Eliz. Fields | 31 | | N. C. |
|     | Thos. J. Fields | 4 | | Ga. |
|     | Mary J. Fields | 1 | | Ga. |
| 38. | Peter Connell | 49 | Farmer | S. C. |
|     | Susannah Connell | 44 | | Ga. |
|     | Simon Connell | 20 | Farm laborer | Ga. |
|     | Jas. S. Connell | 18 | Farm laborer | Ga. |
|     | Sarah K. Connell | 16 | | Ga. |
|     | Richard A. Connell | 12 | | Ga. |
|     | William E. Connell | 10 | | Ga. |
|     | Susan M. E. Connell | 7 | | Ga. |
|     | Martha J. Connell | 5 | | Ga. |
|     | Nancy A. Connell | 2 | | Ga. |
| 39. | Joseph J. Richter | 33 | Farmer | Bavaria |
|     | Wetstel M. Richter | 25 | | Ga. |
|     | Marg. A. Richter | 4 | | Ga. |
|     | Wright F. Richter | 3 | | Ga. |
|     | John A. Richter | 2 | | Ga. |

| | Name | Age | Occupation | Birth-place |
|---|---|---|---|---|
| 40. | David Alligood | 23 | Farmer | Ga. |
| | Ascention Alligood | 23 | | Ga. |
| | Eli B. Alligood | 1 | | Ga. |
| 41. | Elender Alligood | 53 | | Ga. |
| | James Alligood | 19 | Farm laborer | Ga. |
| | Thos. Alligood | 17 | Farm laborer | Ga. |
| 42. | Samuel J. Hart | 25 | Farmer | Ga. |
| | Sarah J. Hart | 16 | | Ga. |
| | Flora H. Hart | 6/12 | | Ga. |
| | Hardy Hancock | 28 | Farm laborer | Ga. |
| 43. | Martha A. Collier | 34 | Weaver and seamst. | Ga. |
| | David H. Collier | 10 | | Ga. |
| | Joel A. Collier | 7 | | Ga. |
| | Piety C. Collier | 4 | | Ga. |
| 44. | James Horne | 23 | Common laborer | Ga. |
| | Susan Horne | 25 | | Ga. |
| | Elafin Horne | 6 | | Ga. |
| | Gilly Ann Horne | 5 | | Ga. |
| | William G. Horne | 3 | | Ga. |
| | Lucy E. Horne | 10/12 | | Ga. |
| 45. | Daniel Lawson | 45 | Laborer | Ga. |
| | Mary Lawson | 37 | | Ga. |
| | Lamanda Lawson | 17 | | Ga. |
| | Nancy E. Lawson | 8 | | Ga. |
| | Sarah J. Lawson | 6 | | Ga. |
| | Ann A. Lawson | 4 | | Ga. |
| | Julia P. Lawson | 1 | | Ga. |
| 46. | Joshua J. Warren | 37 | Farm laborer | Ga. |
| | Marg. A. Warren | 22 | | Ga. |
| | John Warren | 8 | | Ga. |
| | Mary C. Warren | 7 | | Ga. |

## THE CENSUS OF 1860

| | Name | Age | Occupation | Birth-place |
|---|---|---|---|---|
| | James W. Warren | 4 | | Ga. |
| | Ruben W. Warren | 2 | | Ga. |
| | Joseph D. Warren | 10/12 | | Ga. |
| 47. | Linton Carlton | 39 | Farmer | N. C. |
| | Catharine Carlton | 36 | | Ga. |
| | Isaac Carlton | 18 | Farm laborer | Ga. |
| | Nancy Carlton | 13 | | Ga. |
| | Wright Carlton | 11 | | Ga. |
| | Alfred Carlton | 5 | | Ga. |
| | John B. Carlton | 3 | | Ga. |
| | Pauline Townsend | 16 | Domestic | Ga. |
| | Abel P. Hutchison | 34 | School teacher | S. C. |
| | Aaron Carlton | 16 | Scholar | Ga. |
| 48. | Geo. W. Tucker | 34 | Farmer | Ga. |
| | Telitha Tucker | 35 | | N. C. |
| | Nancy Tucker | 14 | | N. C. |
| | Rebecca Tucker | 12 | | N. C. |
| | Mary Tucker | 8 | | N. C. |
| | John Tucker | 10 | | N. C. |
| | Malatha Tucker | 6 | | N. C. |
| | Telitha Tucker | 4 | | N. C. |
| | Louisa Tucker | 5 | | N. C. |
| | Henry A. Tucker | 6/12 | | N. C. |
| 49. | Mack L. Gay | 37 | Farmer | Ga. |
| | Mary K. Gay | 32 | | Ga. |
| | Mary J. Gay | 5 | | Ga. |
| | John Gay | 3 | | Ga. |
| | Samuel Gay | 1 | | Ga. |
| 50. | James J. Hinto | 23 | Farmer | S. C. |
| 51. | Joel P. Register | 44 | Grocer | N. C. |
| | Elva Register | 43 | | N. C. |
| | John T. Register | 14 | | Ga. |

| | Name | Age | Occupation | Birth-place |
|---|---|---|---|---|
| | Nancy C. Register | 12 | | Ga. |
| | Marg. C. Register | 8 | | Ga. |
| | Louisa Register | 5 | | Ga. |
| | John Sloan | 26 | Common laborer | Ga. |
| 52. | Robert Bearden | 30 | Grocer | S. C. |
| | Sarah Ann Bearden | 21 | | S. C. |
| | Moses J. Guyton | 29 | Merchant | Ga. |
| 53. | Henry C. Tucker | 55 | Primitive Baptist | Ga. |
| | Rebecca Tucker | 26 | | Ga. |
| | Henry S. Tucker | 20 | Farm laborer | Ga. |
| | Mary Ann Tucker | 16 | | Ga. |
| | Martha Tucker | 14 | | Ga. |
| | Jane Tucker | 12 | | Ga. |
| | Eliz. Tucker | 10 | | Ga. |
| | Hiram Tucker | 8 | | Ga. |
| | James S. Tucker | 7 | | Ga. |
| | Saphronia Tucker | 6 | | Ga. |
| | Margaret Tucker | 4 | | Ga. |
| | Isaac Tucker | 4 | | Ga. |
| | Joel Tucker | 3 | | Ga. |
| | Ansel Tucker | 1 | | Ga. |
| | (Unnamed) Tucker | 1/12 | | Ga. |
| 54. | Riley Potter | 57 | Farmer | Ga. |
| | Martha Potter | 36 | | Ga. |
| | John W. Potter | 16 | Farm laborer | Ga. |
| | Bosdell Potter | 14 | | Ga. |
| | Sarah Potter | 12 | | Ga. |
| | Wilkinson Potter | 10 | | Ga. |
| | Martha Potter | 8 | | Ga. |
| | Lucinda Potter | 6 | | Ga. |
| | Eliza Potter | 4 | | Ga. |

## THE CENSUS OF 1860

| | Name | Age | Occupation | Birth-place |
|---|---|---|---|---|
| 55. | John Tucker | 27 | Farmer | Ga. |
| | Susan A. Tucker | 25 | | N. C. |
| | Susan Jane Tucker | 3 | | Ga. |
| | Nancy I. Tucker | 1 | | Ga. |
| | Thos. Stevenson | 24 | Farm laborer | N. C. |
| 56. | Sam. Gay | 33 | Farmer | Ga. |
| | Melinda Gay | 25 | | Fla. |
| | Martha J. Gay | 3 | | Ga. |
| | William H. Gay | 2 | | Ga. |
| | Thomas H. Gay | 6/12 | | Ga. |
| 57. | Richard Tucker | 24 | Farmer | Ga. |
| | Civil Tucker | 16 | | Ga. |
| 58. | John G. Coleman | 38 | Farmer | S. C. |
| | Laura H. Coleman | 28 | | Ga. |
| | John G. Coleman | 7 | | Ga. |
| | Virginia C. Coleman | 4 | | Ga. |
| | William R. Coleman | 1 | | Ga. |
| 59. | Willis Price | 23 | Farmer | Fla. |
| | Marg. Price | 42 | | Ga. |
| | Lydia M. J. Price | 11 | | Ga. |
| | William P. Price | 7 | | Ga. |
| 60. | David Bland | 39 | Farmer | Ga. |
| | Nancy C. Bland | 35 | | N. C. |
| | William B. Bland | 14 | | Ga. |
| | George W. Bland | 5 | | Ga. |
| | Francis M. Bland | 1 | | Ga. |
| 61. | Lewis Harrel | 63 | Farmer | Ga. |
| | Litha Harrel | 63 | | S. C. |
| | Litha Harrel | 23 | | Ga. |
| | Mary Harrel | 21 | | Ga. |

|     | Name | Age | Occupation | Birth-place |
|-----|------|-----|------------|-------------|
|     | Rhoda Harrel | 20 | | Ga. |
|     | Amos Turner | 16 | Farm laborer | Ga. |
|     | Sally Hawkins | 96 | | S. C. |
| 62. | Jeremiah T. Hancock | 21 | Farmer | Ga. |
|     | Alafin Hancock | 24 | | S. C. |
|     | Jeremiah N. Hancock | 2/12 | | Ga. |
| 63. | Henry Hancock | 55 | Farmer | Ga. |
|     | Mary Hancock | 45 | | Ga. |
|     | Henry W. Hancock | 23 | Farm laborer | Ga. |
|     | Martha A. Hancock | 17 | | Ga. |
|     | Sarah A. Hancock | 15 | | Ga. |
|     | Selista A. Hancock | 10 | | Ga. |
| 64. | Stephen Hancock | 53 | Common laborer | Ga. |
|     | Blancet Hancock | 47 | | Ga. |
|     | Henry Hancock | 18 | Farm laborer | Ga. |
|     | Hampleton S. Hancock | 13 | | Ga. |
|     | Martha S. Hancock | 9 | | Ga. |
| 65. | Nathaniel Giles | 50 | Farmer | Ga. |
|     | Mary Giles | 46 | | Ga. |
|     | Sarah J. Giles | 24 | | Ga. |
|     | Emily F. Giles | 23 | | Ga. |
|     | Fariba C. Giles | 22 | | Ga. |
|     | Martha A. Giles | 19 | | Ga. |
|     | Jacob J. Giles | 17 | Farm laborer | Ga. |
|     | Melinda M. Giles | 12 | | Ga. |
|     | Mary A. V. Giles | 10 | | Ga. |
|     | David B. Giles | 7 | | Ga. |
|     | Elijah H. Giles | 5 | | Ga. |
| 66. | Hardy Carlton | 44 | Farmer | N. C. |
|     | Barbara Carlton | 35 | | N. C. |
|     | Mary A. Carlton | 12 | | Ga. |
|     | Eliz. J. Carlton | 7 | | Ga. |

## THE CENSUS OF 1860

|  | Name | Age | Occupation | Birth-place |
|---|---|---|---|---|
|  | Sarah C. Carlton | 1 |  | Ga. |
|  | Sarah Jones | 26 | Seamstress | Ga. |
|  | Jacob W. Taylor | 39 | Carpenter | N. C. |
|  | Mary E. Taylor | 32 |  | N. C. |
|  | James S. Taylor | 12 |  | N. C. |
|  | Mordica Taylor | 9 |  | N. C. |
|  | Hencilla A. Taylor | 4 |  | N. C. |
| 67. | William Fulwood | 27 | Farm laborer | Ga. |
|  | Eliz. Fulwood | 25 |  | Ga. |
|  | Vernon M. Fulwood | 1 |  | Ga. |
| 68. | Isaac I. Royal | 56 | Farmer | Ga. |
|  | Nancy Royal | 49 |  | Ga. |
|  | Daniel Royal | 20 | Farm laborer | Ga. |
|  | Thos. A. Royal | 16 | Farm laborer | Ga. |
|  | Martha F. Royal | 13 |  | Ga. |
|  | Nancy M. Royal | 11 |  | Ga. |
|  | Ezekiel A. Royal | 5 |  | Ga. |
| 69. | David Mims | 69 | Farmer | Ga. |
|  | Laurana Mims | 35 |  | Ga. |
|  | Naomi Mims | 21 |  | Ga. |
|  | Eliza Mims | 17 |  | Ga. |
|  | Isaac Royal | 18 | Farm laborer | Ga. |
|  | John Mims | 25 | Farm laborer | Ga. |
|  | Susan A. Mims | 24 |  | Ga. |
|  | John T. Mims | 4 |  | Ga. |
|  | Sarah A. A. Mims | 3 |  | Ga. |
|  | Celestia E. Mims | 2 |  | Ga. |
| 70. | George S. Faison | 51 | Farmer | Va. |
|  | Eleanor A. Faison | 45 |  | Ga. |
|  | Robert W. Faison | 17 | Farm laborer | Ga. |
|  | Averilla D. Faison | 11 |  | Ga. |

| | Name | Age | Occupation | Birth-place |
|---|---|---|---|---|
| | Clara A. Faison | 8 | | Ga. |
| | John B. S. Faison | 7 | | Ga. |
| | Chas. W. Faison | 2 | | Ga. |
| 71. | James NeSmith | 35 | Farmer | Ga. |
| | Eliz. NeSmith | 33 | | Ga. |
| | Elijah G. T. NeSmith | 4 | | Ga. |
| | Elander J. P. NeSmith | 2 | | Ga. |
| 72. | Thos. Jordan | 82 | Past-laborer | S. C. |
| | Dicy Jordan | 71 | | Va. |
| 73. | Daniel O. Saffold | 52 | Farmer | Ga. |
| | Nancy Saffold | 30 | | Ga. |
| | Cena A. C. Saffold | 20 | | Ga. |
| | John T. Saffold | 10 | | Ga. |
| | Richard R. Saffold | 7 | | Ga. |
| | Martha Ann Saffold | 6 | | Ga. |
| | Henry H. Saffold | 4 | | Ga. |
| | Samuel S. Saffold | 1 | | Ga. |
| 74. | Absolom Baker | 51 | Farmer | Ga. |
| | Martha A. Baker | 29 | | Ga. |
| | Lydia A. D. A. Baker | 16 | | Ga. |
| | Jarrett J. Baker | 10 | | Ga. |
| | Zilpha E. Baker | 8 | | Ga. |
| | Absolom Baker | 6 | | Ga. |
| | Martha A. Baker | 4 | | Ga. |
| | Millard F. Baker | 1 | | Ga. |
| | Thos. Tillman | 21 | Farm laborer | Ga. |
| 75. | David Highsmith | 27 | Farmer | Ga. |
| | Leah Highsmith | 26 | | Ga. |
| | Jessie Highsmith | 5 | | Ga. |
| | Martha Ann Highsmith | 5 | | Ga. |
| | Peggie A. Highsmith | 9/12 | | Ga. |

## THE CENSUS OF 1860

|     | NAME | AGE | OCCUPATION | BIRTH-PLACE |
|-----|------|-----|------------|-------------|
| 76. | Elijah Tillman | 28 | Farmer | Ga. |
|     | Mary Tillman | 28 | | N. C. |
|     | Mary M. Tillman | 8 | | Ga. |
|     | Sallie A. R. Tillman | 6 | | Ga. |
|     | John H. Tillman | 4 | | Ga. |
|     | James Tillman | 1 | | Ga. |
| 77. | Henry Gay | 40 | Farmer | Ga. |
|     | Sarah E. Gay | 41 | | Ga. |
|     | James H. Gay | 14 | Farm laborer | Ga. |
|     | John Gay | 14 | | Ga. |
|     | Ruth J. Gay | 13 | | Ga. |
|     | Mary Gay | 12 | | Ga. |
|     | Martha Gay | 12 | | Ga. |
|     | Eliz. Gay | 9 | | Ga. |
| 78. | Richard J. Norman | 23 | Farmer | Ga. |
|     | Fariba A. R. Norman | 21 | | Ga. |
| 79. | James J. Redd | 34 | Carpenter | Ga. |
|     | Martha B. Redd | 36 | | Ga. |
|     | Sarah F. Redd | 12 | | Ga. |
|     | Harriet A. E. Redd | 10 | | Ga. |
|     | John Redd | 7 | | Ga. |
|     | May R. Redd | 4 | | Ga. |
| 80. | Jacob F. Reichert | 40 | Sheriff | Wurtemburg |
|     | Rebecca Reichert | 36 | | Ga. |
|     | Sarah M. Reichert | 16 | | Fla. |
|     | John D. Reichert | 14 | | Ga. |
|     | Julia A. Reichert | 13 | | Ga. |
|     | Louis W. Reichert | 10 | | Ga. |
|     | Henrietta Reichert | 8 | | Ga. |
|     | William Reichert | 6 | | Ga. |
|     | Alexander S. Reichert | 3 | | Ga. |

| Name | Age | Occupation | Birth-place |
|---|---|---|---|
| 81. Wilson McMullin | 51 | Steam mill hand | S. C. |
| Martha McMullin | 50 | | Ga. |
| John McMullin | 14 | | Ga. |
| Nancy McMullin | 13 | | Ga. |
| William McMullin | 11 | | Ga. |
| Julia Ann McMullin | 6 | | Ga. |
| 82. Abraham Gay | 27 | Farmer | Ga. |
| Mary E. Gay | 25 | | N. C. |
| Nancy J. Gay | 5 | | Ga. |
| Sarah C. Gay | 5/12 | | Ga. |
| Hiram Gay | 24 | Farm laborer | Ga. |
| John Bloodworth | 18 | Farm laborer | Ga. |
| 83. Jeremiah B. Norman | 38 | Farmer | Ga. |
| Sarah A. E. Norman | 35 | | Ga. |
| Ruth E. Norman | 13 | | Ga. |
| James T. Norman | 11 | | Ga. |
| Julia A. E. Norman | 9 | | Ga. |
| Susan L. Norman | 8 | | Ga. |
| Jeremiah Norman | 7 | | Ga. |
| John S. Norman | 6 | | Ga. |
| Matthew H. Norman | 4 | | Ga. |
| Zilpha Norman | 10/12 | | Ga. |
| Joseph J. Norman | 27 | Common carpenter | Ga. |
| 84. David A. Gillis | 20 | | Ga. |
| Arena Gillis | 22 | | Ga. |
| 85. Andrew Coker | 28 | Farmer | Ga. |
| Eliz. Coker | 21 | | Ga. |
| Frances M. Coker | 5 | | Ga. |
| John P. Coker | 3 | | Ga. |
| Malta A. Coker | 10/12 | | Ga. |
| 86. Joe Castleberry | 30 | Farmer | Ga. |
| Anna Castleberry | 30 | | Ga. |

## THE CENSUS OF 1860

|     | Name | Age | Occupation | Birth-place |
|---|---|---|---|---|
|     | Henry Castleberry | 8 | | Ga. |
|     | Louis H. Castleberry | 6 | | Ga. |
|     | Susan Castleberry | 5 | | Ga. |
|     | Letha Castleberry | 3 | | Ga. |
|     | Jeremiah B. Castleberry | 1 | | Ga. |
| 87. | James W. Dukes | 27 | Farmer | Ga. |
|     | Lany J. Dukes | 22 | | N. C. |
|     | Julia Ann Dukes | 1 | | Ga. |
| 88. | Early O. Green | 37 | Common laborer | Ga. |
|     | Eliz. Green | 32 | | Ga. |
|     | Mary Green | 9 | | Ga. |
|     | Thos. Green | 8 | | Ga. |
|     | Sylvania Green | 5 | | Ga. |
|     | John Green | 2 | | Ga. |
|     | Henry Green | 2/12 | | Ga. |
| 89. | Flornoy Clark | 35 | Farmer | Ga. |
|     | Eliza E. Clark | 7 | | Ga. |
| 90. | Noel G. Clark | 36 | Farmer | Ga. |
|     | Nancy Clark | 34 | | Ga. |
|     | Georgia Ann Clark | 10 | | Ga. |
| 91. | John R. M. Lindsey | 31 | Farmer | Ga. |
|     | Sarah A. M. Lindsey | 31 | | S. C. |
|     | Mary E. Lindsey | 9 | | S. C. |
|     | Benj. F. Lindsey | 8 | | S. C. |
|     | Winny M. Lindsey | 3 | | S. C. |
|     | John A. James | 17 | Farm laborer | S. C. |
| 92. | Henry Crosby | 30 | Farmer | Ga. |
|     | Patience Crosby | 30 | | Ga. |
|     | John W. Crosby | 10 | | Ga. |
|     | Ezekiel Crosby | 7 | | Ga. |
|     | Eliz. Crosby | 2 | | Ga. |

## HISTORY OF COLQUITT COUNTY

|     | NAME | AGE | OCCUPATION | BIRTH-PLACE |
|-----|------|-----|------------|-------------|
| 93. | Seaborn Weeks | 34 | Farmer | Ga. |
|     | Nancy Weeks | 29 | | Ga. |
|     | Saphrona Weeks | 8 | | Ga. |
|     | John T. Weeks | 6 | | Ga. |
|     | Thos. M. Weeks | 4 | | Ga. |
|     | Martha A. Weeks | 3/12 | | Ga. |
| 94. | Eliz. James | 52 | Weaver | S. C. |
|     | Martha J. James | 15 | | Ga. |
|     | Sarah A. E. James | 12 | | Ga. |
|     | Katharine A. James | 10 | | Ga. |
| 95. | Jacob Kinard | 42 | Farmer | Ga. |
|     | Lucretia Kinard | 40 | | Ga. |
|     | Sina Kinard | 20 | | Ga. |
|     | George Kinard | 16 | Farm laborer | Ga. |
|     | Eliz. Kinard | 12 | | Ga. |
|     | Nancy Kinard | 10 | | Ga. |
|     | Martin Kinard | 8 | | Ga. |
|     | Sela Kinard | 6 | | Ga. |
|     | Lydia Kinard | 5 | | Ga. |
|     | David Kinard | 2 | | Ga. |
| 96. | Thos. Monegan | 48 | Ditcher | Ireland |
|     | Sarah Monegan | 37 | | Ga. |
|     | Sarah Hagan | 18 | Domestic | Ga. |
| 97. | John Lawson | 77 | Farmer | N. C. |
|     | Harriet Lawson | 53 | | Ga. |
| 98. | James R. Douglas | 32 | Farmer | Ga. |
|     | Maria Douglas | 39 | | Ga. |
|     | Mary A. Douglas | 13 | | Ga. |
|     | Geo. W. Wilkes | 11 | | Fla. |
| 99. | John M. Livingston | 32 | | Ga. |
|     | Nancy Livingston | 31 | | Ga. |
|     | Nancy N. Livingston | 10 | | Ga. |

## THE CENSUS OF 1860

|      | Name                       | Age | Occupation    | Birth-place |
|------|----------------------------|-----|---------------|-------------|
|      | Samuel E. Livingston       | 9   |               | Ga.         |
|      | John M. Livingston         | 7   |               | Ga.         |
|      | (Unnamed) Livingston       | 3   | (Female)      | Ga.         |
|      | Love D. A. P. Livingston   | 1   |               | Ga.         |
| 100. | Benj. Weeks                | 40  | Farmer        | Ga.         |
|      | Sarah Weeks                | 39  |               | Ga.         |
|      | Josiah Weeks               | 16  | Farm laborer  | Ga.         |
|      | Sarah A. Weeks             | 14  |               | Ga.         |
|      | Julia A. Weeks             | 13  |               | Ga.         |
|      | Michael L. Weeks           | 12  |               | Ga.         |
|      | Samson Weeks               | 11  |               | Ga.         |
|      | Benj. C. Weeks             | 10  |               | Ga.         |
|      | Mary E. Weeks              | 6   |               | Ga.         |
|      | Paton P. Weeks             | 3   |               | Ga.         |
|      | Thos. J. Weeks             | 2   |               | Ga.         |
|      | Flornoy Weeks              | 1   |               | Ga.         |
| 101. | Michael Weeks              | 75  | Past-laborer  | S. C.       |
|      | Malichi NeSmith            | 27  | Farmer        | Ga.         |
|      | Susan L. NeSmith           | 24  |               | Ga.         |
| 102. | John D. Dawson             | 56  | Farmer        | S. C.       |
|      | Rhoda Dawson               | 47  |               | Ga.         |
|      | Samuel D. Dawson           | 26  |               | Ga.         |
|      | Alston Rivers              | 28  | School teacher| S. C.       |
|      | William E. Rivers          | 11  |               | Ga.         |
| 103. | Geo. W. Hearndon           | 27  |               | Ga.         |
|      | Anna Weeks                 | 44  | Domestic      | Ga.         |
| 104. | Thos. Weeks                | 47  | Farmer        | Ga.         |
|      | Sarah B. Weeks             | 46  |               | S. C.       |
|      | James W. Weeks             | 14  |               | Ga.         |
| 105. | Wm. C. Bennet              | 35  | Farmer        | S. C.       |
|      | Piety Bennet               | 24  |               | Ga.         |
|      | Thos. A. Bennet            | 5   |               | Ga.         |
|      | Wm. C. Bennet              | 2   |               | Ga.         |

132    HISTORY OF COLQUITT COUNTY

|  | Name | Age | Occupation | Birth-place |
|---|---|---|---|---|
| 106. | James Weeks | 25 | Farmer | Ga. |
|  | Charles P. Weeks | 23 | Farmer | Ga. |
| 107. | Solomon P. Mims | 31 | Farmer | Ga. |
|  | Sarah A. Mims | 28 |  | N. C. |
|  | Henry M. Mims | 3 |  | Ga. |
|  | Joseph J. Mims | 2 |  | Ga. |
|  | Eliz. J. Mims | 9/12 |  | Ga. |
|  | Henry C. Quitt | 14 |  | N. C. |
| 108. | Joseph Mims | 78 | Farmer | N. C. |
|  | Elfira Mims | 65 |  | N. C. |
| 109. | Matthew Mims | 40 | Farmer | Ga. |
|  | Mary Ann Mims | 34 |  | Ga. |
|  | David W. Mims | 13 |  | Ga. |
|  | Sarah A. E. Mims | 11 |  | Ga. |
|  | Mary C. Mims | 10 |  | Ga. |
|  | Emily Mims | 6 |  | Ga. |
|  | Julia A. Mims | 4 |  | Ga. |
|  | Wm. J. Mims | 2 |  | Ga. |
|  | Laurana Mims | 34 | Domestic | Ga. |
| 110. | Wm. R. Dawson | 47 | Farmer | S. C. |
|  | Richard P. Dawson | 55 | Farm laborer | S. C. |
|  | Nancy Dawson | 25 |  | Ga. |
|  | Virgil T. Dawson | 3 |  | Ga. |
|  | William R. Dawson | 2/12 |  | Ga. |
| 111. | Andrew Dorman | 49 | Farmer | Ga. |
|  | Susan Dorman | 39 |  | Ga. |
|  | Louisa Dorman | 20 |  | Ga. |
|  | George W. Dorman | 19 | Farm laborer | Ga. |
|  | Daniel A. Dorman | 17 | Farm laborer | Ga. |
|  | Martha E. Dorman | 15 |  | Ga. |
|  | Benanel B. Dorman | 13 |  | Ga. |
|  | Henry C. Dorman | 11 |  | Ga. |

## THE CENSUS OF 1860

| | Name | Age | Occupation | Birth-place |
|---|---|---|---|---|
| | Sarah R. Dorman | 9 | | Ga. |
| | William T. Dorman | 7 | | Ga. |
| | Joseph N. Dorman | 4 | | Ga. |
| | Harriet M. E. Dorman | 2 | | Ga. |
| 112. | John A. Tillman | 20 | Farmer | Ga. |
| | Harriet Tillman | 18 | | Ga. |
| 113. | George W. Baker | 47 | Farmer | Ga. |
| | Lucinda Baker | 40 | | Ga. |
| | Maria Baker | 23 | | Ga. |
| | Wm. W. Baker | 21 | Farm laborer | Ga. |
| | Emily Baker | 19 | | Ga. |
| | Jordan Baker | 17 | Farm laborer | Ga. |
| | Polly Baker | 14 | | Ga. |
| | Missouri Baker | 12 | | Ga. |
| | John Baker | 10 | | Ga. |
| | Susan Baker | 8 | | Ga. |
| | Lucinda Baker | 6 | | Ga. |
| | Kansas Baker | 4 | | Ga. |
| | James B. Baker | 1 | | Ga. |
| 114. | Moses C. Norman | 34 | Blacksmith | Ga. |
| | Louisa Norman | 24 | | Ga. |
| | Ruth E. Norman | 7 | | Ga. |
| | James M. Norman | 6 | | Ga. |
| | Wm. H. H. Norman | 5 | | Ga. |
| | Martha J. Norman | 4 | | Ga. |
| | Dica A. Norman | 2 | | Ga. |
| | Jessie F. Norman | 1 | | Ga. |
| | Martha Norman | 29 | Domestic | Ga. |
| | William J. Norman | 1 | | Ga. |
| | Martha A. N. Norman | 4/12 | | Ga. |
| 115. | James M. Norman | 65 | Farmer | Ga. |
| | Ruth Norman | 60 | | S. C. |

|  | Name | Age | Occupation | Birth-place |
|---|---|---|---|---|
|  | Zilpha R. Norman | 24 |  | Ga. |
|  | Harrison Norman | 19 | Farm laborer | Ga. |
|  | Nancy E. Norman | 16 |  | Ga. |
|  | Joel S. Norman | 21 | Wheelwright | Ga. |
| 116. | Willis Jordan | 46 | Laborer | Ga. |
|  | Aurena Jordan | 36 |  | Ga. |
|  | Disa C. R. Jordan | 11 |  | Ga. |
|  | Jonathan J. T. Jordan | 8 |  | Ga. |
|  | Arcada Jordan | 7 |  | Ga. |
|  | Joseph E. H. Jordan | 6 |  | Ga. |
|  | Patsy E. Jordan | 1 |  | Ga. |
| 117. | Burell A. Baker | 25 | Farmer | Ga. |
|  | Disa A. R. Baker | 27 |  | Ga. |
| 118. | Matthew C. Dukes | 55 | Farmer | Ga. |
|  | Julia Ann Dukes | 52 |  | N. C. |
|  | Matthew M. Dukes | 22 |  | Ga. |
|  | Julia Ann Dukes | 18 |  | Ga. |
|  | Phebe J. Dukes | 16 |  | Ga. |
|  | Pelatin Dukes | 13 |  | Ga. |
|  | Emaline A. Dukes | 12 |  | Ga. |
| 119. | Wm. B. Robinson | 39 | Farmer | Ga. |
|  | Eliz. Robinson | 55 |  | S. C. |
|  | Wm. T. Robinson | 13 |  | Ga. |
|  | John Johnson | 83 | Methodist Es. | Hanover |
|  | Hamit Johnson | 30 | Domestic | S. C. |
| 120. | Isaac C. Smith | 28 | Farmer | Ga. |
|  | Lydia M. J. Smith | 28 |  | Ga. |
| 121. | Saul Mercer | 41 | Farmer | Ga. |
|  | Martha Mercer | 33 |  | Ga. |
|  | James Mercer | 16 |  | Ga. |
|  | Susan Mercer | 13 |  | Ga. |

## THE CENSUS OF 1860

|      | NAME | AGE | OCCUPATION | BIRTH-PLACE |
|------|------|-----|------------|-------------|
|      | Cordelia Mercer | 11 | | Ga. |
|      | Benj. W. Mercer | 9 | | Ga. |
|      | Mary Ann Mercer | 7 | | Ga. |
|      | Roxy A. E. Mercer | 4 | | Ga. |
|      | Laura J. Mercer | 2 | | Ga. |
|      | Noah Mercer | 9/12 | | Ga. |
| 122. | John Mercer | 32 | Laborer | Ga. |
|      | Amanda Mercer | 26 | | Ga. |
|      | Sarah F. Mercer | 4 | | Ga. |
| 123. | Jane Gay | 60 | | Ga. |
|      | Matthew Gay | 20 | Farm laborer | Ga. |
|      | Mary J. Gay | 17 | | Ga. |
|      | James W. Bloodworth | 13 | | Ga. |
| 124. | John Tillman | 60 | Farmer | Ga. |
|      | Sarah Tillman | 55 | | N. C. |
|      | Rachel Tillman | 16 | | Ga. |
|      | James H. Tillman | 15 | Laborer | Ga. |
|      | Susan J. Tillman | 12 | | Ga. |
|      | Georgia A. E. Tillman | 10 | | Ga. |
|      | Roxy Ann Tillman | 5 | | Ga. |
|      | Fariba Mercer | 90 | | N. C. |
|      | Leroy Mauldin | 20 | Farm laborer | Ga. |
| 125. | John S. Williamson | 29 | Blacksmith | N. C. |
|      | Mary E. Williamson | 23 | | Ga. |
| 126. | James Robinson | 60 | Farmer | S. C. |
|      | Martha Robinson | 60 | | S. C. |
|      | Susan Robinson | 19 | | Ga. |
|      | Lucy Robinson | 17 | | Ga. |
|      | James Mercer | 11 | | Ga. |
| 127. | James J. Robinson | 25 | Farmer | Ga. |
|      | Sarah Robinson | 21 | | Fla. |

## HISTORY OF COLQUITT COUNTY

| | Name | Age | Occupation | Birth-place |
|---|---|---|---|---|
| 128. | Stuart S. May | 39 | Farmer | Ga. |
| | Susannah May | 39 | | Ga. |
| | Rusheon May | 19 | | Ga. |
| | Mary W. May | 14 | | Ga. |
| | William W. May | 11 | | Ga. |
| | John A. May | 8 | | Ga. |
| | Lindsey M. L. A. May | 6 | | Ga. |
| | Joel C. May | 3 | | Ga. |
| | Edmund May | 1 | | Ga. |
| 129. | Joshua Tillman | 50 | Farmer | Ga. |
| | Mary Tillman | 48 | | Ga. |
| | Joshua J. Tillman | 25 | Farm laborer | Ga. |
| | Richard E. Tillman | 19 | Farm laborer | Ga. |
| | Berry J. Tillman | 18 | Farm laborer | Ga. |
| | Eliz. A. J. Tillman | 15 | | Ga. |
| | Absalom Tillman | 14 | | Ga. |
| | Joseph T. Tillman | 12 | | Ga. |
| | Nathaniel J. Tillman | 10 | | Ga. |
| | Georgia A. L. Tillman | 8 | | Ga. |
| 130. | Joshua Lee | 72 | | N. C. |
| | Nancy Lee | 60 | | N. C. |
| | Frances M. Lee | 24 | Farm laborer | Ga. |
| | Hepsy Lee | 22 | | Ga. |
| | Asenath Lee | 21 | | Ga. |
| 131. | John W. Robinson | 26 | Farmer | Ga. |
| | Mary Robinson | 25 | | Ga. |
| | Charles Robinson | 8 | | Ga. |
| | Mary Robinson | 6 | | Ga. |
| | John Robinson | 4 | | Ga. |
| 132. | Philip Hiers | 66 | Farmer | S. C. |
| | Kesiah Hiers | 56 | | S. C. |
| | Solomon Hiers | 23 | Farm laborer | Ga. |

## THE CENSUS OF 1860

|      | Name | Age | Occupation | Birth-place |
|------|------|-----|------------|-------------|
|      | Rebecca A. Hiers | 18 | | Ga. |
|      | Eliza Hiers | 17 | | Ga. |
|      | Michael Hiers | 16 | Farm laborer | Ga. |
|      | Martha A. E. Hiers | 13 | | Ga. |
| 133. | Durham Hancock | 73 | Farmer | Ga. |
|      | Mary Ann Hancock | 50 | | N. C. |
| 134. | James W. Hiers | 21 | Farmer | Ga. |
|      | Rachel Ann Hiers | 22 | | Ga. |
|      | Mary A. K. Hiers | 7/12 | | Ga. |
| 135. | Joshua Brownin | 66 | Farmer | N. C. |
|      | Lydia Brownin | 56 | | Ga. |
|      | Eliz. Brownin | 23 | | Ga. |
|      | Sarah Brownin | 15 | | Ga. |
|      | Charles Brownin | 2 | | Ga. |
|      | Elbert Brownin | 2 | | Ga. |
| 136. | Daniel Hiers | 25 | Farmer | Ga. |
|      | Phebe Hiers | 25 | | N. C. |
|      | Andrew H. Hiers | 3 | | Fla. |
|      | James E. Hiers | 2 | | Fla. |
|      | Daniel C. Hiers | 2/12 | | Ga. |
|      | Louisa Dorman | 20 | Domestic | Ga. |
| 137. | Lucius M. Wingate | 23 | Farmer | N. C. |
|      | Eliz. Wingate | 63 | | N. C. |
|      | Ann M. Wingate | 29 | | N. C. |
| 138. | John T. Norman | 30 | Farmer | Ga. |
|      | Nancy Norman | 25 | | Ga. |
|      | Sallie A. Norman | 6 | | Ga. |
|      | Vena Norman | 5 | | Ga. |
|      | Eliz. Norman | 3 | | Ga. |
|      | James W. Norman | 1 | | Ga. |
|      | Joseph Harrison | 33 | | N. C. |

|      | Name | Age | Occupation | Birth-place |
|------|------|-----|------------|-------------|
| 139. | John A. Alderman | 32 | Farmer | Ga. |
|      | Emily S. Alderman | 33 | | Ga. |
|      | Nancy A. R. Alderman | 10 | | Ga. |
|      | Sarah A. Alderman | 9 | | Ga. |
|      | William J. Alderman | 7 | | Ga. |
|      | Susan A. Alderman | 6 | | Ga. |
|      | John A. Alderman | 4 | | Ga. |
|      | Disa E. Alderman | 3 | | Ga. |
|      | Daniel H. Alderman | 1 | | Ga. |
| 140. | John W. Weldon | 43 | | Ga. |
|      | Eliz. Weldon | 26 | | Ga. |
|      | John J. Weldon | 8 | | Ga. |
|      | Henry E. Weldon | 2 | | Ga. |
|      | Nancy J. Weldon | 6/12 | | Ga. |
| 141. | Jacob H. Croft | 25 | | S. C. |
|      | Jerona A. Croft | 19 | | Ga. |
|      | Jacob H. Croft | 5 | | Ga. |
|      | Neal Brownin | 20 | Farm laborer | Ga. |
| 142. | Chas. A. Hiers | 35 | Farmer | S. C. |
|      | Mary A. Hiers | 31 | | Ga. |
|      | Nancy Ann Hiers | 12 | | Ga. |
|      | Mary Ann Hiers | 10 | | Ga. |
|      | Philip P. Hiers | 8 | | Ga. |
|      | Angeline Hiers | 6 | | Ga. |
|      | Lucy Ann Hiers | 4 | | Ga. |
|      | Matthew Hiers | 3 | | Ga. |
|      | Susan Hiers | 2 | | Ga. |
| 143. | George W. Croft | 26 | Farm laborer | S. C. |
|      | Sarah Croft | 32 | | S. C. |
|      | Georgia Ann Hunter | 10 | | Ga. |
|      | Berrien Croft | 3 | | Ga. |
|      | Mary C. Croft | 2 | | Ga. |

## THE CENSUS OF 1860

| | NAME | AGE | OCCUPATION | BIRTH-PLACE |
|---|---|---|---|---|
| 144. | David B. Norman | 37 | Farmer | Ga. |
| | Susannah Norman | 37 | | S. C. |
| | David V. A. Norman | 13 | | Ga. |
| | Aaron A. Norman | 11 | | Fla. |
| | Nancy Ann Norman | 10 | | Fla. |
| | Moses X. Norman | 8 | | Fla. |
| | Roxy A. C. Norman | 6 | | Ga. |
| | Susannah C. Norman | 4 | | Ga. |
| | (Unnamed) Norman | 1 | | Ga. |
| 145. | John Manning | 33 | Farmer | Ga. |
| | Eliza Manning | 28 | | Ga. |
| | William Manning | 11 | | Ga. |
| | Haywood Manning | 8 | | Ga. |
| | Nancy A. Manning | 5 | | Ga. |
| | Louisa Manning | 4 | | Ga. |
| | Jackson Manning | 2 | | Ga. |
| 146. | William W. Burgess | 25 | Farmer | Ga. |
| | Susan C. Burgess | 20 | | S. C. |
| | William T. Burgess | 2 | | Ga. |
| 147. | Chas. H. Johnson | 70 | Farmer | England |
| | Eliz. Johnson | 62 | | Ga. |
| | Mary E. Johnson | 18 | | Ga. |
| | Jonathan J. Johnson | 16 | | Ga. |
| | Margaret Godwin | 30 | Seamstress | Ga. |
| 148. | Eliab Roberts | 33 | Farm laborer | Ga. |
| | Sarah A. Roberts | 27 | | Ga. |
| | Mary A. Roberts | 10 | | Ga. |
| | Alderman Roberts | 8 | | Ga. |
| 149. | Nathaniel Croft | 50 | Farmer | S. C. |
| | Mary A. Croft | 45 | | S. C. |
| | Eliz. Croft | 21 | | S. C. |
| | Wm. N. Croft | 18 | Farm laborer | S. C. |

|  | Name | Age | Occupation | Birth-place |
|---|---|---|---|---|
|  | Frances M. Croft | 15 | Farm laborer | S. C. |
|  | Henry J. Croft | 13 |  | S. C. |
|  | Jacob J. R. Croft | 11 |  | Ga. |
|  | John D. C. Croft | 9 |  | Ga. |
|  | James H. Croft | 7 |  | Ga. |
|  | Robert C. Croft | 5 |  | Ga. |
|  | Sarah A. V. Croft | 3 |  | Ga. |
|  | Leroy E. Croft | 2 |  | Ga. |
|  | Martin S. Croft | 1 |  | Ga. |
| 150. | John N. Croft | 25 | Laborer | S. C. |
|  | Martha A. Croft | 23 |  | S. C. |
|  | David N. Croft | 9/12 |  | Ga. |
| 151. | Susan Thompson | 37 | Free Negro cook | Ga. |
|  | William Thompson | 21 | Free Negro waggoner | Ga. |
|  | Delia Thompson | 18 | F. N. field hand | Ga. |
|  | Arthur Thompson | 16 | F. N. | Ga. |
|  | Charles Thompson | 14 | F. N. | Ga. |
|  | Moses Thompson | 12 | F. N. | Ga. |
|  | Ruffin Thompson | 10 | F. N. | Ga. |
|  | Ruben Thompson | 7 | F. N. | Ga. |
|  | Joseph Thompson | 3 | F. N. | Ga. |
|  | James Thompson | 7/12 |  | Ga. |
| 152. | Mitchell J. Alderman | 22 | Farmer | Ga. |
|  | Mary D. Alderman | 18 |  | Ga. |
|  | Jonah Alderman | 6/12 |  | Ga. |
| 153. | George F. Hearndon | 45 | Farmer | Ga. |
|  | Eda Hearndon | 34 |  | N. C. |
|  | John W. Hearndon | 15 | Farm laborer | Ga. |
|  | Eliz. A. C. Hearndon | 13 |  | Ga. |
|  | Martha A. Hearndon | 9 |  | Ga. |
|  | James F. Hearndon | 4 |  | Ga. |
|  | Mary M. Hearndon | 2 |  | Ga. |

## THE CENSUS OF 1860

| | Name | Age | Occupation | Birth-place |
|---|---|---|---|---|
| 154. | John A. Pope | 36 | Farmer | N. C. |
| | Nancy Pope | 34 | | Ga. |
| | Elender E. Pope | 6 | | Ga. |
| | James W. Pope | 4 | | Ga. |
| | Francis J. Pope | 1 | | Ga. |
| 155. | Wesley Pope | 23 | Farm laborer | Ga. |
| | Mary J. Pope | 23 | | Ga. |
| | Willis W. Pope | 4 | | Ga. |
| | Horace J. Pope | 1 | | Ga. |
| 156. | Joseph D. Hicks | 37 | Farmer | N. C. |
| | Mosely J. Hicks | 61 | Farmer | N. C. |
| | James J. Hicks | 28 | Farm laborer | Ga. |
| | Amanda C. Hicks | 25 | | Ga. |
| 157. | Asa Lewis | 27 | Farmer | Ga. |
| | Nancy Lewis | 25 | | Ga. |
| | Susan Lewis | 2 | | Ga. |
| | William H. Lewis | 8/12 | | Ga. |
| 158. | John Selph | 51 | Farmer | Ga. |
| | Sarah A. Selph | 25 | | Ga. |
| | George W. Selph | 25 | Carpenter | Ga. |
| | John W. Selph | 22 | Farm laborer | Ga. |
| | Polly Selph | 21 | | Ga. |
| | Thomas Selph | 18 | | Ga. |
| | James Selph | 16 | | Ga. |
| | Samuel Selph | 13 | | Ga. |
| | Warren Selph | 11 | | Ga. |
| | Sarah Selph | 9 | | Ga. |
| | Jessie Selph | 6 | | Ga. |
| | Nancy E. Selph | 5/12 | | Ga. |
| 159. | Georgia Ann Barwick | 41 | Seamstress | Ga. |
| | Henry C. Barwick | 12 | | Ga. |
| | Martha Ann Barwick | 7 | | Ga. |
| | Susan Barwick | 4 | | Ga. |

| | Name | Age | Occupation | Birth-place |
|---|---|---|---|---|
| 160. | William Murphy | 37 | | N. C. |
| | Hester Murphy | 30 | | Ga. |
| | Henry T. Murphy | 9 | | Ga. |
| | Sallie A. Murphy | 6 | | Ga. |
| | Bird Murphy | 3 | | Ga. |
| | Isaac Murphy | 2 | | Ga. |
| | Eliz. A. Murphy | 1/12 | | Ga. |
| | Eliz. Sloan | 21 | | Ga. |
| | David Sloan | 17 | Farm laborer | Ga. |
| 161. | Calvin Murphy | 34 | Farmer | N. C. |
| | Mary E. Murphy | 30 | | Ga. |
| | Phebe Murphy | 13 | | Ga. |
| | Benj. Murphy | 12 | | Ga. |
| | Nancy Murphy | 11 | | Ga. |
| | William Murphy | 8 | | Ga. |
| | Perry Murphy | 6 | | Ga. |
| | Shadrach Murphy | 3 | | Ga. |
| | Martha Murphy | 1 | | Ga. |
| 162. | James Murphy | 32 | Farmer | N. C. |
| | Eliz. Murphy | 21 | | Ga. |
| | Calvin Murphy | 4 | | Ga. |
| | Eliz. J. Murphy | 2 | | Ga. |
| | William P. Murphy | 10/12 | | Ga. |
| | Jeptha Turner | 13 | | Ga. |
| | Martha Turner | 15 | | Ga. |
| 163. | James Brown | 30 | Farmer | Ga. |
| | Eliza Brown | 30 | | Ga. |
| | Andrew Brown | 7 | | Ga. |
| | Edmund D. Brown | 10/12 | | Ga. |
| | Nathan Barwick | 16 | Farm laborer | Ga. |
| 164. | Shadrack Wells | 63 | Farmer | N. C. |
| | Phebe Wells | 51 | | N. C. |
| | John W. Wells | 25 | Farm laborer | Ga. |

## THE CENSUS OF 1860

| | Name | Age | Occupation | Birth-place |
|---|---|---|---|---|
| 165. | Henry Murphy | 63 | Farmer | N. C. |
| | Mahalie Goff | 42 | | N. C. |
| | Isaiah Goff | 19 | Farm laborer | Ga. |
| | Butler Williams | 18 | Farm laborer | S. C. |
| 166. | John W. Kelly | 47 | Farmer | S. C. |
| | Martha M. Kelly | 48 | | S. C. |
| | James I. Kelly | 22 | Farm laborer | S. C. |
| | Eliza Ann Kelly | 20 | | Ala. |
| | Martha E. Kelly | 19 | | Ala. |
| | Missouri Kelly | 17 | | Ga. |
| | Harriet E. Kelly | 15 | | Ga. |
| | John T. Kelly | 13 | | Ga. |
| | Susan Kelly | 11 | | Ga. |
| | Timothy Kelly | 9 | | Ga. |
| | Saphrona Kelly | 7 | | Ga. |
| 167. | Henry Murphy, Jr. | 55 | Farmer | N. C. |
| | Elender Murphy | 39 | | N. C. |
| | William P. Murphy | 16 | | Ga. |
| | Eleazer Murphy | 12 | | Ga. |
| | Sarah W. Murphy | 7 | | Ga. |
| | David J. Murphy | 3 | | Ga. |
| | James Turner | 25 | Farm laborer | Ala. |
| 168. | Shadrack Beasley | 30 | Laborer | S. C. |
| | Sophia Beasley | 29 | | Ga. |
| | Florence A. Beasley | 4 | | Fla. |
| | Mary F. Beasley | 1 | | Ga. |
| 169. | John A. Hancock | 24 | Farmer | Ga. |
| | Eliza Hancock | 19 | | Ga. |
| | Mary E. Hancock | 1 | | Ga. |
| 170. | John Hancock | 63 | Farmer | N. C. |
| | Eliza Hancock | 45 | | Ga. |
| | Thos. Hancock | 12 | | Ga. |

| Name | Age | Occupation | Birth-place |
|---|---|---|---|
| John Hancock, Jr. | 10 | | Ga. |
| Mitchell Hancock | 6 | | Ga. |
| Taylor Hancock | 2 | | Ga. |
| (Unnamed) Hancock | 1/12 | | Ga. |
| 171. Levi Cox | 48 | Farmer | N. C. |
| Polly Cox | 30 | | N. C. |
| Ellen Cox | 17 | | Ga. |
| Jasper Cox | 15 | Farm laborer | Ga. |
| Jackson Cox | 10 | | Ga. |
| Sally Cox | 8 | | Ga. |
| Eliza Cox | 6 | | Ga. |
| Nancy P. Cox | 3 | | Ga. |
| William F. Cox | 3 | | Ga. |
| Seaborn Willis | 28 | Farm laborer | Ga. |
| 172. Thos. White | 54 | Farmer | S. C. |
| Martha White | 41 | | Ga. |
| Matthew White | 15 | Farm laborer | Ga. |
| Susan White | 13 | | Ga. |
| Frances White | 11 | | Ga. |
| Adeline White | 9 | | Ga. |
| Victoria White | 7 | | Ga. |
| Nancy E. White | 2 | | Ga. |
| 173. James Hancock | 26 | Farm laborer | Ga. |
| Susan Hancock | 20 | | Ga. |
| 174. Fielding G. Suber | 30 | Farmer | S. C. |
| Emily Suber | 24 | | Ga. |
| William Suber | 4 | | Ga. |
| 175. Harrison E. Suber | 28 | Farm laborer | S. C. |
| Mary Suber | 26 | | Ga. |
| Charles Suber | 3 | | Ga. |
| William Suber | 1 | | Ga. |

## THE CENSUS OF 1860

|   | NAME | AGE | OCCUPATION | BIRTH-PLACE |
|---|---|---|---|---|
| 176. | Archibald Lee | 72 | Farmer | S. C. |
|   | Jeptha Lee | 31 | Methodist | Ga. |
|   | Eliza A. Lee | 20 |   | Ga. |
|   | Jonathan Lee | 18 | Farm laborer | Ga. |
|   | Matilda S. Lee | 4 |   | Ga. |
| 177. | James S. Barrow | 40 | Farmer | Ga. |
|   | Benetia A. Barrow | 30 |   | Ga. |
|   | Marg. A. E. Barrow | 17 |   | Ga. |
|   | Tamar Barrow | 13 |   | Ga. |
|   | James G. T. Barrow | 11 |   | Ga. |
|   | John W. Barrow | 7 |   | Ga. |
|   | Wm. A. Barrow | 3 |   | Ga. |
|   | Martha H. Barrow | 1 |   | Ga. |
|   | Lafayette A. Barrow | 1/12 |   | Ga. |
| 178. | Wm. Barwick | 34 | Farmer | Ga. |
|   | Sarah A. E. Barwick | 32 |   | Ga. |
|   | Sarah A. W. Barwick | 14 |   | Ga. |
|   | Almeea S. Barwick | 10 |   | Ga. |
|   | Elbert A. Barwick | 8 |   | Ga. |
|   | Theodore A. Barwick | 6 |   | Ga. |
|   | Emma E. Barwick | 4 |   | Ga. |
|   | James M. Barwick | 2 |   | Ga. |
| 179. | Wm. Alligood | 33 | Farmer | Ga. |
|   | Eliza Alligood | 32 |   | Ga. |
|   | Mary Alligood | 8 |   | Ga. |
|   | Robert H. Alligood | 4 |   | Ga. |
|   | (Unnamed) Alligood | 4/12 |   | Ga. |
| 180. | Jacob Resencranse | 50 | Farmer | Switzerland |
|   | Joseph A. Resencranse | 20 | Farm laborer | Switzerland |
|   | Barbara Resencranse | 14 |   | Ga. |
|   | Henry Resencranse | 10 |   | Ga. |
|   | Julia A. Resencranse | 8 |   | Ga. |

|  | Name | Age | Occupation | Birth-place |
|---|---|---|---|---|
| 181. | Jared I. Gandy | 21 | Farmer | Ga. |
|  | Mary M. Gandy | 22 |  | Switzerland |
|  | Idealilly Gandy | 1/12 |  | Ga. |
| 182. | Murphy Lanier | 55 | Farmer | N. C. |
|  | Temple Lanier | 48 |  | N. C. |
|  | John Lanier | 23 | Blacksmith | Ga. |
|  | Hardy Lanier | 21 | Farm laborer | Ga. |
|  | Gibson Lanier | 19 | Farm laborer | Ga. |
|  | Thomas Lanier | 16 | Farm laborer | Ga. |
|  | Timothy Lanier | 14 |  | Ga. |
|  | Marion B. Lanier | 9 |  | Ga. |
| 183. | Thos. J. Stansill | 23 | Farmer | Ga. |
| 184. | James M. Gunn | 22 | Steam mill hand | Ga. |
|  | Nancy Gunn | 16 |  | Ga. |
| 185. | John B. Harris | 25 | Farm laborer | Ga. |
|  | Desdemona Harris | 23 |  | Ga. |
|  | Joseph B. Harris | 5 |  | Ga. |
|  | Nancy J. Harris | 3 |  | Ga. |
|  | Rufus C. Harris | 1 |  | Ga. |
| 186. | Reason J. Marlow | 37 | Steam mill hand | Ga. |
|  | Laura J. Marlow | 25 |  | Ga. |
|  | Martha E. Marlow | 11/12 |  | Ga. |
| 187. | Harriet E. Mauldin | 51 | Seamstress | Ga. |
|  | America Mauldin | 17 |  | Ga. |
|  | Richard Mauldin | 16 | Steam mill hand | Ga. |
|  | Samuel Mauldin | 15 | Farm laborer | Ga. |
| 188. | Geo. W. Evans | 48 | Miller—steam mill | Ga. |
|  | Olive Evans | 41 |  | Ga. |
|  | John B. Evans | 21 | Steam mill hand | Ga. |
|  | Zilpha Evans | 19 |  | Ga. |
|  | James Evans | 17 |  | Ga. |

## THE CENSUS OF 1860

|  | Name | Age | Occupation | Birth-place |
|---|---|---|---|---|
|  | Daniel Evans | 15 |  | Ga. |
|  | Sarah Ann Evans | 12 |  | Ga. |
|  | Joseph R. E. Evans | 9 |  | Ga. |
|  | Eli W. Evans | 7 |  | Ga. |
|  | Mary M. Evans | 4 |  | Ga. |
|  | George P. Evans | 1 |  | Ga. |
| 189. | Joel S. Graves | 48 | O. S. P. | Vt. |
|  | Eunice Graves | 47 |  | N. Y. |
|  | Roxianne Graves | 22 | Teacher common s. | Fla. |
|  | Nathan Graves | 17 | Farm laborer | Fla. |
|  | Spencer Graves | 16 | Farm laborer | Fla. |
|  | Charles Graves | 13 |  | Fla. |
|  | Cherry H. Graves | 11 |  | Ga. |
|  | Cyrus Graves | 8 |  | Ga. |
|  | Alice Graves | 4 |  | Ga. |
|  | Ruth Graves | 57 | School teacher | Vt. |
|  | Sarah Thompson | 21 |  | Fla. |
|  | William J. Thompson | 1 |  | Ga. |
|  | Eliza Franklin | 14 |  | Ga. |
|  | Lucy Franklin | 10 |  | Ga. |
| 190. | Gilford Kent | 22 | Steam mill hand | Ga. |
|  | Martha Kent | 22 |  | Ga. |
|  | James N. Kent | 7/12 |  | Ga. |
| 191. | James McMullin | 23 | Steam mill hand | Ga. |
|  | Sarah McMullin | 29 |  | Ga. |
|  | Emily McMullin | 1 |  | Ga. |
| 192. | Wright Flowers | 58 | Farmer | Ga. |
|  | Eliz. Flowers | 57 |  | Ga. |
|  | Oliver N. Flowers | 24 | Farmer | Ga. |
|  | James B. Flowers | 20 | Farm laborer | Ga. |
|  | Amanda E. Flowers | 19 |  | Ga. |
|  | Wm. Porter | 6 |  | Ga. |

| | Name | Age | Occupation | Birth-place |
|---|---|---|---|---|
| 193. | Matthew Tucker | 33 | Farm laborer | Ga. |
| | Eliz. Tucker | 29 | | Ga. |
| | Nancy J. Tucker | 5 | | Ga. |
| | Richard B. Tucker | 4 | | Ga. |
| | Mary A. Tucker | 1 | | Ga. |
| 194. | Josiah Johnson | 28 | Wheelwright | N. C. |
| | Rebecca M. Johnson | 24 | | Ga. |
| | Jonah Johnson | 2 | | Ga. |
| | Manda Johnson | 3/12 | | Ga. |
| | Elkanah Johnson | 22 | Farm laborer | Ga. |
| 195. | Wm. E. Jordan | 23 | Laborer | Ga. |
| | Leonora Jordan | 22 | | Ga. |
| | David Jordan | 2 | | Ga. |
| | Thos. R. Jordan | 10/12 | | Ga. |
| 196. | Jessie Carlton | 55 | Farmer | N. C. |
| | Rhoda Carlton | 47 | | N. C. |
| | Thos. Carlton | 20 | Farm laborer | Ga. |
| | Mary Ann Carlton | 17 | | Ga. |
| | Phebe Carlton | 15 | | Ga. |
| 197. | Henry Scott | 34 | Farmer | Ga. |
| | Martha Scott | 31 | | Ga. |
| | Wm. B. Scott | 14 | | Ga. |
| | Green B. Scott | 10 | | Ga. |
| | James Scott | 7 | | Ga. |
| | Lawson Scott | 5 | | Ga. |
| | Georgia Ann Scott | 2 | | Ga. |
| | Savannah Scott | 2/12 | | Ga. |
| 198. | Nancy Bryant | 50 | | Ga. |
| | Calvin Bryant | 26 | Farm laborer | Ga. |
| | Martha A. Bryant | 20 | | Ga. |
| | Lavinia Bryant | 17 | | Ga. |

## THE CENSUS OF 1860

| | Name | Age | Occupation | Birth-place |
|---|---|---|---|---|
| | John Bryant | 15 | | Ga. |
| | Susan J. Bryant | 12 | | Ga. |
| | Henry B. Bryant | 8 | | Ga. |
| 199. | William Duggin | 61 | Farmer | N. C. |
| | Priscilla Duggin | 50 | | N. C. |
| | Polly Duggin | 33 | | Ga. |
| | Martha E. Duggin | 21 | | Ga. |
| | Edmund Duggin | 18 | Farm laborer | Ga. |
| | Sarah J. Duggin | 17 | | Ga. |
| | Josephine Duggin | 11 | | Ga. |
| | Susan Duggin | 10 | | Ga. |
| | Rebecca Duggin | 10 | | Ga. |
| | John Duggin | 8 | | Ga. |
| | Francis Duggin | 4 | | Ga. |
| 200. | John Johnson | 30 | Farmer | S. C. |
| | Nancy Johnson | 25 | | Ga. |
| | John Johnson | 4 | | Ga. |
| | Nancy Ann Johnson | 1 | | Ga. |
| | Henry P. Johnson | 1/12 | | Ga. |
| | William E. Johnson | 20 | Farm laborer | Ga. |
| | Katherine Johnson | 50 | Domestic | S. C. |
| 201. | James M. West | 48 | Farmer | N. C. |
| | Katherine West | 45 | | Ga. |
| | Eliz. Hearndon | 20 | Domestic | Ga. |
| 202. | Peter O. Wing | 43 | Ordinary Col. Co. | Maine |
| | Eliz. A. Wing | 22 | | Ga. |
| | Sarah Wing | 2 | | Ga. |
| 203. | Amos Turner | 59 | Clerk S. Court | N. C. |
| 204. | Moses Thompson | 51 | Farmer | Ga. |

CHAPTER XXI

## Colquitt's Slaves in 1860

WHEN THE FEDERAL CENSUS of 1860 was taken, the only provision made for counting slaves was a statement of their owner and their age and sex. The name of the slave was not given at all.

Under the laws of the State of Georgia, it was forbidden, at that time, to teach any member of the negro race to read or write. Penalty for infraction of this law was fine for white violators and whipping for negro violators. Possibly the only reason for counting the slaves at all was to meet the provision of the Constitution of the United States for additional Congressmen from slave States, based on the number of slaves in such States. For this purpose, a slave was equal to three-fifths of a white person.

The census of 1860 shows that at that time 27 slave owners owned 110 slaves in Colquitt County—52 males and 58 females. The largest number of slaves held by any single owner was held by Charles H. Johnson, who is shown by this census to have been the owner of 24 slaves, occupying three slave houses. Mr. Johnson was 70 years old in 1860, and he reported that he was born in England. His first years were spent "Before the Mast"; and, by the way, he was a contemporary of Author Richard H. Dana, the author of "Two Years Before the Mast"; and he must have been a very interesting character during the time in which he lived in Colquitt. He reported himself to Census Marshal Wing as being 70 years old in 1860. It is an established fact that after that date he lived 26 years. Some of his grandchildren are still alive and they say that he died in 1886. We believe that he has the record for longevity among the males who have lived and died in Colquitt County. We have already noticed in connection with the census of 1860 that Marshal Wing found Sally Hawkins up in the Weeks settlement in Colquitt who confessed "up" to being 96 years old.

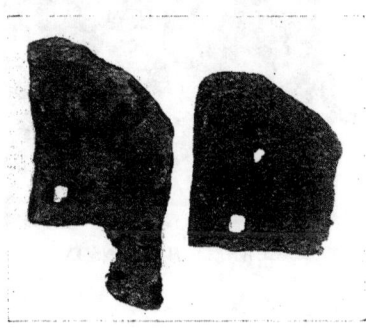

Remnants of two hand forged plows made on the Johnson Estate in slavery days.

Pioneer Johnson is said to have had a flair for establishing clearings on the "bottom lands" of the Okapilco Creek which ran through his plantation down in the southeast corner of Colquitt. These clearings still exist—some of them, although they have not been farmed for more than a generation. Recently some of his grandsons exhumed from one such field two plow-points which were in use during slavery. We append pictures of these plows—or "plow-points" as they would now be called. Fully one-half of the original metal content has rusted away. It is believed that these are the only existing farming implements ever in use in Georgia by slave labor. One of these plows was a "half-shovel," and the other was a "twister." (The twister is the one with the "whing," as we Crackers sometimes pronounce the word "wing.")

We also insert as part of this article a cut of the residence erected by Charles H. Johnson in the early 1840's, which is still standing. It was a double log-pen two-story building, and for fifty years after its erection was the most pretentious residence in the Colquitt County territory.

Finally, we are pleased to be able to submit to "all and singular," a cut made from a copy of a daguerreotype of Pioneer Johnson himself. As will be seen, Patriarch Johnson was a handsome man in his time, reminding one of George Washington. We are very glad to have obtained this photograph which comes to us through the courtesy of Mrs. Enoch Vann, a granddaughter of Mr. Johnson.

CHARLES H. JOHNSON

The Johnson Residence in 1840. From free hand drawing made by M. STEEPLE of Augusta, during the civil war.

## CHAPTER XXII

# The Georgia-Northern Railway

FROM 1818, the date of the Jackson-Seminole Treaty, ceding Southwest Georgia to Georgia, to the year 1893, stretches three-quarters of a century, and during this period Colquitt County made practically no progress. On the day this is written (June 10, 1936), we interviewed a grandson of one of the Colquitt pioneers who came here in 1836. This pioneer was not illiterate when he came here from North Carolina, but could read and write. The interviewed grandson is eighty years old, and cannot read or write. Of course conditions as to education began to improve a little with the establishment of Georgia's public school system, so that practically every one born since 1870 can read and write at least a little.

The thing that happened to change all things in Colquitt County was the shriek of a locomotive's whistle, sounding at the county-site on February 26, 1893. On that date C. W. Pidcock drove the first train into Moultrie, on tracks just completed from Pidcock, a station on the A. C. L. Ry., thirty miles to the south.

This event has been the most important thing that has happened to the Colquitt territory since the Indians, under Jackson's iron pressure, gave away twenty counties to Georgia. Here is how this boon to Colquitt came to pass.

On June 6, 1892, C. W. Pidcock, and his father, the late Hon. James Nelson Pidcock, organized the Boston and Albany Rail Road Co. Together they met some local business men in Boston, Ga., who owned a legislative charter for the "Boston and Albany Rail Road Co.," although nothing had been done toward its construction by the owners. The Pidcocks, father and son, on the 6th day of June, 1892, organized the Boston and Albany Railroad Co., naming the late James N. Pidcock, the father of C. W. Pidcock, president; Mr. R. Mallette, vice-president, and C. W. Pidcock, secretary-treasurer and superintendent. After this organization, the Boston and Albany Railroad Co., purchased the logging tram of the Quitman Lumber Co., which tram line extended from a small station on the A. C. L. a few miles east of Boston, called "Pidcock," to Hollis, Ga., a distance of twelve miles to the North. This tram-line track they rebuilt, and extended it to Moultrie, Ga., entering Moultrie on the 26th day of the month of February, 1893, Superintendent Pidcock acting as engineer, and E. N. Phelps acting as conductor of this, the first train ever brought into Moultrie from any source. The town had at that time some two or three hundred inhabitants.

The Boston and Albany Rail Road Co., passed into receivership during the big panic in June, 1893; however, Mr. C. W. Pidcock's services were retained by the receiver in the capacity of superintendent until in October, 1894, it was purchased at receiver's sale by James N. Pidcock, Jr., who re-organized it in the same year, as the "Georgia-Northern Railway Company." Mr. J. N. Pidcock, Jr., became president under this re-organization, and served until 1897, when his brother, the late John F. Pidcock, succeeded him as president and served in that capacity until his death in January, 1902.

J. N. Pidcock, Jr., then again became president of the Georgia-Northern Railway Co., and so continued to be until January, 1906, when he sold his Georgia-Northern Railway interests to C. W. Pidcock, who continued to be such president until the date of his death, December 18, 1935.

During all the years of his connection with the Georgia-Northern Railway Co., President Pidcock served it with

C. W. PIDCOCK, SR.

never-tiring energy, especially during the years when he was its chief executive. He was possessed of a knowledge of railroading that few men possessed, being both a theoretical man as well as extremely practical. Mr. Pidcock, during his more than four decades of service to the railroad that he built, acted in every capacity except that of an operator, having been at times, secretary-treasurer, superintendent, general superintendent, vice-president and general manager, conductor, roadmaster, engineer and traffic manager. Mr. C. W. Pidcock and his father, J. N. Pidcock, Sr., were the pioneer railroad men in Colquitt County and were the first men to ever foresee the commercial possibilities of the county and of the whole of Southwest Georgia; and Mr. C. W. Pidcock's connection with the development of the railroad involved the services of practically his whole life-time.

As has already been said hereinabove, Mr. C. W. Pidcock died on December 18, 1935. He was succeeded as president and general manager of the Georgia-Northern Railway by his young son, C. W. Pidcock, Jr., a position which he still holds. The remainder of the official set-up as of the present date, February 20, 1937, is as follows:

F. R. Pidcock, Sr., Executive Vice-President.
Mrs. Besse P. Pidcock, Treasurer.
F. R. Pidcock, Jr., Secretary.
Ed H. Lewis, General Freight and Passenger Agent.
J. F. Hatfield, Superintendent.
I. C. Johnson, Auditor.
J. D. Weston, Jr., General Agent.
J. R. Hackett, Jr., General Agent.
L. G. Cox, Train Master and Car Accountant.
C. B. Patterson, Master Mechanic.
H. F. Hatcher, Commercial Agent.

The Georgia-Northern Railway Co., and its owners have logically participated in the general prosperity of the community, a prosperity which has resulted largely from the

## THE GEORGIA-NORTHERN RAILWAY

courageous foresight of the members of the Pidcock family. Of course the Georgia-Northern Railway Co., and its owners have stressed the transportation business, but they have known always that their business not only tends to build up basic industries but is itself built up and supported by such industries; so they have always accepted suggestion of their Colquitt County neighbors and customers that they contribute of their money and leadership to community enterprises of a worthy nature. Moultrie had its first growth as soon as the Georgia-Northern reached Moultrie. The town had at that time a population of 150. In 1900, it had 2,000. In 1920, the population of the City of Moultrie was a little less than 7,000. At the present date, February 20, 1937, the population of the city including its suburbs is the rise of 14,000 souls. During all the railroad's existence its relations with its employees have always been of the most cordial and friendly nature and there has never been a strike among its laborers.

## CHAPTER XXIII
## Moultrie Speaks

WE HERE REFER to a kind of advertisement printed on map paper, in size about 18″ x 30″, and gotten out in 1895, a copy of which is in our possession at this time. The center of this ad is a cut of the second courthouse of Colquitt County, which is surrounded by printed matter, setting out the advantages of Moultrie and Colquitt County. We attach a copy of this ad at the end of this chapter. We think it is a "hot" piece of advertising. Moultrie and Colquitt have had many a special trade edition since this advertisement; but it sets a swift pace, it will be admitted.

In a border of this ad appears a few advertising items worthy of being set forth here:

"Pearsall and Shipp" deal in Law and Collections.

"The Moultrie Observer" holds itself out as the "leading newspaper in South Georgia," doing this through "W. H. Cooper, editor, publisher and proprietor." Founder, too, of Colquitt's first newspaper.

"A. M. Tyler and Co." advertise "A complete line of clothing, hats, shoes and groceries."

"J. J. Walker, Attorney and Counsellor-at-Law," will take a case in any kind of court.

"W. H. Cooper" will sell a few lots, as a sideline to his newspaper work.

"Christian Wurst" is a blacksmith.

"H. B. Lester" is a lawyer.

"R. C. Ingalls" sells timber and lands.

"The Central House" is, quite appropriately, "centrally located," being run on the present site of the Norman Hotel, by Mrs. J. L. Peeples, a sister-in-law of Mr. D. A. Autrey.

"Fisher Bros."—J. S. Fisher, sheriff, and M. J. Fisher—run a livery stable, a fact rendered more emphatic by a spanking team attached to a buggy, with a whip standing upright in a whip-socket.

"J. P. Smith" is a lawyer. J. L. Hall is ditto.

"D. F. Arthur, Atty.," deals in lands.

"James Holmes" is running a still, as is evidenced by a cut showing a copper still and "worm." No; you're wrong; it's a turpentine still.

"Dukes and Huber" do a contracting business, and manufacture a superior quality of brick.

"Fisher and Smith"—J. S. Fisher and W. B. Smith—build wagons, buggies and carts.

"Beall and McLean"—O. A. Beall and ...... McLean, are general merchants.

"C. C. Harrel"—Quitman, Georgia, and Moultrie, Georgia—runs a general dry goods store at both places, called "The Fair."

"J. B. Norman, Jr.," is a retail dealer in all kinds of foodstuffs and feed-stuffs.

"The Holloway Company" hold themselves out to the world as "Jewelers, and dealers in optical goods, and proprietors of the Poplar Spring Bath-houses, centrally located, where you can always get baths of all kinds." (Query: What has become of "Poplar Springs"?)

"A. B. Peters" says he is a physician and surgeon, and lends color to the assertion by publishing a mortar and pestle, for such cases made and provided.

"W. C. Sessoms" is likewise a physician and surgeon, but minus the mortar and pestle.

Last of all, as we make the round of the ad, is a picture of a young merchant named "W. B. Dukes," who modestly puts out an alias of "The Model American Merchant, Owner and Operator of Five Different Stores." The reader will hear more of "the model merchant," which is the due of both the reader and the merchant.

Note: Upon a review of the above border ads, we find that Dr. C. A. Holtzendorf is a "Dental Surgeon," with office over Dukes and Smith's drug store. Also, that we have overlooked Dr. J. H. Cook, another "dental surgeon," whose office is over the Autrey Building, to have missed them both, is perhaps in the nature of things. One cannot be expected to put one's self out much to find a "dental surgeon."

As we promised, we end this chapter with the advertisement hereinbefore referred to. We do this for the reason that we are rather proud of this piece of advertising. It is the first of many put out since May, 1895, by Moultrie boosters; but we have doubts as to whether it has ever been surpassed.

## Moultrie

Situated away down in south Georgia, in the midst of the wire grass and pines, is one of the most flourishing and prosperous towns of the South.

It has indeed caught the spirit of thrift and enterprise, and is fast forging its way to the front. Three years ago, Moultrie had only 50 inhabitants; now she is a thriving little town of 1200, busy, stirring souls; and her population is increasing daily.

People growing tired of the old barren hills of north Georgia and the Carolinas are seeking new homes in this favored section.

Very little short cotton is raised here now; the long-staple Sea Island can be raised here just as cheap; and, while short cotton is

## MOULTRIE SPEAKS

selling at from four to five cents, long staple brings from twelve to twenty cents a pound; and those who plant it claim that just as much of the long staple can be raised per acre as the short staple. Land here, well tilled, will produce two-thirds of a bale of long cotton per acre; and the farmers of other sections of the South, growing tired of the low prices of short staple cotton, are fast coming to Colquitt County, and taking advantage of her fresh, cheap, productive lands, discarding the cheap short-staple cotton, and devoting their time and energies to the long staple.

This is the home of the watermelon. The finest melons in the world are raised in this section. Immense amounts of melons are shipped every year from south Georgia to the North, and to less favored sections of the United States. One acre here planted in melons and properly cultivated will bring as much in the market as ten acres in corn or cotton.

Another great industry to which our lands and climate are peculiarly adapted is the fruit culture. Peaches, pears, apples, grapes, and all kinds of fruits grow here to perfection. We are only twenty-eight miles southwest of Tifton, the great fruit center.

Some of our most enterprising planters are embarking in the cultivation of fruit. It is astonishing to what perfection sugar cane and potatoes grow here. And the peanut, the oat, and corn, grow here as well as anywhere in the world. The health of this section is proverbial. We are twenty-six miles northeast of Thomasville, the renowned health resort.

Land here can be bought for a mere song. The very best of lands can be had for from $2.50 to $10.00 per acre, though the price of land is constantly rising.

This county has a record for morality and law-abiding that is not exceeded by any county in the South.

Colquitt County was established in 1856—thirty years ago—and during that time, there has never within her borders occurred a lynching, nor has anyone ever been hanged, and but one criminal sent to the penitentiary.

This county has perhaps the finest saw-mill and turpentine timber anywhere to be found, until recently remote from railroads, her timber stands almost in its primeval glory.

Quite a number of turpentine stills are being operated in the county, and sawmill men are coming here to save the timber, as the turpentine men leave it.

Moultrie perhaps ships more naval stores than any other point in the world.

At present, we have but one railroad—the Georgia Northern, which intersects with the Savannah, Florida and Western, at a point thirty-one miles south of here. We hope, however, to soon see both the Tifton and Thomasville and the Columbus Southern extended from Albany to Valdosta. If these roads are built, Moultrie will then have ample railroad connection.

Moultrie has twenty-nine mercantile establishments, all in prosperous condition. She has four livery stables, all running on a paying basis. The Central Hotel, run by Mrs. J. L. Peeples, is one of the best in the South. The climate here is superb. There is an absence of both extreme heat and cold, and out-of-door work is possible the year round. The population in the last two years has increased from 150 to not less than 1400. Fifteen or twenty buildings are in course of construction, and will be erected during the summer. A large modern brick hotel is in contemplation, and it is probable that its doors will soon be thrown open for the entertainment of guests. Stock companies are being formed by northern men, and are buying up lands in this section, preparatory to undertaking fruit culture.

Cattle, sheep, hogs, and goats are permitted to run in the forest unguarded and unsheltered and unfed throughout the year, and yet they thrive and multiply, drawing on Nature's storehouse for their provisions. This is considered an unusually good country for bees, wild flowers growing spontaneously, and the writer can testify that he never saw anywhere richer colored honey.

## CHAPTER XXIV

## Colquitt in 1898

THE PRECEDING CHAPTER deals with Moultrie and Colquitt County in 1895, which was two years after the first railroad reached Moultrie. We are now to deal with our subject as we found it in 1898. Our first personal contact with Colquitt was on the second day of June, 1898. We had been admitted to the bar twelve days before, at Ellijay, Georgia, by Judge George F. Gober, of the Blue Ridge Circuit. We visited our wife's kin at Arlington and at Camilla, and with her, drove over from Camilla in a two-horse hack, coming through Hartsfield, and the section that is now Funston. We arrived at Moultrie at high noon, and took dinner with W. H. Budd, the Methodist preacher, and went into a rented house belonging to Mr. J. F. Monk. The next day, we took dinner with Mr. H. C. MacKenzie, whose wife was a relative. Mr. John H. Smithwick, our professional partner to be, had preceded us one day, having left Cherokee County about the same time we did; but he came direct to Moultrie.

In a biography of William Tecumseh Sherman appears the account of how his parents, both college people, went West as advised to do by Horace Greeley, and settled at Lancaster, Ohio. The book says, "It was a good place to build up a law practice. The county was new, and there was much title and transfer work, as well as land litigation. Also, there were several saloons, which furnished a lot of criminal practice."

This exactly describes conditions in Colquitt County in 1898. Plenty of title litigation, and much real estate transferring. Also, there were nine saloons. Also there was a criminal killing about every four weeks, and we did not count Negroes. It was a young lawyer's paradise, if he

164   HISTORY OF COLQUITT COUNTY

knew how to charge and collect a fee. The prosperity sounding out of the advertisement described and quoted in a preceding chapter was rising right on. W. B. Dukes, the "model merchant," was still running his five stores. He was Moultrie's leading merchant alright, his main store being situated on the northeast corner, formed by the intersection of the streets where Friedlander's store is now located. Monk Murphy and Co., a partnership composed of Miles Monk, Sr., Henry Murphy and J. F. Monk, was operating a general store, where the Moultrie Cafe is now located. Jack Walker, the lawyer, was gone, as was Attorney Lester. John A. Wilkes had just come to Moultrie, and formed a partnership with J. L. Hall. H. C. MacKenzie and J. D. MacKenzie were practicing law in partnership. Drs. Sessums and Peters sole members of the medical profession in 1895, had been joined by a Dr. Ellis, whose office was on the ground floor of a building in the middle of the block immediately south of the courthouse square. He had a mounted human skeleton in his consultation office. Dr. Holtzendorf, plying the profession of dentistry in 1895, was gone in 1898. Dr. J. H. Cook, however, was still in Moultrie.

W. C. Vereen, who lived on his turpentine farm in northwest Colquitt in 1895, had moved to Moultrie, in 1896, and lived in a two-story frame building, on the present site of his elaborate brick residence.

The Moultrie Banking Company, which was not in existence in 1895, was here and going good on June 1, 1898, with W. W. Ashburn, president; W. C. Vereen, vice-president, and J. H. Clark, cashier. J. B. Norman, Jr., owner of a grocery business in 1895, had closed this business in June, 1898. There were only two brick buildings in Moultrie in 1898, and none in 1895. Antone Huber was laying brick on the second story of his two-story building, situated then and now on the west side of the courthouse square. Battle Bros., a firm composed of George and Joe J. Battle, had a kind of livery stable and wagon and buggy business where the Sunday school extension of the First Baptist Church of Moultrie now stands.

JAMES MURPHY, Colquitt Reconstruction Leader.

The Battles were very eccentric, on occasion. For instance, late in the year 1898, this firm put in a stock of undertakers' supplies in their store, and advertised that part of their business by suspending a full-sized black coffin to a beam extending out over the sidewalk at right angles to their warehouse. In a night or two, the coffin was missing; and was presently found over in the Ocapilco swamp, filled with mud. Some fifteen year later, Joe Battle had a livery stable and a live-stock warehouse running back north from First Avenue, East, and back to the present Friedlander store. In course of time, he cut off on the side of his warehouse a storeroom, for a stock of milliners' supplies; and in a day or two, across the whole front of his building and high up above the roof, was a big sign in box-car letters, carrying the words, "J. J. Battle, Millinery and Mules."

By 1898, J. B. Norman, Jr., Hon. Martin F. Amorous, and Major Bacon had acquired extensive timber interests on the eastern side of Colquitt County, and had built a tramway to their sawmills which were located about fourteen miles east of Moultrie. From Sparks, a station on the G. S. & F. Ry., and then decided to extend it to Moultrie, having taken out a charter for it, under the name of Sparks, Moultrie and Gulf Railroad. This had been done in the middle of 1898, and daily schedules had been put on between Moultrie and Sparks. Henry Parrish presided in its Moultrie depot, which was near the present A. B. & C. depot. By 1898, a good many thousands of acres of timbered lands had been worked for turpentine, especially that portion within hauling distance of Sparks. The men who had worked this turpentine were J. B. Norman, Jr., W. H. Barber, Duncan Sinclair, W. B. Connoley and a Mr. DeVane. Mr. W. C. Vereen came to Colquitt for the purpose of going into the naval stores business in the neighborhood of Pineopolis, only to find that Mr. DeVane had already preempted it. As a result Mr. Vereen went to the northwestern part of the county, and secured a bonanza in virgin, workable timber.

Others who were at work in the naval stores business in 1898 in Colquitt were A. C. Darling, and James Holmes, operating separate stills in the eastern suburbs of Moultrie. D. A. Autrey, with a hundred thousand dollar investment, at Autreyville, in southern Colquitt, and Major John K. McNeil toward the southeast corner of Colquitt, was doing an extensive naval stores business, in connection with his son, Thos. McNeil.

There was held in Colquitt County, on June 6, 1898, an election for State and county offices. Perhaps it was a primary; but anyhow, there was no registration and Negroes voted in droves.

The candidates for governor were Robt. Berner, Spencer Atkinson and Allen D. Candler. Pearsall and Shipp managed for Atkinson, while McKenzie and McKenzie sponsored Candler's interests in Colquitt. Candler spoke, just before the election, at the courthouse. High light of the speech—

"And fellow citizens," he squeaked, "I'm against taking taxes from the poor for the upkeep of the University of Georgia, for the purpose of teaching dudes to dance. My observation has been that, about the time you learn a boy the meaning of the Latin hic, haec, hoc, he forgets the meaning of gee, haw, Buck." The audience roared in glee, and Bob Shipp, Atkinson's manager in Colquitt, said to those around him, "Let's go, boys, the old man's got the county."

In the afternoon of June 6, we acted as a clerk to the election managers, this machinery was seated in one of the rooms on the ground floor of the old courthouse, and on the south side. The voters came up the walk from the south of the courthouse square, and handed their tickets, marked and folded, through a window. Presently, in some excitement, a turpentine operator, brought up forty-three Negroes on the walk. He stood at the head of the column, and as a Negro would walk up, he handed him a marked ticket and watched him while he stuck it in the window. The column reached nearly, if not quite, through the turn-stile on the south side of the square. Two white flankers walked up and down the column, to prevent the opposition to the ticket being voted by the men from getting any of them away from their boss-man.

"Can that man vote all those Negroes?" we asked of lawyer Bob Shipp, who with us was in the room where they were voting.

"It's a pretty safe bet he can," answered Shipp.

"Well, if I were running for anything, I'd like to have the support of that gentleman," we mused.

Just about that time, a man tried to yank one of the "voters" out of the line, when, with great promptness, one of the flankers shot him. The shot was not fatal, but it was temporarily effective all around; and after this, the turpentine man was not interfered with any further in his politics. The turpentine operator is still alive, a resident of a nearby county; and the man who got shot is still going. But we are under the impression that he has quit fooling with another man's political "rights."

In 1898, there were no paved sidewalks in Moultrie, although some planked sidewalking is remembered in front of the stores, over in front of the south side of the courthouse square. The streets around the square were very sandy, and much cut up with the traffic. About 1904, the city authorities spread a coating of native red clay over the surface of the streets around the square; and Attorney John A. Wilkes told us that he had just overheard a visiting woman say, "There'll be no endurin' the people of Moultrie henceforth, now that she has clayed her streets." John thought the remark was in poor taste, and attributed it to envy. Said he thought that she must have come from either Camilla or Tifton.

## CHAPTER XXV

## Old Greenfield

JOEL C. GRAVES was Colquitt's first manufacturer. He was a native of Vermont, who in 1838 had moved to Monticello, Florida. In the beginning of 1857, he trekked northward again; saw Colquitt County; bought timbered lands lying to the south of Moultrie, and finally built a dam across ——— Creek, about eight miles south of Moultrie, and near the Pavo road, where he erected a gristmill, and put in a set of wool cards, and built a barrel factory—a "bucket shop," as it was called by Graves' neighbors. All these enterprises were housed in a three-story frame building. Their motive power was steam.

This shop manufactured from native hardwoods, such as cypress and the gums, black and sweet, barrels, tubs, and small kits. If we except a few gristmills and wool cards, this was Colquitt's first manufacturing establishment.

Presently, he made a contract with the Confederacy for supplying the army and navy with barrels for use in shipping syrup and meats to the armies from this section. Also, it furnished an excellent reason for keeping Graves' two sons from under the provisions of the "Conscript Act."

At one time during the life of this contract, some fifty to sixty laborers, all taken from the vicinage, worked for Mr. Graves. Of course, when the war was over, the contract was no longer effective; and the local market for barrels, tubs, and buckets did not suffice to keep the bucket shop going.

So Mr. Graves borrowed some money from his three brothers, and finally paid off this indebtedness by deeding some of his Colquitt timber lands to them. One of his brothers was killed at the Battle of Resaca in 1864, leaving some fifteen hundred to two thousand acres of these lands to his wife and two daughters.

Mr. Joel C. Graves was a Presbyterian minister; and when he changed his residence to a place which had no church organization of that faith and order, he would proceed to create such organization; and, when he found it necessary, he would erect the church building. This explains why for seventy-two years, there has been standing in the midst of Mr. Graves' former land-holdings in Colquitt County, a brick church building. It long has been called "The Old Greenfield Brick Church"; and was built from brick burned from clay taken from a deposit near Mr. Graves' mill. This was the first brick structure ever erected in Colquitt County, and the only one, till another, a jail, was erected in Moultrie in 1892.

Since Mr. Graves' family, including his "in-laws," constituted all the Presbyterians resident in Colquitt County at the time Mr. Graves built his church, they, of course, constituted his organization. After Mr. Graves moved away from this section, the church building came to be used in a desultory way for both Methodists and Missionary Baptists, residing in the neighborhood. Especially, after Dr. Baker E. Watkins, a neighbor of the Graves, and a Methodist, and Rev. A. C. Stephenson, a noted Baptist preacher, who lived in Thomas County for fifty years, held forth with more or less regularity in the brick church.

Mr. Graves, a year or two after the war, moved his residence to a point about four miles from Ty Ty, in Worth County, where he was engaged in duplicating his work at Greenfield (including a Presbyterian church building), when he died there, in 1867, and was brought back to Greenfield graveyard for burial, among the "rude forefathers of the hamlet," not many steps from the last resting place of his former friend and associate, Dr. Baker E. Watkins, Methodist preacher, member of Georgia's Constitutional Convention of 1865, and father of two of Colquitt's representatives in the House of Representatives in the General Assembly of Georgia. Dr. Baker E. Watkins' grave, with that of his wife, has fallen into much disrepair. Doubtless it will soon be put in proper shape, as the Moultrie McNeil Chapter of the U. D. C. has constituted itself guardian for Greenfield churchhouse and graveyard. This fact is profoundly gratifying, since it is always painful to find graveyards have become "neglected spots."

The 1860 census shows that Ruth Graves, a native of Vermont, age 51, and by profession a common-school teacher, was an inmate of the residence of Joel S. Graves, at Old Greenfield. It also shows that Roxy Ann Graves, age 23, a native of Florida, who had the same profession, likewise lived with Joel S. Graves. The former was a sister of Mr. Graves, and the latter his daughter. We have omitted to say that, in addition to Presbyterian church building, Mr. Graves was said to always build a school building. And this is what he did, at "Old Greenfield." The brick building at that place was divided into two rooms. One was for religious services, and the other was used as a school room. Both Ruth and Roxy Graves taught, at times, in that section of the building. We incline to the view that their work was of a very high order of excellence. And we are sure that the same can be said of Mr. Graves' preaching. He is said to have been a zealous proselyter for his church, although it was open for preachers of other faiths and orders.

## CHAPTER XXVI

## Some Important Visitors to Colquitt County

We were once, for an hour or two, a guest at the home of the venerable J. B. Norman, Sr., at Norman Park. We took up part of the time in asking him about the past history of the county. Among other things, we asked for the names of noted men who had made public speeches at Moultrie. He said that Benj. H. Hill was the first man of any prominence to make a set political speech in the county. It was in his campaign for the governorship in 1856, when he was the nominee of the know-nothing, or American, party, against Superior Court Judge Joseph E. Brown, of the Blue Ridge Circuit, who was the nominee of the Democratic party. Mr. Hill was the special guest of Mr. Norman, who entertained him at his house overnight, brought him to Moultrie for his speech, and then carried him across the country in his buggy for a speech there.

"Did he make a good speech here?" I asked.

"Well, I thought he did," said he, with characteristic moderation.

"Did Joe Brown visit the county?"

"No."

"Who managed for Brown?" I asked.

"Henry Gay," answered my host.

"Who carried the county?" I wanted to know.

"Brown carried the county," he answered, with placid resignation.

## IMPORTANT VISITORS TO COLQUITT CO. 173

Bob Taylor, the celebrated lecturer, former Governor of Tennessee, United States Senator, and the hero of many a rough-and-tumble political campaign, once came to Moultrie for a paid lecture. We sat with him in the judge's stand at the courthouse, while we waited for his audience to assemble. Presently, he bent over and said to us, in a low tone of distress:

"I am about dead of stage fright."

"Oh, you can't be in earnest!" we said, "with all your experience, and before this little audience in this out-of-the-way place."

"Well, it's true," said he; "I am never free from it; and the attacks are more painful, as I grow older."

Woodrow Wilson, who did nothing in the way of a speech impromptu, suffered from the same malady; and it is said that he had to have medical treatment for an unusually severe attack, on the night he addressed the joint session of the Congress, recommending our entrance into the World War.

* * * * *

Sam Jones, the evangelist, lectured more than once in Moultrie. His lecture delivered in the old brick warehouse, situated on 1st Street, S. E., was an epochal deliverance, resulting in the destruction of ten saloons, and a revolution in the habits and moral reactions of an entire town and county.

* * * * *

We heard Mrs. Gen. George Pickett deliver a paid lecture under the auspices of the Alkahest Lyceum Bureau, about 1920. It was under a tent, near where now stands the Baptist S. S. annex. She was a well-groomed, handsome woman; and her subject was "Pickett's Charge at Gettysburg." This military maneuver was the most conspicuous instance of disciplined valor the modern world ever saw; and, a few years before, we had walked over the ground covered by Pickett's 18,000 veterans. Lordy, lordy, we'll never hear a speech more thrilling than this woman's description of that memorable event.

\* \* \* \* \*

Some twenty years ago, we heard Dr. W. L. Pickard, at that time president of Mercer University, and always after maturity an able and scholarly Baptist minister, preach in Moultrie from the following text:

"Being found and fashioned as a man, He humbled Himself, and became obedient unto death, even the death of the Cross. Wherefore, God also hath highly exalted Him, and given Him a name which is above every name: That at the name of Jesus, every knee should bow of things in Heaven, of things in earth, and things under the earth, and that every tongue should confess Him Lord, to the glory of God the Father."

It was a great discourse made by the doctor, who had had only one child, and that a son, who died years before. Our "raised spirit" walked in glory with him during that hour; and the experience helped us to reach the permanent conclusion that of all classes of public speakers, the Christian minister has the least excuse for being commonplace.

\* \* \* \* \*

Woodrow Wilson was never in Colquitt; but he delivered an address at Albany, in 1912, in behalf of his campaign for the presidential nomination of the Democratic party. The Georgia Northern Railway sent up a special train. The speech was not up to his ancient form, we think, being too cautious. We were impressed, however, by the remark general on the train as we returned, "Why, he's a good man!"

None of us had any idea of the tremendous power he was to exert through the whole earth, within the next eight years.

## IMPORTANT VISITORS TO COLQUITT CO.

Mrs. Rebecca Felton, wife of the celebrated orator William H. Felton, of Cartersville, Ga., and the first woman ever to be sworn in as a senator of the United States spent one night in Moultrie. It was in the Spring of 1865, when she came into town from the south, whither she had refugeed with her boy in order to escape the attentions of Gen. Tecumseh Sherman. She spent the night at the double-pen log house of Mr. and Mrs. Peter O. Wing, which stood on the present site of the Daniel drug store in the northwest corner of the intersection of Main Street and 1st Avenue, South, and the next morning she proceeded by carriage to Albany.

\* \* \* \* \*

William Jennings Bryan, soon after his retirement from Wilson's cabinet in 1916, made a paid lecture at Moultrie at 2 P. M. one afternoon. His subject was some modification of his great staple lecture, entitled "The Prince of Peace." He lectured on this subject three times in a single day—at Camilla, at 11 A. M.; at Moultrie at 2 P. M.; and at Thomasville at 8 P. M.

A few of us went out to Hartsfield to meet him on his way to Moultrie. We knew pretty well when to expect him at Hartsfield, and so stopped there; and we had waited only a few minutes when his car rolled swiftly down the slight elevation just west of the stores. We waved him down, and he stopped, took a few steps in order to get to our car; and forthwith, Hartsfield was never to be the same place any more; such is the power of a great spirit over even inanimate things.

As we drove out toward Moultrie, Mr. W. C. Vereen called his attention to the fact that they both were delegates to the Baltimore Democratic Convention in 1912. "Ah, yes," said Mr. Bryan, "and do you remember my Morgan-Ryan Resolution?"

"Oh, very well, of course," said Mr. Vereen.

"Well," said Mr. Bryan, "I'll remember that scene as long as I remember anything—the rage into which the opposition lashed itself. Upon the platform, Tom Taggart running up and down. He looked as if he wanted to say something, but didn't know what it was. His eyes were all bulged out."

Mr. Bryan was impressed by the farm land through which we passed, and said so. We are convinced now that we could have sold him a nice block of Colquitt real estate, had we tried. He kept admiring the land and asking about the ruling prices.

When we reached the Ochlochnee bridge, we were compelled to stop our car, so that a farmer might get off with his two-mule team.

"Who is that man?" said Mr. Bryan.

"Of what consequence can that be to you?" we asked. "You are not going to see him again."

"I am impressed with his face," said he. "Do you know him, and is he a good man?"

It was a good man; and we so told him. He was Mr. John Gay, grandson of Henry Gay, Colquitt's life-long pioneer Democrat. He now lives at Ellenton, in Colquitt County.

Mr. Bryan was running late when we reached Moultrie; and advanced swiftly at the head of his escort committee to the courthouse, where his crowd was waiting. There was a beggar-man sitting on the sidewalk, with his tin cup. The "Great Commoner" stopped, took out his bill fold, and peeled one of them off and dropped it in the cup. Then followed suit the members of the committee. It was a red letter day for the beggar-man.

After the lecture, Mr. Z. H. Clark, treasurer for the local lecture bureau, handed Mr. Bryan a check for his contract price. He demurred, saying, "I think you did not take in that much."

"Mr. Bryan, we keep our contracts down here in the South," said Mr. Clark.

"Well, we sometimes break ours up North," said Mr. Bryan, "and I am going to break this one, so you keep the check, and deduct all proper expenses, and send me the balance. As a trained lecturer, I know that $200 is too much."

That night he gave $100 to a local campaign for the Y. M. C. A. at Thomasville.

## CHAPTER XXVII

# Being More About the Women

It has already been said, herein, that the pioneer women of Colquitt got a rather raw deal at the hands of Fate, when their menfolks brought them to the wilds of Colquitt. It has been seen how such men as Elder Crawf. Tucker carried their guns to their Saturday meetings, for the purpose of bringing down a deer or a wild turkey, which they might run across on their way home. And practically every man was a hunter, and worked at it. For instance, John Tucker, big land-owner and politician in a local way, killed, so it is still said, more deer than any man that was ever in the county, frequently hunting with Robert Bearden, his neighbor and friend.

Then the men went rather often to such market towns as Albany, Thomasville, St. Marks, Tallahassee and Columbus; but their women generally stayed at home with the children and "the stuff." Too, the men have been seen to have had some rather agreeable contacts with Judge Hansell and the visiting lawyers, twice a year at the "Big Court"; but from these the women were strictly barred. In fact, a real nice woman thought it grossly improper for a woman to go about the courthouse, when court was in session.

Then, from the time Bob Bearden and "Aunt Sallie" opened a general store at Moultrie, in the fifties, alcoholics were obtainable, at low prices, and practically all the men drank, more or less. But the women did not drink, for one reason that the men would not stand for it. The reason for this general objection was that they knew that prudence goes out, as liquor goes in; and they wanted no doubt to exist as to the matter of the fatherhood of the children.

However, the women generally used snuff, or plumply chewed tobacco more or less on the sly, generally agreeing among themselves that "Terbacker shore is a heap of company to a body." Then, too, as has already been observed, herein, while the monotony and the isolation of life to the housewives was terrible, a remedy was found in the average big family of the period. The women "raised their company."

At all this, however, at the beginning of the present century, statistics showed a larger percentage of farmers' wives in the lunatic asylums of this nation than of any other class of our population, the reason being that the business of being a backwoods farmer's wife, and cooking his meals for forty or fifty years, three times per day, including leap years, is likely to become a bit wearing on the nerves. Anyhow, it is our firm opinion that, when the true historian comes along, he is going to decide to drop consideration of the doings of the men; and write several books about the farmers' wives of this land. So feeling, we are going to keep telling about these pioneer women of Colquitt right on to the end of this chapter, at least. Out of the hundreds of these women, we introduce just a few:

Susan A. Tucker, wife of John Tucker, and daughter-in-law of Patriarch Crawford Tucker, was before marriage Susan A. Stephenson, born near Raleigh, N. C., on September 28, 1835, coming to Colquitt, soon after her birth, with her parents. Notwithstanding her handicaps, she reared a fine family of children. Of course, neither she nor her children had much education, as there were no schools within reach; but her pictures show her to have been modest and dignified. We also know all this from the fact that she gave to Colquitt a lot of fine girls. It was a good day's work for Colquitt when John Tucker went a sparking of her.

The reader, if he has followed us closely, already knows how Susan Jane Tucker (alia dicta "Babe") stands with this historian. We have seen how John Tucker, her father, pitched the biggest wedding party for her that Colquitt ever saw—before or since. We have seen how Susan Jane took life as it came to her, staying by her man till his death, in 1896. John Tucker, before her marriage, boasted that she could run a straighter furrow than any man on the farm. It is still told how that when a colt fell into a well on the home place, she superintended getting it out, claimed it for herself in virtue of this accomplishment, and took it away as a part of her marriage portion; while, just the other day, a man told us that, on occasion, she would drive a two-horse team to Thomasville and back with her own hands, in order to obtain a load of supplies.

It will occasion no surprise, therefore, when the reader is told that, in the interval between the death of her husband, in 1896, and her own death, in 1932, no sheriff ever levied a paper on anything on her farm, and no mortgage ever encumbered any of her property. Best of all, she finished raising her eleven children in the years of her widowhood, and turned them all out into Colquitt's citizen-body, as creditable members. She was born, in 1857, being the first-born of her parents; and during her last years was full of good works and alms-deeds. Having been called "Susan Jane" and "Aunt Babe" by scores of her relatives and neighbors, a whole country-side called her "Mammy," during several years next preceding her death. This tribute is paid to her memory, with all the gladness in the world.

* * * * *

Ruth Tillman Norman, the wife of James M. Norman, was born in South Carolina, on September 18, 1798, and died at the home of her daughter, Mrs. A. J. Strickland, in Colquitt County, on March 8, 1884, having survived her hus-

## BEING MORE ABOUT THE WOMEN 181

band a full twenty years. She was the mother of the six Normans whose group picture is placed at the end of this chapter, and of a seventh son, John Tillman Norman, who reached adulthood, reared a family, and died in the year that Moultrie was incorporated. She also had five daughters, as follows: Emily Susannah (Mrs. John A. Alderman), Dica (Mrs. Burrell Baker), Hettie (Mrs. Henry Gay), Elizabeth M. (Mrs. A. J. Strickland), and Zilpha (spinster).

When it is considered that a woman in her day had only one career open to her—namely, looking after her household duties, and rearing children, and that this is still her highest work, Ruth Tillman Norman must in the light of her record as a mother be rated as one of Colquitt's great women. Her kindred have for nearly a century been builders in the county; and this applies to both her own descendants and to her brothers and sisters and their descendants. She was a sister to John Tillman and Joshua Tillman, both Colquitt pioneers, and she is therefore a great aunt of W. M. Tillman, the present Chairman of Colquitt's Board of County Commissioners. She sleeps by the side of her husband, in the Pleasant Grove Primitive Baptist Cemetery, two miles from Moultrie, on the Adel road.

\* \* \* \* \*

Sarah Ann Norman, born a Dukes, in 1825, was the wife of Jeremiah Bryant Norman, senior, who was the oldest son of pioneer James Mitchell Norman. This couple had children as follows: Ruth E., James T., Julia A., Susan L., Sarah Ann, Zilpha, Jeremiah Bryant, junior, John S., Matthew H., M. D., R. L., and V. F. All these children reached maturity and married off, except John and Matthew, both of whom died within a few days of each other, as young children, in 1860. All the surviving sons became leaders among the citizens of Colquitt County in finance, politics, and religious affairs. The four daughters married, and helped to train large families of children, as follows: Julia married G. F. Newton; Sarah Ann married George Clark; Zilpha married Jeremiah Tillman; Susan married Miles Monk, Sr., and Emily Susannah married John A. Alderman. It is safe to say that no woman has made a larger contribution to permanent values in Colquitt County that has Sarah Ann Dukes Norman. She was born in 1825, in what was then Irwin County, in territory that was soon afterwards incorporated in Lowndes. This writer saw her once in her home at Norman Park. It was not long before her death. She is buried by the side of her husband at Pleasant Grove Church, near Moultrie.

\* \* \* \* \*

Julia Norman was the third child of Jeremiah B. Norman, Sr., and his wife Sarah Ann Norman, of whom we treat in the paragraph of this chapter next above. She was born in 1851, and after the close of the Civil War, she married George F. Newton, a young soldier, who went to the war from Brooks County, left an arm at Gettysburg, and came a-courtin' Julia when he got home.

We have hitherto held that the acid test of womanhood is her achievement in the way of "borning" and rearing children. In this regard, Julia A. Newton was not one whit behind her mother. Without any exception, her 10 children are blameless citizens of the communities in which they reside. Luckily for Colquitt, most of them reside within her limits.

Julia Ann Newton was a kind of Primitive Baptist saint. Luther Stallings, who lived in her house for more than a year, one time, says that she had the best controlled mind and nerves of any person he ever saw—that she never condoned wrong in any particular, but at the first signs of repentance, she began to make concessions to the wrong-doer, saying, "Well, we cannot tell the strength of the temptation," or "He

## BEING MORE ABOUT THE WOMEN 183

might have been swept away when he was not on guard." A group of the contemporaries of her older children, speaking of her the other day, agreed, "Should we get to Heaven, we expect to find her, looking like she did for a generation of Sundays at Pleasant Grove Church; black dress, black poke bonnet, head slightly down on one side, looking intently over her specs at the Primitive Baptist preacher, as he was holding forth."

\* \* \* \* \*

From all accounts, practically the same thing can be said of her sister, Susan L. Norman, who was the second wife of Miles Monk, Jr., and of another sister, Sarah Ann Norman, who married Rev. G. F. Clark. Same type of children— same big families—same devotion to the cause of the Lord.

\* \* \* \* \*

Mary McNeil was a native of Cheraw, S. C., being a daughter of Major Neil McKay McNeil and his wife, Jane Johnson Pegues. She married W. C. Vereen, a young business man of Cheraw, S. C., casting in her fortunes with his at a time when to be broke was the hallmark of South Carolina aristocracy. The fact that she went cheerfully along with her husband into the woods of first Douglas, then Montgomery, and finally Colquitt County, where for six years she shared the cares and anxieties of a turpentine operator with him, entitles her to a place in the list of Colquitt's Pioneer Women.

This historian came to Colquitt, June 2, 1898, just a few months before the death of Mrs. Vereen, so that he has no recollection of ever seeing her. He was asked to accompany Hon. M. J. Pearsall, a friend of the Vereens, to her funeral rites at the old Presbyterian Church. He did not understand all the circumstances, but enough got into his knowledge to impress him that this death was calculated to sweep the tenderest emotions of the human heart. There is yet present in our memory pictures of seven children in various stages of immaturity, running down to infants in arms. Also, the indications of her popularity among the citizens of the town, who filled the church and its approaches. Also tender memories of Mr. Pearsall, who was himself to meet a tragic death a few years later.

* * * * *

These noted women of Colquitt County have been picked out with some diffidence. A diffidence which grows out of our knowledge that there have been scores, and perhaps hundreds of other Colquitt women who in their backwoods homes have pursued the even tenor of their way, too much engrossed by the pressure of immediate duties to think of anything else, the majority of whom await the Resurrection of the Last Day in unmarked graves. But at that time they will be all right; for

> "While Valour's haughty champions wait
> Till all their scars are known,
> Love walks unchallenged through the gate,
> And sits beside the Throne."

Six Sons of JAMES M. and RUTH TILLMAN NORMAN. *Left to right:* Sitting, JOE J., JOEL, BRYANT. *Standing:* RICHARD, MOSES C., W. H. H., JOHN T. NORMAN.

CHAPTER XXVIII

# Christian Churches in Colquitt

*"Heaven and Earth shall pass away;
But My Word shall not pass away."*
—JESUS THE LORD.

THE PILGRIM FATHERS, who settled New England, were not more prompt to provide for religious worship than the pioneer settlers of the Colquitt section, and, by the way, there is a remarkable resemblance between their theology. Only in case of the Colquitt pioneer, he was not called a Puritan, but a "Primitive Baptist." The Normans, the Tuckers, the Hancocks, the Bakers, the Hires, the Tillmans—all these and practically all their neighbor settlers belonged to this "faith and order."

They had the congregational system of church government; but at that, practically all of them were loosely joined together in "associations."

Calvinists, they were, as much as the Puritans or the Scotch Covenanters. Once a month, their services were held, con-

Old Greenfield Church, 1936

sisting of two days each. On Saturdays all church business was attended to, and preaching was had at eleven A.M. Saturday morning. On Sunday morning, the rite of Baptism was performed at the nearest water convenient for immersion; then, back to the Church-house for a Sunday sermon. Listening to a sermon was called, in the minutes of these meetings, "sitting under the droppings of the Sanctuary." The audiences gave rapt attention, as the records show, and as tradition affirms, three generations after their preachers went into "the tongueless silence of the grave."

We are inclined to think that the "Baptist Church of Christ, Sardis," is the first church building ever erected to God in the Colquitt territory. From inspection of early minutes of this church organization now religiously kept by Mr. Lawrence Norman, Clerk of this church at present, we know that his great-grandfather Artexerxes B. Norman was Clerk in the first years after its organization; and that his great-great-uncle, James M. Norman, was its second Clerk. The minutes of this organization, largely written by these Normans and John Tillman, constitute a very remarkable set of ancient documents. Here follows a copy of the minutes of one of the regular monthly meetings:

"Jan. 24, 1835.

"The Church of Christ at Sardis met; and after sitting under the dropping of the Sanctuary—as we hope for the comfort of the

## CHRISTIAN CHURCHES IN COLQUITT 187

people of God, and the alarming of sinners—by Rev. Joel Pate, then and after our beloved pastor, we came into conference.

"1. First invited visiting brethren to seats with us.

"2. Inquiry was made after absences.

"3. A door was opened for the reception of members. One came forward—Timothy Bryant—and was received by experience of Grace.

"4. On motion we agreed to come to a close. Done in order.

"J. M. Norman C. C.

"Met Sabbath morning for the ordinance of Baptism. Then returned to the meeting house; and our beloved pastor spoke from Tim. 1:15 to an attentive congregation. J. M. N., C. C."

On September 27, 1837, the minutes of this congregation shows that two "letters of correspondence" were sent out— one to Bethany, and the other to Bethsaida. (Bridge Creek.) Henry C. Tucker and A. B. Norman were named messengers to convey the letter to Bethsaida; and Elijah Duke and H. C. Tucker were sent to Bethany. This minute record is also signed "James M. Norman, C. C." Here is found the first record that we have been able to find about the Bridge Creek Church. Tradition partly runs to the idea that Bridge Creek is the oldest church ever organized in the County. We think, however, that the weight of tradition favors Sardis for this honor. Anyhow, we know definitely from this record, that the church named Sardis was organized in July, 1834. The Sardis congregation celebrated the hundredth anniversary of its founding in 1934.

A very large graveyard is maintained at this church-house. Possibly two hundred marked graves. A larger number appears to be unmarked.

The graveyard at Bridge Creek is about the same size as that of Sardis. Among other early notables, Elder Henry Crawford Tucker, one of the founders of this church, and for many years its minister, sleeps in the Bridge Creek graveyard, under the branches of the swamp growth of Bridge

Bethsaida Grave Yard at Bridge Creek

Creek, which branches are festooned with gray Spanish moss, surrounded by scores of his numerous tribe, as he awaits the resurrection of the "Chosen." It is one of the beautiful cemeteries we have seen.

The last time we saw it, the sun was sinking behind the swamp growth, out of which came the love notes of a mourning dove, the whole tending to fill the soul with the peace which is the assured end of "the upright man."

Pleasant Grove Primitive Baptist Church is situated on the old Moultrie and Adel road, about two miles east of Moultrie. While much younger than Sardis or Bridge Creek, it is fully eighty years old itself. And its graveyard is the largest in the County, if we except Moultrie. In this cemetery are buried most of the Normans, included James Mitchell Norman and his wife Ruth Tillman Norman. James M. Norman was born March 18, 1792, in Washington's second administration, and died September 12, 1864, at "Coker's Place," on the old Albany road—six miles north of Moultrie. His wife was born September 18, 1798, and died March 8, 1884. The graves of this couple are in much disrepair, and a marker ought to be set up to prevent their complete disappearance.

Live Oak Primitive Baptist Church is some five or six miles north of Moultrie, on the west side of the old Moultrie-Albany road. Here, side-by-side, are the graves of John Tucker and his wife, Susan A. Stevenson Tucker. A handsome marble monument marks their last resting place. It was erected by the pious instincts of their numerous posterity, and will withstand the ravages of time for centuries. It is a credit to the whole tribe. A final observation: All these and practically all other Primitive Baptist congregations in the County have a beautiful yearly custom of assembling at the churches for the purpose of annual worship and homecoming, and the clearing off of the graveyards. At present, all the graveyards which we have mentioned in this chapter are impressively clean and free from weeds and debris.

### Board of Christian Education

| Rev. W. A. Kelley | Phillip Covington | Mrs. O. O. Owens |
| Mrs. L. R. Barber | Mrs. W. A. Kelley | W. F. McCall |
| Mrs. Robt. Travelute | R. S. Register | M. L. Lee |

E. P. Thompson....................................Chairman Board of Stewards
W. H. McKay.......................................................................... Treasurer
I. C. Johnson........................................Chairman Finance Committee
W. R. Neal..................................................................Church Lay Leader
W. A. Blasingame................................................District Lay Leader
Mrs. L. R. Barber....................President Woman's Missionary Society
Miss Eleanor Blanton............................Church Clerk and Treasurer

Sardis Primitive Baptist Church

CHAPTER XXIX

# The Moultrie Methodist Church

THE FLORIDA CONFERENCE of the Methodist Episcopal Church, South, held its annual session at Bainbridge, Georgia, in the year 1856, the exact date being January 10th. It was composed of the Tallahassee, Madison, Jacksonville and Tampa Districts of Florida, and the Bainbridge, Thomasville and Saint Mary's Districts in south Georgia. Bishop Andrew

First Methodist Episcopal Church, South

presided, and made assignments to the Thomasville District for the year 1856, as follows:

P. P. Smith, presiding elder; Thomasville Church—F. R. C. Ellis; Duncanville—Milton C. Smith; Grooverville—C. Raford; Grand Bay—A. Davis; Alapaha—P. Murdock; Flint River—T. J. Johnson; Fletcher Institute—R. H. Lucky; Ochlocknee Mission—J. W. Jackson.

## THE MOULTRIE METHODIST CHURCH

The post office at Moultrie was called "Ochlocknee" at that time, and had been for five years previous. The present town of Ochlochnee, in Thomas County, being then unknown; and so the Moultrie community was served by Missionary J. W. Jackson. This was the first effort of the Methodist organization to do work in Colquitt County. It is possible that Colquitt County had already been created before Missionary Jackson reached his appointment. We have no accounts of the minutes of the Florida Conference for the years 1857 and 1858. The minutes of the annual meeting of this conference for 1859 and 1860 make no mention either of Ochlocknee or Moultrie; however, they show that on May 8, 1861, the Florida Conference met at Quincy, Florida, and that "Moultrie Mission" had assigned to it the same J. W. Jackson, and that he worked under R. H. Lucky, presiding elder of the Thomasville District.

It is safe to say that Missionary Jackson did his preaching in some private residence during his 1856 assignment; and that during his conference year of 1861, he used the new two-year-old courthouse as a church.

There is a blank in Methodist history in Moultrie from 1861 to sometime about 1878, when Mrs. Carrie Culpepper called a meeting of Methodist-minded folks, at the courthouse of Colquitt County, for the purpose of organizing a church at Moultrie. The membership was composed of Lawrence A. Hall and his family, which included Mr. A. B. Hall, who resides in Moultrie yet and holds the distinction of being the oldest living member of the Moultrie Church. The meeting also included Mrs. Martha Carlton, part of the family of Frank Nelson, and two or three others.

By 1883, Rev. A. D. Patterson and his family had moved to Moultrie from Nashville, Georgia, as had George W. Hooker, who came from Thomas County. It is likely that George Faison had lived at Moultrie more than twenty years.

Certainly the census shows that he and his family were residents here in 1860. The Pattersons, the Hookers and the Faisons, all identified themselves with the new organization, about 1883. By this time too, a little church building had been erected near the present site of the City Hall, and a Sunday school had been organized. Mr. Patterson preached at this church in a desultory way, as did Revs. George Stewart, Moses C. Smith and M. H. Galloway.

By 1892, "Moultrie Mission" was recreated by the Georgia Conference. It was composed of the little church at Moultrie, "Old Greenfield," and "Weeks' Chapel." R. S. McCord was the first preacher in charge, and H. Stubbs was the presiding elder. This assignment was made for 1894. Here follows a list of preachers assigned to the Moultrie Methodist Church since then:

| | |
|---|---|
| 1896—R. P. Fain | 1913—W. H. Kerr |
| 1897—C. W. Littlejohn | 1914—E. M. Overby |
| 1898—W. H. Budd | 1918—A. W. Reese |
| 1902—C. H. Branch | 1921—W. F. Smith |
| 1903—W. D. McGregor | 1923—Reece Griffin |
| 1904—J. C. Flanders | 1925—    Parker |
| 1907—J. H. Mather | 1927—L. P. Tyson |
| 1908—J. W. Wooten | 1931—T. H. Thompson |
| 1909—L. W. Colson | 1934—W. A. Kelley |
| 1911—J. M. Glenn | |

Since the organization of the church in Moultrie, three buildings have been erected: First, a large frame building, taking the place of the original meeting place. This was erected in about the year 1892. In 1903, a brick building was erected on the present site of the City Hall, during the pastorate of Mr. Budd. Under the pastorate of Mr. Overby, the present beautiful and commodious edifice was erected on the southeast corner of First Street, South, and Fourth Avenue, Southeast. Mr. and Mrs. M. M. Kendall donated the site. Prominent among the contributors toward

# THE MOULTRIE METHODIST CHURCH

the erection of this church were Dr. G. F. Taylor, R. M. Morrison, M. L. Lee and S. P. Turnbull.

The present membership of this church is 1,100. The Sunday school organization, which is really older than the church organization itself, has a membership of 660. The present superintendent is Mr. C. H. McCall.

### BOARD OF STEWARDS

| | |
|---|---|
| E. P. Thompson | W. A. Blasingame |
| E. Z. Crowley | P. J. Sineath |
| W. F. McCall | M. L. Lee |
| W. H. McKay | Dr. C. L. Dean |
| Dr. R. H. Rogers | T. H. Willis |
| T. E. Lewis | W. E. Young |
| R. B. Wright | J. F. Lockwood |
| T. G. Walters | T. P. Carithers |
| R. McB. Pryor | I. C. Johnson |
| W. B. Dasher | James West |
| Dr. R. M. Joiner | F. O. Heard |
| G. W. Brantley | M. L. Battle |
| I. L. Morrison | R. S. Register |
| B. B. Blalock | H. A. Williams |
| B. K. North | J. M. Smith |
| E. G. Taylor | J. L. Holman |
| W. R. Neal | Dr. T. H. Chesnutt |
| L. O. Rogers | Dr. H. M. McGehee |

CHAPTER XXX

# Moultrie's Missionary Baptist Church

THE FIRST BAPTIST CHURCH of Moultrie was constituted on May 30, 1880, the official presbytery being composed of Reverends T. A. White, A. C. Stephenson, S. E. Blitch, and Moses Ward. Nine persons entered the organization, which was housed in a very unpretentious building, about half a block east of the site of the present courthouse.

First Missionary Baptist Church

About 1894, the church entered into its new building, a commodious frame structure about two blocks east of the southeast corner of the courthouse square. This was outgrown by 1903, when a brick building was erected at the corner of Main St., S., and First Avenue, the same being one block south of the southwest corner of the courthouse square. Other buildings have been erected on the church property; so that this plant is worth, at present values of real estate, as much as $125,000. It is the most complete thing of its kind to be found in any town twice the size of Moultrie in Georgia, including a splendid auditorium, a commodious parsonage, and a third building which houses the

## MOULTRIE'S MISSIONARY BAPTIST CHURCH

Sunday school, of more than 1200 people. Several state-wide organizations have been housed by the buildings of the Moultrie Baptist Church.

Among the early church clerks were: A. Scarborough, J. G. Culpepper, W. H. Spivey, D. F. Arthur, V. W. Touchstone, J. T. Killen, and C. B. Allen.

Among the early Sunday school superintendents were: S. G. Gregory, A. Bailey, J. L. Hall, W. A. Aaron, J. R. Hall, M. D. Allen, and Z. H. Clark.

The following ministers of the Gospel have served this church as pastors: A. C. Stephenson, S. E. Blitch, E. H. Bryan, T. A. White, J. M. Waller, A. M. Bennet, Carl W. Minor, A. C. Cree, J. M. Haymore, J. E. Hampton, F. H. Farrington, Walter P. Binns, J. M. Roddy, and R. C. Gresham.

The church was organized as a result of missionary work of the Mercer Association, in cooperation with the State Board which sent out Rev. A. C. Stephenson as a missionary. This was not the only work of this kind done by Mr. Stephenson, nor is it the only Baptist church organized through his efforts. He was a citizen of Thomas County; and he participated in the local option elections in that county and in surrounding counties.

Rev. Solomon Elihu Blitch was another pioneer evangelist of south Georgia. Born in Effingham County, licensed to the ministry in Sept., 1875, ordained May 21, 1876, he served at various times as pastor at Sumner, Ty Ty, Isabella, Lesley, Andersonville, Ellaville, Enigma, Willacoochee, Pearson, etc. For years he was missionary of the State board, during which time he laid the foundations for many churches in south Georgia. Mr. Blitch was converted under the preaching of Rev. J. D. Evans, and was called to ordination by the Pleasant Hill Church in Colquitt County, which was his first pastorate.

Rev. Asa Castleberry Stephenson, born in South Carolina in 1835, and came with his parents to Georgia in 1849, united the Double-branch Church in Franklin County, which church later ordained him to the ministry, served in the Confederate Army, and settled in Thomas County after the war, where he traveled and preached for a while without compensation. The Moultrie Church was a feeble band when he first came to it as pastor.

Rev. E. H. Bryan had served during his ministry several churches of the Mercer Association. He was pastor at times of the churches of Big Ochlochnee, Buck Creek, Hopewell, and Mount Carmel.

Rev. Thos. Alexander White, who died Oct. 1, 1919, was born about the year 1848, and was reared in Oxford, Georgia. He was a member of Gordon's Brigade during the war. Taken prisoner at Fort Steadman, he was kept in prison until the close of the war, during which time he read a small testament given him by J. B. Taylor, afterwards missionary to Italy. He was converted in 1866, at Salem Church, Newton County, where he was made a deacon at nineteen years of age, in which office he continued to serve until 1875, when he was ordained to the ministry by presbytery of Quitman Baptist Church. During the forty-four years of his ministry, he served many churches: Bainbridge, Boston, Meigs, Cairo, Coolidge, Moultrie, and many country churches. He did much building w o r k, changing preaching stations into churches. He accumulated considerable property during his career, and having no children, he requested his wife to leave their property at her death to the orphans' home at Hapeville. One of his living monuments is the Moultrie Church, and the church and community is to be thankful that it was honored in its early history by being associated with this "Apostle of the Piney-woods."

J. M. Waller had charge of the Moultrie Church during the transition from barrooms to prohibition. Our information is that he was born in humble circumstances and had meager opportunities for the improvement of his mind—"but privation and toil could neither deaden nor dull the spiritual aspirations and large hopes that stirred in his breast." Entering college late in life, he was graduated in 1888, winning high esteem with faculty and students for faithfulness and loyalty. His zeal was apostolic; and he had all the courage of one of the early Christian martyrs. He was one of the leaders in the campaigns in 1898 and subsequent years to rid Colquitt County of barrooms, when it meant something to assume such leadership; but he went at it with all his ransomed powers, being at the same time an Irishman and a Christian, he was afraid of nothing. The church under his ministry and that of A. M. Bennet had its heroic era.

Speaking of the "Heroic Age" of this church organization, we are reminded that Rev. A. M. Bennet followed Mr. Waller, and was as much responsible as he for the fighting conditions that stirred the church. It was under his pastorate that the work commenced under Mr. Waller was consolidated and completed. We rode the county in the same buggy with him, in the last and successful Local Option campaign. Mr. Bennet died suddenly at one of the meetings of his church, somewhere in the West, during the present year.

At present, the Moultrie Church has 1525 members, and maintains a Sunday school which has an enrollment of 1360. Dr. C. G. Watson has been the Superintendent of the Sunday school continuously for the past twenty-one years. The board of deacons of the church is composed of the following members: C. J. Austin, C. B. Allen, L. R. Barber, C. Q. Trimble, C. G. Watson, E. O. Sinclair, E. R. King, H. H. Whelchel, F.

R. Pidcock, C. O. Smith, J. Frank Norman, L. L. Moore, A. N. Davis, and Alex Hall.

Miss Ruby Young is Pastor's Assistant, Moultrie Church; Mrs. O. F. Creech is Organist and Choir Director and S. M. DuPree, Church Clerk.

The Colquitt County Baptist Association is composed of twenty-five active churches. Leon F. Hobby is Moderator, H. M. Melton, Vice-Moderator, E. W. Rhoden, Clerk and Treasurer.

## CHAPTER XXXI

## Moultrie Presbyterian Church

MOULTRIE is the courthouse town of Colquitt County in Georgia. A Presbyterian Church was organized here, in the Baptist Church, on October 3, 1892, by Rev. T. J. Allison, the Evangelist of Savannah Presbytery. He enrolled the following persons as members thereof, viz.:

John A. Millsap from Ashpole Church, N. C.
Mrs. Mary E. Millsap from Ashpole Church, N. C.
Mrs. Mollie E. Millsap from Ashpole Church, N. C.
William B. McPhaul from Ashpole Church, N. C.
Mrs. Nannie L. McPhaul from Ashpole Church, N. C.
James A. McKay from Ashpole Church, N. C.
William C. Vereen from First Church, Atlanta, Ga.
Mrs. Mary Vereen from First Church, Atlanta, Ga.
Major N. McK. McNeill from Cheraw Church, S. C.
Mrs. Jane J. McNeill from Cheraw Church, S. C.
Mrs. Sallie Heath from Cheraw Church, S. C.
Miss Ellen McNeill from Camilla Church, Ga.
Burgess A. Rowland from Ashpole Church, N. C.
A. N. McDonald from Lumber Ridge Church, N. C.
Walter L. Wilson from Mayesville Church, S. C.
Miss Carrie McNeill on profession of faith.

William C. Vereen and William B. McPhaul were elected, ordained and installed Ruling Elders. John A. Millsap was elected and installed a Deacon and James A. McKay was elected, ordained and installed a Deacon. By a unanimous vote, *Moultrie* Presbyterian Church was the name chosen for this new organization. The organization was perfected and the church built and dedicated in June, 1893. Rev. J. B. Mack, D.D., evangelist of Synod of Georgia, acting as Moderator. Dr. Mack continued to preach at intervals during 1893. The first communion service was held in this church March 25, 1894. The elements were administered by Dr. J. B. Mack. The day was a very stormy one, as it rained hard and incessantly, yet there was a good congregation present. Dr. Mack was followed by the following ministers: Rev. W. A. Wynne, G. L. Cook, and N. M. Templeton during 1894 and 1895. Revs. Malcolm MacGilliary, J. P. Word, and L. T. Way, during 1896-7-8-9. In 1900 Rev. W. H. McMeen came as stated supply and remained until November, 1901. He was followed by Rev. J. C. Tims, who came as regular pastor, February 1, 1902.

When the first building was erected it was the concensus of opinion that Moultrie, following "the star of empire" would grow towards the west. This proved to be a mistake. The building was finally sold, and for a while the congregation worshipped in the Methodist Church.

First Presbyterian Church

During 1903 a lot was secured and a beautiful manse erected. The esthetic tastes of the occupants soon found expression in a row of camphor trees which they planted along the front of the house. These in their garb of beautiful evergreen leaves soon almost hid the manse from sight.

At a session meeting in 1910 Elder Vereen stated that he did not think the Shorter Catechism was studied as it should be in the Sabbath School and he made an offer of $5.00 to each one in the Sabbath School who would recite the Catechism by the next Christmas. This offer has been renewed from time to time, having been an open offer now for twenty-six years (1936).

Largely through the efforts of a Presbyterian Sunday School teacher (Mr. W. J. Vereen), who endeavored to give to his class of boys a place for supervised play and instruction, the nucleus from which has grown the present Y. M. C. A. was started.

During 1910 the need of larger equipment was clearly recognized, and the pastor, Rev. J. G. Venable, called a meeting to consider the matter. The beautiful building in which services are now held, costing over $30,000.00, was the result. The new church was built and dedicated without cutting down any of the regular contributions.

Sunday, September 29th, the last service was held in the old frame church. It was a sad day to many, but the change was inevitable. Its history was a glorious one. Within its unpretentious walls God had been glorified, but now that its work was done, it was to pass away and disappear. The new church, located on the corner of First Street, S. E., and Fifth Avenue, S. E., was occupied for the first time, October 6, 1912. It was a glorious day for the church life of Moultrie. A grand union service was held both morning and evening, when the church was dedicated to the service of God, and the pastor was installed.

The original sixteen members, only one of whom is now alive, has increased to about four hundred at the present time (1936) and many have been dismissed in the passing years to other churches. The Sunday School from a membership of twenty has grown to about two hundred and ten. The entire history of the church has been a record of faith and practical common sense.

During Mr. Meacham's ministry the church celebrated her twenty-fifth anniversary. A letter received by the pastor from Rev. S. L. Morris, D.D., Executive Secretary of Home Missions in the Presbyterian Church of the United States, gave some interesting facts about the history of the church. One paragraph of this letter is quoted here: "I remember on one occasion preaching to your people on Home Missions, and at the conclusion, Mr. W. C. Vereen, of his own motion, arose and moved that the congregation support an evangelist in the West, and the motion was seconded by Mr. C. W. Pidcock, backing his address with a subscription of $500.00. In a few moments, the church subscribed $1,600.00 and supported the Rev. W. T. Matthews, as evangelist in Oklahoma. Through the instrumentality of Rev. Matthews quite a number of churches were organized in Oklahoma, and he practically developed the one Presbytery into the present Synod of Oklahoma. I want your people to know that the Moultrie church is thus the mother of churches in Oklahoma and that you never invested anywhere any money that has brought in greater returns to the Presbyterian Church than the support you gave our work in Oklahoma."

During Mr. Dick's pastorate a Sunday School annex was built, that the young children might have better Sunday School training. This building was dedicated on June 20, 1931.

The following ministers served as, what is known in the Presbyterian Church as, a Stated Supply during the years 1894-95; Reverends W. A. Wynne, G. L. Cook, and N. M. Templeton. During the years 1896-97-98-99: Reverends L. T. Way, Malcom MacGilliary, and J. P. Word. During the period 1900 to 1901: Rev. W. H. McMean.

The following regular pastors have served the church since 1901:

## MOULTRIE PRESBYTERIAN CHURCH

Rev. J. C. Tims, from Feb. 1, 1902 to Feb. 1, 1907.

Rev. J. G. Venable, from Oct. 1, 1907 to Nov. 1, 1911.

Rev. J. W. Tyler, D.D., from April, 1912 to July, 1914.

Rev. J. B. Meacham, from Nov., 1914 to Aug. 1, 1920.

Rev. D. W. Brannen, D.D., from Nov. 1, 1920 to Feb. 22, 1923, the date of his death.

Rev. A. D. Wauchope, from June 1, 1923 to Nov., 1926.

Rev. A. W. Dick, from Feb. 1, 1927 to Feb. 1, 1932.

(Rev. A. M. Gregg, stated supply, from June 1, 1932 to October, 1932.)

Rev. M. A. MacDonald, from Feb. 1, 1933, and is still serving as pastor in 1936.

The present (1936) Board of Ruling Elders of the church is as follows:

| | |
|---|---|
| W. C. Vereen | W. F. Westbrook |
| D. A. Autrey | S. W. Prince |
| Ben VanDalsem | L. A. Slade |

The present (1936) Board of Deacons is as follows:

W. J. Vereen, Chairman
M. C. Farley, Treasurer

| | |
|---|---|
| J. A. McHargue | G. Darbyshire |
| Charles J. Knapp | Willie Withers |
| J. S. Johnson | E. R. Bryan |
| M. W. Majors | W. R. Latham |
| I. R. Aultman | C. B. Patterson |

D. G. Phillips

Director of Young People..........................Mrs. George Mau
Director of Junior Young People................Mrs. T. H. Chestnut
Director of Music...........................................Miss Lucile Autrey
Superintendent of Sunday School..............Mr. Ben VanDalsem
President, Women's Auxiliary.....................Mrs. J. B. Pinckard
Approximate membership of church.........................................400
Approximate membership of Sunday school...........................210

City of Moultrie Officials

*Standing:* Geo B. Hunt, Chief of Fire Department; Geo. A. Shaver, Clerk and Treasurer; Hoyt H. Whelchel, Attorney; Ernest P. Pinson, Supt. Water and Light Dept.; Paul J. Sineath, Tax Collector; L. L. Smith, Chief of Police; Dr. T. L. Wright, City Inspector; Berry L. Lanier, Sanitary Inspector; J. M. Leverette, City Engineer. *Sitting:* Chas. W. Cook, Chairman Police Committee; Geo. F. Huber, Chairman Street Committee; J. Wiley Belvin, Chairman Water and Light Committee; Evans Reynolds, Chairman Finance Committee; A. V. Johnson, Chairman Fire and Building Committee; Hon. J. Frank Norman, Mayor of the City of Moultrie.

## CHAPTER XXXII

# Colquitt's Educational Facilities

### MOULTRIE CARNEGIE LIBRARY

THE MOULTRIE CARNEGIE LIBRARY was established in 1908, largely as a result of the efforts of Mr. John E. Howell, who secured an appropriation of $10,000.00 from the Carnegie Library Fund. He was chairman of the first library board, and ever zealous for its interests. This board was created by the authorities of the City of Moultrie. The ordinance is dated February 5, 1907, and shows that the Council pledged itself to pay $100.00 a month to maintain the library. It also provided for a Board of Directors, consisting of the following names: John E. Howell, C. B. Allen, C. W. Pidcock, W. C. Vereen, W. H. Barber, J. B. Norman, Jr., J. F. Monk, and W. A. Covington.

The Carnegie people demanded, as a condition precedent to giving the $10,000.00, that a building be erected on a centrally located lot, at a corner. Such a lot was found, and the owners, M. D. Norman, and J. B. Norman, Jr., contributed one-third of the value of the lot, Mr. Z. H. Clark gave another third, and several smaller contributions made up the remainder of the purchase price. The library was opened to the public in the year 1908. It is maintained at present by joint contributions of the City of Moultrie and Colquitt County. In supplying the building with adequate books, many contributions have been made, the largest being $1,200 contributed by the Moultrie Kiwanis Club fifteen years ago.

The first librarian was Mrs. W. C. McKenzie, to whose executive ability much credit is due for the organization of the institution. Mrs. McKenzie held the position of librarian from 1908 to 1919, during a part of which time Miss Ola Mae Monk served as her assistant. Miss Lois Adams was librarian from 1919 to 1923. The period of 1924-25 was covered by Miss Annabel Conner (now Mrs. Hoyt Whelchel). After her, Miss Louise Aycock (now Mrs. Allen Furman), Miss Velma Goode, and Mrs. W. E. Young, have served in that capacity. Mrs. Young is the present efficient librarian.

The library has extended its service to citizens of the County as a whole, and is an institution of permanent value as an educational force to the entire community.

## Young Men's Christian Association

The project of the Y. M. C. A. for Moultrie was first suggested at the annual meeting of the Chamber of Commerce, on March 2, 1916, by Mr. F. R. Pidcock. Mr. H. Daugherty was the first General Secretary (December 1, 1916).

The building was completed October 1, 1917. In April, 1919, Mr. J. H. Kenny was elected Assistant Secretary.

In the summer of 1921, the regular work for men and boys was reinforced by the commencement of work for ladies and girls, and a residence building hard by the building of the Y. M. C. A. This activity has been continuous, since that time.

In 1923 Mr. Daugherty left the Association, so that he might take charge of Methodist Orphans' Home, at Macon; and J. H. Kenny succeeded him as General Secretary, a position which he has held continuously till the present.

During the whole of its history, the Moultrie Y. M. C. A. and Y. W. C. A. have functioned one hundred per cent.

## Norman Institute

Norman Institute was founded in 1900, by Hon. J. B. Norman, Jr. It is located at Norman Park, Georgia, a village of some 1,200 inhabitants, located on the A. B. and C. Railroad, about ten miles from Moultrie, in the direction of Tifton, Georgia.

After Mr. Norman had procured buildings to be erected, and had provided for a substantial endowment fund, he died, in ..... His heirs have from time to time made other contributions, as have other Colquitt County friends. At this time, Norman Institute is a part of the Mercer system of educational institutions, and is controlled by a board of trustees appointed by Norman Park Baptist Church, various Baptist Associations and the Georgia Baptist Convention.

Norman Institute has a Christian faculty, every member of which is college-trained; second, excellent equipment for science; third, an excellent department for the training of pupils in domestic science and household arts. And the ambition of the present management is to make Norman Institute second to none as a junior college, and a fashioner of character. Its work spreads far beyond the County of Colquitt; but it is as a factor in the upbuilding of Colquitt that we are considering it, now.

## Colquitt's Public School System

In 1872, the Statewide movement for free public schools for the children of Georgia was launched. The credit for the establishment of the system and its incorporation in the Georgia Constitution of 1868, has already been placed in this History. In Colquitt, at least, the term was at first only sixty days, and lasted from "Laying-by time" till "Fodder-pulling time." The curriculum covered the "three R's"— Reading, Writing, and Arithmetic; the Constitution of 1868 providing for free education of all persons resident in the State between the ages of six and twenty-one years old, and "in the elementary branches of an English education."

Dr. Baker E. Watkins, hereinbefore referred to, as a local Methodist preacher, and Colquitt's first resident physician, was elected Colquitt's first County School Commissioner. He held for four years; and his was the task of organization. Henry Gay came next, with twelve years of service. Then came N. M. Marchant, who served sixteen years, being himself the first youth ever matriculated at the University of Georgia from Colquitt County, and who still remains with us, past eighty years of age, and still a man of taste and culture. Other commissioners have been: Hon. J. H. Smithwick, Mr. John E. Howell, Prof. Lee S. Dismuke, Prof. O. A. Thaxton, Prof. Frank Clark, and Prof. L. O. Rogers—the last named being the present incumbent. All these men have been excellent workmen, and each has contributed his share to the upbuilding of Colquitt's splendid system of public schools. Miss Amanda McDonald taught the first free school term ever organized in the City of Moultrie. Daughter she was of James McDonald, of "down about Pavo," and a leading man of Thomas County, for more than a generation; wife she was to be of W. H. Gibson, popular citizen of Colquitt for twenty years, and mother she was to be of sons Joe, Dan, Carl, Frank, and Eustace Gibson, and of daughters Mary Gibson Knapp, and Annie Gibson Green.

Some of the other teachers during the early days of the system were: A. D. Patterson, L. A. Hall, N. M. Marchant, Montgomery M. Folsom, H. R. Hutchinson, Thomas Breedon, John Gibson, John A. Wilkes, and Daniel Lawson.

At present, there are sixteen consolidated schools in Colquitt County, as follows: Autreyville, Berlin, Center Hill, Cool Springs, Crossland, Culbertson, Ellenton, Funston, Hartsfield, Norman Park, Ocapilco, Reedy Creek, Rock Hill, Rose Hill, Sunset, and Ty-Ty.

# COLQUITT'S EDUCATIONAL FACILITIES

The tenth and eleventh grades of all consolidated schools are sent for their work to Moultrie High School, Doerun High School, or to Norman Park Junior College.

By special contract, all pupils residing within a radius of five miles from Doerun, are sent to Doerun public schools for all their work. This, although Doerun schools exist under legislative enactment, operates in practice to render this system itself another consolidated school.

There are twenty-nine buses in use in connection with Colquitt's school system, carrying 3,160 pupils to and from school.

The total enrollment of pupils in attendance at the public schools of Colquitt County at the beginning of the Fall Term 1936 is 7,074 whites, and 1,870 colored.

One of the Moultrie High School Buildings

## CHAPTER XXXIII

# Women's Clubs

### JOHN BENNING CHAPTER DAUGHTERS OF THE AMERICAN REVOLUTION

UNDER PROPER authority, the John Benning Chapter, Daughters of the Revolution was organized on November 1, 1910, with twelve members, with Mrs. W. C. Vereen, Organizing Regent, such authority being signed by Mrs. Julia G. Scott, President-General, and Mrs. John M. Graham, State Regent of Georgia.

Charter Members: Mrs. Jennie Vereen Bell, Mrs. Bonnell Strozier Bivins, Miss Jean Patton Cameron, Mrs. Virginia Carroll Cree, Mrs. Harriet Holtman Chase, Mrs. Stella Ray Howell, Mrs. Emily Kline Shipp, Mrs. Jessie Vereen Smithwick, Miss Pearl Vereen, Mrs. Ellen Vereen, Mrs. Adelle N. Way, Mrs. Lottie Thompson Vereen.

### MOULTRIE-MCNEILL CHAPTER DAUGHTERS OF THE CONFEDERACY

The Moultrie-McNeill Chapter of the Daughters of the Confederacy was organized at the home of Mrs. J. R. Hall, in March, 1903. Mrs. W. S. Humphreys, now deceased, was organizer and first president.

The charter members of this Chapter were: Mrs. W. S. Humphreys, Mrs. W. C. Vereen, Mrs. J. D. McKenzie, Mrs. D. A. Autrey, Mrs. Kate Crenshaw, Mrs. R. L. Shipp, Mrs. Everett Daniel, Mrs. J. R. Hall, Mrs. P. B. Allen, Mrs. H. C. McKenzie, Miss Jennie Vereen, Mrs. W. J. Matthews, Mrs. S. F. Way, and Mrs. D. A. Fish.

The local chapter of the U. D. C. has the distinction of being oldest and the largest women's organization in Moultrie. It has at all times worked at the various undertakings looking to the preservation of the ideals of the general organization. At all times, since its organization, it has sought out the comfort and welfare of the surviving soldiers of the Southern Confederacy. It has especially on Southern Memorial Day served these survivors and theirs with a dinner, and put on a program of education for the young of the County. The beautiful monument that stands on the southwest corner of the public square is in memory of the Confederate soldiers, and was erected through the efforts of the local chapter of the U. D. C. in 1909.

### The Worth While Club

The Worth While Club was organized in the early fall of 1907, for social and educational purposes, with thirty-five members. Its club room is over the Moultrie Carnegie Library, which is sufficiently large to accommodate the club meetings and social affairs, and a membership of fifty actives.

The club joined the National Federation in 1909, and is organized along the following lines: Home Economics, Library Extension, Community Service, Forestry, Fine Arts, Child Welfare, Industrial and Social Relations and Literature.

CHAPTER XXXIV

## The Moultrie Banking Company

THE PRESENTMENTS returned at the November Term, 1835, by the Grand Jury of Thomas County show that that County had on hand $753.87 in notes and cash, deposited in various banks, three of which were in Florida, one in Alabama, and one in Macon, Georgia. There was no bank in Thomas County at that time, and the nearest bank to Thomasville was the "Magnolia Bank of Magnolia, Florida." Here the town of Thomasville opened its first bank account.

At the May term, 1836, of the Superior Court of Thomas County, the Grand Jury called attention to bad roads generally, and especially the roads between Thomasville and Magnolia.

Magnolia was situated up the Saint Marks River, and across it, opposite the present site of Newport. It is gone now; but it was a flourishing town then.

There was no bank in Thomas County until 1861, when the "Cotton Planters' Bank" was established in Thomasville. There was very little business with banks on the part of the people of the Colquitt section of Thomas County, so long as it was in the "pastoral" stage. Even as late as the 1870's, when a Colquitt man wanted a little ready cash, he would go, either to Jack Johnson, Staten May, Ab Baker, or Jim Gay. At such times, the borrower would be asked to sit down in the house and wait a while. The lender would then absent himself a little while, and come back with the money. By 1890, the turpentine and lumber business was developing in Colquitt County, and better banking facilities were found to be necessary, and so, on the .... day of ..........,

## THE MOULTRIE BANKING COMPANY

1896, a charter was obtained for a bank to be known as the "Moultrie Banking Company." Associated in this undertaking were W. W. Ashburn, Z. H. Clark, W. C. Vereen, M. J. Pearsall, J. F. Spivey, John McK. McNeil, and J. B. Norman, Jr. W. W. Ashburn was the first president, and so remained until his death in 1906. W. C. Vereen was elected active vice-president, and so remained until president Ashburn's death, when he was elected president. This position he has continuously held from the date of his election to the present day. Z. H. Clark was originally elected cashier of the bank, and so remained until the date of his death on May, 1916, when M. L. Lee became cashier, who has held this position continuously until the present. The original capitalization of the bank was $25,000.00, and the actual cash paid in was $15,000. The bank has continued to grow, as is shown by practically every one of its financial reports during the last forty years.

Until the last report, under date of September 30, 1936, shows it has passed into the class of "three million dollar banks." The financial condition of this bank, as of September 30, 1936, is as follows:

Moultrie Banking Co.

## CONDENSED FORM OF STATEMENT
## MOULTRIE BANKING COMPANY
### MOULTRIE, GEORGIA
### September 30, 1936

As Called for by State Superintendent of Banks

### Assets

| | | |
|---|---:|---:|
| Loans and Discounts | $ | 718,327.29 |
| Stocks | | 12,955.00 |
| U. S. bonds owned— | | |
|   Direct and Guaranteed | $1,082,187.50 | |
| State, County and Municipal bonds | 133,734.14 | |
| Other bonds owned | 29,087.50 | |
| Advances on cotton | 83,475.69 | |
| Cash on hand and in banks | 992,222.97 | |
| Total cash assets | | 2,320,707.80 |
| Banking house and fixtures | | 67,062.30 |
| Other real estate | | 18,306.90 |
| Other assets | | 229.81 |
| Total | | $3,137,589.10 |

### Liabilities

| | |
|---|---:|
| Capital Stock | $ 200,000.00 |
| Surplus and profits | 315,431.03 |
| Reserve funds | 12,381.20 |
| DEPOSITS | $2,609,776.87 |
| Total | $3,137,589.10 |

DEPOSITS INSURED UNDER THE U. S. GOVERNMENT PLAN

### Officers

| | |
|---|---:|
| W. C. Vereen (elected 1906) | President |
| F. R. Pidcock | Vice-President |
| W. J. Vereen | Vice-President |
| E. M. Vereen | Active Vice-President |
| M. L. Lee | Cashier |
| M. C. Farley | Assistant Cashier |
| C. H. Lewis | Assistant Cashier |

# THE MOULTRIE BANKING COMPANY

### Directors

| | |
|---|---|
| G. J. Austin | F. R. Pidcock |
| J. Bennison | H. P. Plair |
| H. Jones | Elkin G. Taylor |
| M. L. Lee | E. M. Vereen |
| R. M. Morrison | W. C. Vereen |
| G. W. Newton | W. J. Vereen |
| R. L. Norman | C. G. Watson |

J. R. Hall, Jr.

### Clerical Force

Miss Sarah McPhaul, Savings Department
George O. Mobley, Teller
J. Ferrell Lockwood, Teller
W. H. McCoy, Jr., Bookkeeper
H. Carlton Lockwood, Bookkeeper
J. Floyd Monk, Bookkeeper.

A bank being a public institution; and in more ways than one belonging to the public, must, like Caesar's wife, be constantly "above suspicion." And this is exactly what could be truthfully said of the Moultrie Banking Company during every day of its more than forty years of active life. This has resulted from the fact that its founders were themselves men of highest personal probity; and its managers have at all times jealously maintained its high traditions. This fact is a ground of proper pride, not only for the stockholders, but for the whole of Colquitt County.

## CHAPTER XXXV

## Moultrie National Bank

THE BANK WAS ORGANIZED January 3, 1928. The applicants for a charter were R. J. Corbett, R. A. Cooper, John T. Norman, A. G. Whitehead, and Lewis Edwards.

The first official set-up was:

R. J. Corbett..................President
John T. Norman..................Vice-President
Lewis Edwards..................Cashier
Charles F. Cook..................Assistant Cashier

### DIRECTORS

R. J. Corbett      John T. Norman
R. A. Cooper      A. G. Whitehead
Lewis Edwards

The present official set-up of this institution is:

Waldo DeLoache..................President
R. A. Cooper..................Vice-President
J. S. Harris..................Vice-President
H. S. Cohen..................Vice-President and Cashier
Leroy Dubberly..................Assistant Cashier
Marian McKay..................Assistant Cashier

### DIRECTORS

L. R. Barber      Louis Friedlander
Leo T. Barber      J. S. Harris
Chas. W. Cook      I. C. Johnson
R. A. Cooper      L. L. Moore
Waldo DeLoache      E. O. Sinclair

## MOULTRIE NATIONAL BANK

### Last Official Financial Statement

Resources:

| | |
|---|---:|
| Loans and Discounts | $ 336,931.10 |
| Bonds | 277,286.14 |
| Stock Federal Reserve Bank | 3,900.00 |
| Banking House | 7,000.00 |
| Furniture and Fixtures | 5,600.00 |
| Other Real Estate | 2,085.57 |
| Cash on Hand and Due from Banks | 548,138.14 |
| Total | $1,180,940.95 |

Liabilities:

| | |
|---|---:|
| Capital | $ 100,000.00 |
| Surplus | 30,000.00 |
| Undivided Profits | 32,581.16 |
| Reserves | 3,000.00 |
| Deposits | 1,015,359.79 |
| Total | $1,180,940.95 |

It will readily appear that the Moultrie National Bank has been keeping step with the prosperity that has been general in Colquitt County since the organization of the institution. Within less than nine years from the date of its organization it has become a "Million Dollar Bank;" and such is the energy and character of its officers we are warranted in predicting that it is destined to be an increasingly prominent factor in the future development of our great county.

Moultrie National Bank

## CHAPTER XXXVI

# Moultrie Cotton Mills

1. Date of organization: April 4, 1900.
2. Personnel of first official set-up:

W. C. Vereen..................................................President
W. W. Ashburn...........................................First Vice-President
M. D. Norman............................................Second Vice-President
Z. H. Clark................................................Secretary-Treasurer

### DIRECTORS

W. W. Ashburn             D. N. Horne
W. C. Vereen              Miles Monk
T. I. McNeill             D. Sinclair
D. S. Smith               M. J. Pearsall
C. E. Holmes

3. Present official set-up:

W. C. Vereen..................................................President
W. J. Vereen............................Vice-President and Treasurer
L. L. Dickerson.............................................Secretary

### DIRECTORS

W. C. Vereen              F. R. Pidcock
W. J. Vereen              M. L. Lee
L. R. Barber

4. The Moultrie Cotton Mills was organized with a subscribed capital stock of $100,000.00, with authority to increase to $500,000.00. The original capital has been increased from time to time and a large part of surplus earnings have been carried to undivided profits and used in purchasing new machinery and enlarging buildings.

Work on the buildings of the mill began in June, 1900. The mill was completed and active operations commenced

April 7, 1901, with 5,000 spindles and 160 looms, together with all other preparatory machinery and power plant of sufficient size to double the capacity of the mill when needed. The equipment of the mill at this time is 12,000 spindles and 300 looms, the capacity having been increased three times since operations first began.

The mill has run almost continuously since it started in April, 1901, until the present time except for a period of about three weeks in 1935 together with about four or five weeks previously in order to install a new engine and power plant.

Moultrie Cotton Mills

During the first year of the mill's operations about 1,500 bales of cotton were used. In 1936 the amount of cotton consumed was about 6,500 bales, and during the year 1937, with new machinery added, it is expected that about 8,000 bales will be used.

Since 1933 the mill has been using two shifts of hands, running night and day. The mill employs at present about three hundred and twenty-five persons, most of whom have been with the company for many years.

## MOULTRIE COTTON MILLS

The goods manufactured are, for the most part, sheetings, drills, and osnaburgs. In the early years after the organization of the mill, a considerable portion of the goods was sold in China. For many years past, however, the entire product has been sold in the United States.

During the first few years of the operations of the mill the production was about 2,600,000 yards per annum for cloth of various kinds. In 1936 the production of cloth is approximately 10,400,000 yards with new equipment which is being installed. In 1937 the production of goods should amount to about 15,000,000 yards of cloth.

Salaries, wages, cash paid for wood for fuel, for the year 1936 amounted to $189,000.00. Amount paid for cotton during the year 1936 is $390,000.00.

## CHAPTER XXXVII

## The Moultrie Packing Company

As HAS BEEN SEEN hereinbefore, the Pastoral Era in Colquitt County commenced gradually to give place to the Industrial and Manufacturing Era in 1890, with the coming of the railroads from the Coast Line and from the Georgia, Southern and Florida, on the East. By 1898, the turpentine and sawmill industries were in full flower through practically the whole county. In other words, the magnificent yellow pine timber had been leased up in generally what would be considered short term leases. Anyhow, by 1910, the end of the timber industry was in sight; and people began to discuss what was to follow the exhaustion of the timber. As a matter of fact, nothing could be foreseen except the bringing of the cut-over lands under the plow for purely agricultural purposes and there was only one crop that promised any cash returns of any magnitude. At any rate, citizens who were unable or indisposed to move away commenced the process of opening up the lands to cultivation.

And then a very serious thing happened. Rumors were spreading that coming out of Mexico and advancing toward the East by great annual leaps, was an insect pest which swept growing cotton off the face of the earth, and threatened the whole future of this section.

Possibly on account of this distressing foreboding of disaster, the propaganda began to trickle in for a readjustment of the land industries, looking to the substitution of stock and hog raising for cotton, as a money crop. As a consequence of this propaganda, and as a part of it, the people of Southwest Georgia began to discuss the location of "packing plants" for the processing of meats in this section. Gradually this propaganda assumed respectable proportions in Colquitt County—due to the fact that some of its citizens had been in the northwest and had given some study to the meat packing industry in that section. It was a condition of necessity that compelled consideration of this matter by the industrial leaders of Colquitt County, and so finally a mass meeting was called at Moultrie, and after some discussion, W. C. Vereen, W. H. Barber, and R. M. Morrison, citizens of the County at the time, were named as a committee to investigate the whole matter, going for that purpose to the northwest, and carefully studying the situation. These gentlemen had for a long while been citizens of Colquitt County, and had established pretty fair reputations for ultra-conservatism; but their report made to the citizens' meeting, upon their return, established the fact that they were capable of taking pretty liberal chances, on occasion. In other words, they reported favorably as to the enterprise; and backed their judgment by leading the subscription list to the stock.

There is not space here to set forth the importance of this action and its consequences. It is sufficient to say that twenty-four years after the Moultrie Packing Company was organized, it has revolutionized agriculture and industry in the whole of Southwest Georgia. Swift and Company, of course, operate it now, but it is extremely unlikely that this fact would have happened but for the courageous action of the organizers of the Moultrie Packing Company.

The present owners are not disposed to talk much about their business, which is their right; but our investigation has developed the fact that the operation of this plant gives employment to some 600 people at weekly wages of not less than $12 per week. The pay-roll during at least four months of the year amounts to $18,000 per week. The banner week was one of the weeks of the present season, in which the farmers of this section brought livestock to Moultrie, and went home with $240,000.00 in their pockets. This is enough to ruminate on, while we submit the first official set-up of the Moultrie Packing Company, so that the generations to come may at least know the names of these pioneers in the packing industry in Southwest Georgia:

### Officers

| | |
|---|---|
| W. C. Vereen | President |
| W. H. Barber | Vice-President |
| Z. H. Clark | Secretary and Treasurer |

### Directors

| | |
|---|---|
| W. C. Vereen | C. W. Pidcock, Sr. |
| W. H. Barber | R. J. Corbett |
| J. R. Hall | H. A. Ashburn |
| John A. Carlton | R. M. Morrison |
| W. J. Matthews | |

We are glad to present them to you, ladies and gentlemen of the ages to come, as men who served their day and generation in the widest most comprehensive way. At a most critical period in the history of the County and the Section—when even the stoutest hearts were worried to distraction by dangers that beset the future, they pooled their resources in a movement in which was involved not only their investments but their credits; and all this they did, as this historian knows, not so much as a personal investment but as a prop and support to the very existence of the community in which they lived, and where their dead are buried.

After the establishment and equipment of a plant for the processing of meats, they operated it for two and one-half years, and sold it to Swift & Company; and, what is remarkable about that transaction, they were operating at the time of the sale at a profit and sold the stock after two and one-half years of operation at $125.00, the par value of the same being $100.00.

The Original
Packing Plant
at Moultrie

## SWIFT & COMPANY
### MOULTRIE, GEORGIA

The original Meat Packing Plant at Moultrie was financed by local capital and operated from September 1914 until June 1917 under the name of Moultrie Packing Company with Mr. W. C. Vereen as President.

Swift & Company purchased the plant in June 1917 and have operated it since that time under the name of Swift & Company.

The first Manager for Swift & Company was F. A. Luchsinger, who remained until February 1919, when he was succeeded by the present Manager, Horace McDowell.

The capacity of the packing plant in 1917 was about 25,000 cattle and hogs annually. The plant now has an annual capacity of 100,000 cattle and 600,000 hogs.

The Moultrie Packing Plant pays out to live stock producers approximately six million dollars annually and while they purchase live stock from points all over Florida, Alabama, Georgia, and South Carolina, 75% of their purchases are made from territory within 150 miles of Moultrie.

Moultrie has been the center of the development of the live stock industry of the Southeast due not only to the Swift plant being kept in continuous operation since 1917, but particularly due to the inspirational leadership of Moultrie citizens in encouraging production, not only in Colquitt County, but all over the Southeast.

Swift & Company officials believe the Southeast will develop live stock production many times greater than at present and that eventually the Southeast will produce as much beef and pork as is consumed in southeastern States.

The Swift Moultrie Plant has always made an effort to popularize Peanut Hams and other cuts from peanut fed hogs, considering Peanut Pork superior in quality.

### Present Plant of Swift & Co., Moultrie

CHAPTER XXXVIII

## Crime in Colquitt

UPON A REVIEW of this History, as we are on the point of bringing it to a close, we find that little has been written about crime and criminals. And, since the space agreed upon by us with the publishers has been about taken up already, there seems little that can be done about it; and, after all, this may be just as well.

There is nothing alluring about accounts of crime, especially about crimes of violence.

There are no court records in existence covering Colquitt's history from 1856 to 1881. The fire which burned up the court-house in that year disposed of all court records, and tradition gives us no account of any major crimes during that period.

From 1881 to 1901 was the period of lawlessness in the county's history. This was the beginning of the naval stores and lumber industry. The pay-rolls were comparatively large. There was an influx of Negro labor; and there were from four to eleven saloons. And, as is always the case, the easy access to alcoholic stimulants developed crimes of violence.

But there is nothing of the heroic about crime based on liquor consumption; and nothing is gained, and no useful end is served by chronicling such matters. It is sufficient, we think, to register the fact that when Colquitt County banned the sale of intoxicants in 1902 crimes of violence commenced to decrease; and that they have, by this time, decreased one thousand per cent. In other words, the dockets of the criminal courts show that present Colquitt, with forty

## CRIME IN COLQUITT

thousand population, has less than a third as many crimes of violence as the Colquitt of 1900 with ten thousand inhabitants.

At all and everything, however, Colquitt's statistical records as to crime do not show up so bad by comparison with other sections.

There has never been a white person executed for crime in the county. Three Negro men were hanged at separate times by the sheriff at the old brick jail, carrying out the sentences of the law and two Negro men have suffered electrocution at Milledgeville in accordance with the law. Four men —all Negroes—have been lynched in the county. There has

Moultrie Municipal Building

been only one white person—Henry Harris—convicted and sentenced to death in the history of the county. At the fall term, 1897, of Colquitt Superior Court, Harris was convicted of murdering Henry NeSmith. It was family trouble. The Harris boy had married NeSmith's daughter. The menfolk of both families were in Moultrie one Saturday afternoon. Henry Harris and his son, Bob, went to Finch's bar, on the present site of Henderson Furniture Store, and bought 45 cents worth of whisky, and from there to W. B. Duke's store, on the present site of the Friedlander stores, and bought two cartridges afterwards. The Harrisses drove up to the Ne-Smiths—father and son—and killed the father.

After the trial the wife of Harris carried a big dose of strychnine to her husband's cell and passed it to him and watched him die in tremendous spasms. We saw her in the fall of 1898, walking with her son, Robert; she had just been discharged from prison. She had a complexion like yellow-tanned rawhide—a result of years of field work. Henry NeSmith lies in a marked grave in the "Old Greenfield Church," near the Moultrie and Tallokas road.

## CHAPTER XXXIX

# Colquitt Weather

In October, 1898, at the regular term of the Superior Court, we sat at a table in the dining room of the old "Fish Hotel," in Moultrie. Near us sat Judge Augustin H. Hansell, the venerable judge of the Southern Circuit of Georgia, and a circuit riding Methodist preacher. Judge Hansell had been riding the Southern Circuit a matter of fifty years; and the preacher had been riding preaching circuits during the same length of time. They were discussing the climate of this section of Georgia; and they agreed that they had never known a crop failure on account of weather conditions.

This statement was made some thirty-eight years ago; and during this time we have been familiar with this section. And we have never heard or seen a crop failure in Colquitt County. Which comes pretty close to setting up a record of a hundred years. And we believe the record is unique. Let us analyze our weather:

We are at such a distance from the North Polar sections that any blizzard gets out of heart before it reaches our latitude. We are close enough to the Atlantic and the Gulf as that direct winds are sufficiently cool to render the average summer night cool enough to render a little "kiver" agreeable; while we are at such a distance away that we have never been reached by what might be called direct-blowing storms. And, for a century the rainfall has been ample to mature crops of all kinds, and so distributed through the year that it is possible to make an average of two crops on the same land each year. And the Charleston Earthquake of August, 1886, was not even felt in this County.

In the interest of perfect truth it ought to be said that two destructive storms have come through the County in the past ninety years. "Cyclones," storms like these two are called in Georgia. They play along the face of the country, like an inverted spinning-top, capable of blowing everything off the face of the earth over a strip rarely wider than two or three hundred yards. They were really "whirlwinds" on a big scale, which carry a velocity of four or five hundred miles to the hour in their spinning motion, as they advance along the country to the northeast at a rate of thirty or forty miles per hour.

The first of the two storms of this kind to strike Colquitt came along out of the southwest, at about three o'clock of the afternoon of the second day of March, 1877; and, like all such storms, moved along towards the northeast. It came along between Ochlochnee and Meigs in Thomas County, coming along to the southeast of what is now Funston in Colquitt, and struck the double-pen log residence of Elder Henry Crawford Tucker, a matter of one and one-half miles north of the Moultrie and Camilla paved road. It was going good, too, having thrown prone on the ground thousands of acres of some of the finest yellow-pine timber in Georgia, after it had entered Colquitt. It struck the Tucker double-pen amidships, buckled down a little, and slapped every pound of power it had into the contest. It was a case of the "irresistible force coming in contact with an immovable object," about which we have heard; but when the brief struggle was over, the cyclone went roaring into the Ochlochnee swamp, with every outhouse and tree about the Elder's place prostrate, and most of them in the swamp. But the "Double-Pen" was there—not on account of the fact that the "Elder" had founded it on a rock; but because it was necessary for it to be moved as it stood, if it was to be moved at all. All the logs were joined together by wooden corner pins.

Sheriff Davied Murphy lived some distance south of the Tucker place; and we have heard his sons Henry and Aaron tell how they were called out on the porch of their residence to see this cyclone pass. And how they went with their father the next day to help Elder Tucker gather up the contents of his smokehouse out of the Ochlochnee swamp—hams, shoulders, heads, jowls and sides. For sixty years, this storm has been called by the settlers along its route the "Tucker Hairycane." It was a honey; but it is rather discouraging for a "hairycane" to run into a forest of virgin yellow pines, with residences averaging four or five miles apart, and double-pens, when reached. This one, after crossing the Ochlochnee, proceeded to blow things around on the farm of Isaac Royal. Next, it tackled the farm of Daniel Highsmith. After that, it jumped down on the farm of the Widow Bulloch; and our last accounts trace it to the house of Joe Weeks, and possibly to the premises of Flournoy Clark.

The only other such storm, since the first settlement of this County passed over Moultrie, one morning, some twenty years ago. No one was injured, and only two or three small buildings were blown down. This cyclone was a terrible looking thing; but it was traveling rather high. However, when the next one comes along, it will pass through a denser population, and so may do much harm. Witness the damage worked at Cordele and Gainesville, during March of the present year (1936). And so it would be the part of the highest prudence for each residence to have a storm cellar; and similar precautions taken to protect the children assembled in our ever-increasing school buildings.

WM. HENRY BARBER

## William Henry Barber

W. H. BARBER, one of the most important among the original developers of Colquitt County, was born near Catharine Lake, Onslow County, N. C., on April 8, 1862. His parents, Thomas R. Barber and Alavana (Groves) Barber, were both born in the State of North Carolina, the former near Catharine Lake, February 15, 1826, and the latter at Hamilton, Martin County, February 15, 1833.

Mr. Barber's great-grandfathers, Joseph Barber and Hillary Brinson, were soldiers in the American Army during the Revolutionary War. The Barbers are of Irish extraction, the Brinsons are Scotch, and the Groves family is of English descent.

Thomas R. Barber enlisted in March, 1863, as a private in Company H, Third North Carolina Cavalry, and participated in the engagements at Hanover Court House, Rona Mills, Munk's Neck, Drewry's Bluff and Franklin, Va., and in the military operations around Richmond, remaining in the Confederate service until the close of the conflict. His regiment was a part of W. H. Lee's division of Stuart's Cavalry Corps.

The marriage of Thomas R. Barber and Alavana, the daughter of Wm. E. and Matilda (Kiell) Groves, occurred on February 8, 1857. They became the parents of nine children, five sons and four daughters.

Wm. H. Barber's boyhood was passed during the troublous years following the Civil War, so that his opportunities to acquire an education were rather limited. He remained on his father's farm until August, 1879, when he went to Bertie County, N. C., where he clerked in a country store for about two years. He then went to Kinston, N. C., and worked in a store for one year, and at the end of that time he returned to the old farm home, near Catharine Lake, and attended school for five months. For the next six years he was in the employ of a merchant named M. T. Horne, at Chinquapin, N. C.; and in January, 1889, he came to Worth County, Ga., where he worked on Mr. Horne's turpentine farm for about one year, and at the end of this time he formed a co-partnership with Mr. K. W. Horne for the manufacture of naval stores in Colquitt County, Ga., in which line of industry he remained practically to his death, and in which he achieved phenomenal success.

In 1899, the Citizens Bank was organized at Moultrie, with Mr. Barber as vice-president. Three years later, Mr. Barber was promoted to the position of president of this institution, and held this position to the date of his death. He was one of the original promoters of the Moultrie Telephone Exchange, of the Moultrie Ice and Cold Storage Company, the Moultrie Cotton Mills, and the Colquitt County Cooperage Company. Later in life he acquired enormous interests in the naval stores industry in the State of Florida. In co-operation with a few other daring spirits he undertook an entirely new development in Colquitt County, when a packing plant for the processing of meats was built at Moultrie. This enterprise was perhaps the most important one that was ever started in Colquitt County and was epochal in the industrial history of South Georgia. In the ages to come, therefore, tribute will be paid without stint to Mr. Barber and his associate promoters of this enterprise.

Mr. Barber was married in March, 1892, to Miss Florence F. Parrish, daughter of W. W. Parrish and Roseline Juhan Parrish, of Berrien County, Ga. To this union six children were born, as follows:

LeRoy Barber, Moultrie, Ga.
Myrtle Barber, Moultrie, Ga.

Elizabeth Barber (Mrs. R. O. Watson), Tallahassee, Fla.
Lucy Barber (Mrs. Wilbur Boozer), Tallahassee, Fla.
Florence Barber (Mrs. Foreman Dismuke), Columbus, Ga.

Mr. Barber died suddenly at his home in Moultrie, Ga., on November 12, 1923. Mr. Barber was a life-long member of the Missionary Baptist denomination. He was active in the erection of the present imposing building of the First Baptist Church at Moultrie. For years immediately preceding his death, he served as a member of the Board of Deacons of this church, and as the teacher of the Men's Bible Class in the Sunday School.

This historian was for some years the legal adviser of Mr. Barber, and appends a few anecdotes of a personal nature which will serve to illustrate what he thought of his duties as a member of society:

Once a friend of the writer—an elderly man of somewhat limited means—came to the office of the writer, and asked him how he might raise two or three hundred dollars to pay for a course in pedagogy for his young daughter, who wanted to qualify herself for teaching. "Go to Mr. Henry Barber," we said, "he'll let you have it." "But I have a past-due note at his bank already," said our friend. "All the same," we answered, "go over and see right now—he'll let you have it." A matter of two hours afterwards, we met the two men coming down the sidewalk, arm-in-arm, and looking as friendly as one could wish. "Well, Judge," said our friend, "I got it just like you said." "Yes," said Mr. Barber, "when I first came to this country, and was hired as a turpentine woods-rider, 'The Major' (I always called him 'The Major,' since he was a soldier in the Confederate War) let me run a little open account at his store. Yes, and I always try to take care of 'The Major,' and besides all that his daughter is a very deserving child, and she'll pay me the loan."

At another time, a few of us friends of Mr. Barber—being a little younger than he was—were ragging him a little about being close with his money. He laughed good-naturedly, and said, finally, "Boys, I know that you know I enjoy this kind of conversation as much as you do; but I feel that I ought not to let the occasion pass without telling you for your own good that this very quality of being 'saving' has enabled me during the past week to extend from my personal funds assistance to more than 50 distressed farmers who could get no help from the banks." (This happened during the so-called Hoke Smith panic, in 1908, when the banks suspended payments.)

This writer had an option on a piece of farm property and asked Mr. Barber to find a purchaser, offering him half of his commission. He sold the property, but when it came to making papers, he said the purchaser was Mr. D. N. Horne, and that his past relations with him were such that he could not afford to take his part of the commission, and so asked that it be turned over to Mr. Horne.

In a recent conversation with us, Hon. W. C. Vereen paid very high tribute to the courage of Mr. Barber, as displayed in more than one financial venture in which they both were interested. Mr. Vereen especially remembers Mr. Barber's stubborn courage when things did not look so good as to the future of the Moultrie Packing Co., of which they were both founders and directors. At one time, he says there seemed to be some transfer of holdings of some of the stockholders but not a movement that indicated demoralization on the part of W. H. Barber was ever made by him.

## Frank Jarvis Bivins

THIS CITIZEN OF COLQUITT COUNTY for many years was born near Pineville, Ga., in the County of Marion. He was educated in the common schools of Marion County and was graduated from the Alabama Polytechnic Institute, at Auburn, Ala. Occupation, real estate broker. Profession, civil engineer. At one time cashier of a bank. Independent Democrat. Episcopalian. Kappa Alpha college fraternity. Author of *"Dead Horse In the Spring Branch."*

He was a captain in the Officers' Training Camp at college. He was mayor of Cordele, Ga., about 1896. His father was Martin Luther Bivins, a native of Wilkes County, Ga., who was married on June 1, 1860, and who died in 1879. Martin L. Bivins was a Justice of the Inferior Court in Marion County, fought in the Battle of Atlanta in 1864, and freed his slaves on his own motion as an act of justice. Mother of F. J. Bivins was Marthena Caroline Cox, who was born in 1879, and who was a sister of the founder of Cox College.

Martin Luther Bivins, Sr., was a son of William Bivins, and Miss ...... Hall. William Bivins was a soldier of the Revolution. When LaFayette came to the United States in his old age, about 1825, William Bivins journeyed to Washington, Ga., for the purpose of shaking the hand of his distinguished comrade, which he did.

Frank J. Bivins married Bonnell Strozier in Meriwether County, Ga. She was born in 1879, and still survives. She was graduated from LaGrange Female College. She is a daughter of John Lucillius Strozier, a captain in the Confederate Army, a native of Meriwether County, and a resident there until his death in 1912.

Mother of Bonnell Strozier Bivins was Sarah Carolina Robertson, born in 1845, in Meriwether County, Ga. She was a first-honor graduate of Wesleyan Female College, and now resides at Glennville, Ga., in the full possession of all her mental and physical powers.

Names of the children of F. J. Bivins and Bonnell Strozier Bivins:

Bonnell Bivins, born in 1899.
Martin Luther Bivins, born in 1902.
Jas. McAlpin Bivins, born in 1908.

Frank J. Bivins and his family moved to Moultrie in 1900 and resided there until the date of his death, 1932. He was engaged in the real estate business, and life and fire insurance, and finally in loans. With G. A. Horkan, he organized the "Angelus Mutual Insurance Company" about the year 1910.

## Wesley Futrell Blasingame

THE SUBJECT OF THIS SKETCH was born on April 7, 1869, in Crawford County, Ga. His education was obtained in the common schools and in the dental department of the Southern Medical College in Atlanta. The date of his diploma was 1890. He immediately entered into the practice of dental surgery, and has been in such practice until now.

He is a Methodist, a Democrat, a K. of P., and an Odd Fellow.

The name of the father of W. F. Blasingame was John Wesley Blasingame, born in 1840, in Monroe, Ga. He married in Crawford County, Ga., and died, 1905, at Moultrie. He was first a farmer, then a school teacher, and then a merchant. His wife was Eliz. Vashti Futrell, born in Monroe, and died in 1896 in Yatesville, Upson County, Ga. Her education was derived in the common schools and she devoted much time to uplift and betterment of the "forgotten people" in the community where she lived.

The name of the paternal grandfather of W. F. Blasingame was Powell Blasingame. He was born in Monroe, Ga., he being the son of a French Huguenot immigrant.

The name of the maternal grandfather of W. F. Blasingame was Cicero Futrell, born in Crawford County in 1823; married, 1869; died, 1906, in Crawford County. He was a farmer, and the name of his wife, the mother of W. F. Blasingame, was Rebecca Smith, native of Crawford County, Ga.

W. F. Blasingame was married in October, 1891, in Crawford County. The maiden name of his wife was Lena Rivers Jack, born February 22, 1870, in Upson County, Ga., and died July 8, 1936, in Moultrie. The name of her father was J. W. Jack, born in Upson County, where he was married about 1867. He is now dead. He was a farmer for a great part of his life, but for twenty-five years before his death he was Clerk of Superior Court of Crawford County. The maiden name of the mother-in-law of W. F. Blasingame was Lydia Grace, of Crawford County, who died in 1905.

The children of W. F. Blasingame and his wife, Lena Rivers Jack Blasingame, are as follows:

W. A. Blasingame, born June 27, 1891.
Willie Mae Blasingame, born March 4, 1893.
Chas. Guy Blasingame, born May 10, 1895.

W. A. Blasingame married Miss Mary Sims, daughter of Dr. Sims, of Barnesville, Ga., a dentist. They have the following children: Marilyn, 9; Elizabeth Ann, 6.

Willie Mae Blasingame married W. C. Mather, of Hollywood, Fla., an attorney. This couple have two children: Mae, 14; Jean, 12.

Chas. Guy Blasingame married Miss Ruby Parks, of Meansville, Ga., and this couple has one child: Guy, Jr., 3.

W. A. Blasingame is a well-established business man, a resident of Moultrie, having a flourishing drug business and extensive farming interests.

Guy Blasingame also owns and operates a flourishing drug business here.

## James William Coleman

J. W. COLEMAN, the subject of this sketch, was born on June 15, 1871, at Swainsboro, in Emanuel County, in the State of Georgia. He was educated in the common schools of that county. During his life, he has been extensively engaged in farming, practical mechanics and in construction work, doing well in all.

He is a Primitive Baptist by profession of religious faith, and is a Democrat in politics.

Mr. Coleman invented an animal self-feeder, and received a patent in January, 1924.

He was a District Road Overseer in 1896-1898. He was a District Road Commissioner in 1898-1900. He was a member of the Board of Education of Colquitt County, 1900 to 1906. He was Chairman of the Board of Commissioners of Roads and Revenues from 1906 to 1912. He was a member of the City Council of Moultrie in 1910-1912.

The father of J. W. Coleman was James Elsie Coleman, born on November 18, 1846, in Emanuel County, Ga.; married in May, 1870, in Emanuel County, Ga., and died on April 12, 1928, in Emanuel County, Ga. He was a farmer by profession, and did service in the Confederate army in

## JAMES WILLIAM COLEMAN

1864 and 1865. He invented the "Coleman Long-Staple Gin" in February, 1895.

The maiden name of mother of J. W. Coleman was Lavina Lanier, and she was born on April 11, 1852, in Emanuel County, Ga., and died on April 27, 1932, in Emanuel County, Ga. She was the mother of eight sons and four daughters, of whom seven sons and three daughters are living.

Name of paternal grandfather of J. W. Coleman was William Coleman, born August 10, 1819, in Emanuel County, Ga.; married in 1840, and died on November 7, 1898. He was a successful farmer and mechanic, and a Confederate soldier during the whole of the Civil War. The maiden name of the paternal grandmother of J. W. Coleman was Sarah Sutton, born in Emanuel County, Ga., in 1821, and died in the same county in 1877.

The maternal grandfather of J. W. Coleman was Wm. Lanier, born September 26, 1825; married in 1849, and died on September 24, 1910; all of which events happened in Emanuel County. He was a Confederate soldier from 1863 to 1865. Maiden name of the maternal grandmother of J. W. Coleman was Sallie Clifton, born November 22, 1822, in Bulloch County, Ga., and died on August 9, 1885, in Emanuel County, Ga.

J. W. Coleman was married on January 21, 1894, in Bulloch County, Ga., to Miss Sallie Elizabeth Temples, who was born on February 2, 1871, in Wilkinson County, Ga., and is still living in Colquitt County, Ga. She was a daughter of Hudson Temples, who was born March 15, 1843, in Wilkinson County, Ga., and married on September 13, 1864, in Wilkinson County, Ga. He was a minister of the Gospel for more than 50 years. Maiden name of mother-in-law of J. W. Coleman was Mariah Carr, born in 1844 in Wilkinson

County, Ga., and died January 25, 1876, in Wilkinson County, Ga.

There is now in life one child, the issue of the marriage of J. W. Coleman and Sallie Elizabeth Temples, a daughter named Vista, who was born on April 1, 1899, in Colquitt County, and who is now the wife of Ray S. Hall, prominent citizen of Baker County, Ga. This couple has two children, William Calvin Hall and Bettie Temples Hall.

J. W. Coleman, the subject of this sketch, moved with his wife to Colquitt County in January, 1894; purchased a farm three miles north of Moultrie, and lived on it till 1905. First engaged in farming, and then in lumber manufacturing business, moving to Moultrie in 1905. In 1908 built and operated the first modern cotton ginnery in Colquitt County. He built and operated the first fertilizer mixing plant in the county. Built and operated the first modern cotton and storage warehouse in the county. And generally assisted in the county's development.

## William Alonzo Covington

W. A. COVINGTON was born January 19, 1869, in the backwoods of northwest Cherokee County, Ga., being oldest child of Sidney Stanhope Covington and Honor Adeline Burns, and a grandson of A. J. Covington and Olivia Ellis Covington, and of Henry Burns and Anne Rhine Burns. Both parents of W. A. Covington are natives of Georgia. His paternal grandparents were natives of Rutherford County, N. C., and his maternal grandparents were natives of Spartanburgh district, S. C.

W. A. Covington is a graduate of Reinhardt College (1887), and of Emory College (1896). He is a Methodist, a Mason, a K. of P., a W. O. W., and an Odd Fellow. He

# WILLIAM ALONZO COVINGTON

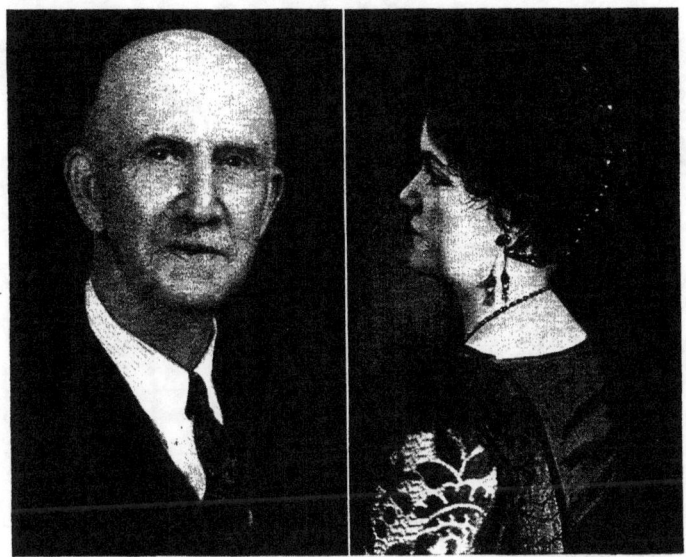

W. A. and Burney S. Covington

has been mayor of Moultrie several terms, and a representative of Colquitt County in the General Assembly of Georgia in 1905, 1906, 1907 and 1908. Also in 1919-20 and in 1923-24. He was the author (with L. G. Hardman), of Georgia's Prohibition Statute of 1907. He is responsible for the action of Georgia's Legislature in the destruction of the Convict Lease System, in 1908.

He came to Colquitt with J. H. Smithwick in 1898, and with him organized a partnership for the practice of law. He was appointed Judge of the City Court of Moultrie by Governor Candler, and served till his election to the Legislature.

W. A. Covington married Miss Burney Sheffield on May 12, 1897, at Arlington, Ga. She is a daughter of Hon. Henry Sheffield, Judge of the Superior Courts of the Pataula Circuit of Georgia, and of his wife, Ida Holder Sheffield. Her progenitors are all prominent among the pioneers of original Early County, Ga. She is an alumna of Wesleyan Female College (1896).

Children of W. A. Covington and Burney S. Covington are:

Sidney S. Covington, died June, 1934.
Dorothy Covington (Mrs. J. L. Pilcher), Meigs, Ga.
Wm. N. Covington, Brooklyn, N. Y.
Philip Stanhope Covington, Moultrie Attorney.
Drew Roberts Covington, died in infancy.
Catherine Covington, died in infancy.

## Waldo DeLoache

THE SUBJECT OF THIS SKETCH was born on March 3, 1898, at Glennville, Tattnall County, Ga. His education was received in the common schools of Tattnall County, and was finished at Mercer University, from which he was graduated in 1919, with the degrees of A.B. and LL.B. He was admitted to the practice of law at the date of his graduation in Macon, Ga. He is a Baptist and a Democrat.

He was a private in the World War, serving in the United States forces at Fort Screven, Ga. He removed to Moultrie, in Colquitt County, immediately after graduation, where in a very short while he built up a very lucrative practice.

In 1931 he was appointed Judge of the City Court of Colquitt County by Governor Richard B. Russell, Jr. He was elected to succeed himself in this office in September, 1934. He resigned in January, 1935, in order to accept appointment as State Director for the Georgia Federal Housing Administration. This office he resigned in December, 1936, and re-entered the practice of law at Moultrie, Ga., and entered the management of his extensive business interests in this section.

Mr. DeLoache was the son of Alexander Joseph DeLoache, who was born September 30, 1854, in Tattnall County, Ga.; married on December 28, 1876, in Tattnall County, Ga., in which county he passed out of this life on August 17, 1930.

The maiden name of the mother of Waldo DeLoache was Sarah Elizabeth Burkhalter, who was born on September 17, 1861, in Tattnall County, Ga., and who still survives.

The name of the paternal grandfather of Waldo DeLoache was Jesse DeLoache, who was born on March 12, 1816, in Tattnall County, Ga.; married in the same county in 1836, and passed out of life in Tattnall County in 1874. He was a soldier in the armies of the Southern Confederacy.

The maiden name of the paternal grandmother of Waldo DeLoache was Elizabeth Smith, of Tattnall County, Ga., who died in that county on March 31, 1890.

The maternal grandfather of Waldo DeLoache was John Michel Burkhalter, who was born February 27, 1825, in Tattnall County, Ga.; married in June, 1848, in the same county, and died on January 8, 1863, at South Newport, while on active duty in the armies of the Confederacy.

The maiden name of the maternal grandmother of Waldo DeLoache was Mary Elizabeth Smith, who was born on January 30, 1831, in Tattnall County, Ga.; died on September 11, 1908, in that county.

Mr. Waldo DeLoache was married on July 28, 1921, in Clay County, Ga., to Miss Clyde Killingsworth, a native of Clay County, Ga., having been born April 5, 1899. She was the daughter of Emmett Walton Killingsworth, who was born March 12, 1866, in Clay County, Ga., and who was married in Clay County, Ga., where he still survives.

The maiden name of the mother-in-law of Waldo DeLoache and the wife of E. W. Killingsworth was Susan Sanders, a native of Clay County, Ga. She survives with her husband.

The children, being the issue of the marriage of Waldo DeLoache and Clyde Killingsworth DeLoache, are:

Waldo DeLoache, Jr., born August 5, 1924, departed this life on April 14, 1933.

Michel DeLoache, born October 3, 1934, who, with his parents, lives at Moultrie, Ga.

Mr. DeLoache is genial and philosophic in his temperament, is an excellent lawyer, and a highly successful business man. He has a healthy interest in the social and political problems; reads extensively, and is a very eloquent public speaker. His friends are very proud, and have every right to be, of his accomplishments in the ordinary activities of a young man of this age, and are well convinced that the most of the achievements of his life are in the future.

Mrs. Waldo DeLoache is deservedly popular among all classes, in Moultrie in her own right, and by virtue of many charms of manner and heart. The entire community has therefore been much pleased at the recent return of the DeLoaches to permanent residence here.

## Montgomery M. Folsom

THE SUBJECT OF THIS SKETCH was born near Hahira, in Lowndes County, Georgia, on January 31, 1857. His grandfather, Randall Folsom, a scholarly man over in Lowndes had a namesake and cousin of the same name, who for many years lived over on the eastern side of Colquitt, and who died there a few years ago, at the great age of ninety-three. All the Colquitt Folsoms are kin to Colquitt's Randall Folsom, and consequently to Montgomery Folsom.

Montgomery also taught school down in the southeast corner of Colquitt for one term, at least. One of his pupils was Frances Edna Croft, daughter of Nathaniel Croft and Mary Anne Hiers Croft, both of whom were born in South Carolina. Montgomery married Frances Edna on November 13, 1879.

All this by way of showing that although strictly speaking, Montgomery Folsom is not one of Colquitt's sons, he might, with perfect justice and propriety, be claimed by Colquitt, as her distinguished son-in-law. This historian saw him only once—in 1891, when he was doing work on one of the Atlanta papers; but we were already familiar with his fine poetry and prose writings. When we moved to Colquitt, we were much pleased to meet the Colquitt County Folsoms, as well as his wife's relatives, the Crofts.

Afterward, we met his wife and some of his fine children in Atlanta, when we were in the legislature from Colquitt County. We once asked Mr. D. MacDonald about him, he, being a cousin of Folsom, and a schoolmate at one time. He stated, among other things, that one day he found Montgomery then a mere child, weeping over a flower, which he had accidentally crushed.

We subjoin here in conclusion of this chapter two of Montgomery Folsom's best poems. If the reader cares to read more about him, we refer him to the Appendix to this book.

### Jeff Hancock's Bull
(By Montgomery M. Folsom)
(Copyrighted in *Scraps of Song* and *Southern Scenes*)

Jeff Hancock's my neighbor. One mornin' last spring
When skeeters were jist a beginnin' to sing,
I went over thar to git one of his plows,
And found him a pennin' a fine bunch of cows.

"What news?" says I, "neighbor, you've jist come from town?"
"No news, 'cept I've arrangements with Brown,
To git my supplies of guanner an' bacon;
He said 'twer the fortieth mortgage he'd taken."

"You've got some fine stock." "Yes, jist look at that calf;
He's the fines' bull yearlin' round 'ere by half;
His horns sets jist right, and do look what a neck!
His daddy's half Jersey, and his mammy's Ole Speck.

"His hair is jist es soft an' es fine as split silk;
I'll let 'im run out an' have all of her milk,
An' then, he'll improve all my cattle, ye know."
"Well, yes," says I, "Jeff, that is shore to be so."

The yarlin', he growed and got powerful fat,
An' 'is hide were es slick es the Parson's new hat;
His horns set es purty as purty could be,
An' the beatenes' neck that ye ever did see.

One day, 'twere along 'bout the middle of June,
An' I were a smokin' an' takin' my noon—
I looked an' seed Jeff come apokin' along,
An' I knowed right imejitly sumthin' were wrong.

"Come in—have a chair—been to dinner?" says I.
"I've been through the motion," says he, mighty sly;
"But as shore's ye're borned, it's a mighty poor eat,
When a feller's got dinged little bread an' no meat.

"That yearlin' is not near so fine es he wus;
His hair it aire sorter beginnin' to fuzz;
His neck aire so spinlin' he never can fight;
His legs aire too long, an' his horns don't set right;

"He are gittin' to be—though I 'spose he aire sound—
The ugliest yearlin' on top o' the ground;
My craps but half made, an' my store account's full,
An' it's do on short rashuns, or butcher that bull."

"Hol' on," says I; "Jeff, ye're in too big a haste;
To kill that bull yearlin' aire absolute waste."
"I know it; but I can't work 'thout eatin', ye know."
"Well, yes," says I; "Jeff, that aire shore to be so."

So this were the end of Jeff's big specerlation,
Improvin' 'is stock with 'is big calkerlation.
They eat up 'is meat, used his tail for a cracker,
An' bartered 'is hide fur some salt an' terbacker.

Now this aire the moral, or else I'm mistaken:
Ye can't have fine stock till ye raise ye're own bacon;
Men's notions aire big when their stummicks are full;
It were skacety of bacon kilt Jeff Hancock's bull.

## Whip Poor Will

### By Montgomery M. Folsom

(Copyrighted in *Scraps of Song* and *Southern Scenes*)

When purpling shadows westward creep,
And stars through crimson curtains peep,
And south winds sing themselves to sleep;
From woodlands heavy with perfume
Of spicy bud and April bloom,
Comes through the tender twilight gloom,
    Music most mellow,
      "Whip po' Will—Will, oh!
        Whip po' Will—Will, oh!
Whip po' Will, Whip po' Will, Whip po' Will—Will, oh!"

The bosom of the brook is filled
With new alarm, the forest thrilled
With startled echoes, and most skilled
To run a labyrinthine race,
The fireflies light their lamps to chase
The culprit through the darkening space—
    Mischievous fellow,
      "Whip po' Will—Will, oh!
        Whip po' Will—Will, oh!
Whip po' Will, Whip po' Will, Whip po' Will—Will, oh!"

From hill to hill the echoes fly,
The marshy brakes take up the cry,
And where the slumbering waters lie
In calm repose, and slyly feeds
The snipe among the whispering reeds,
The tale of this wild sprite's misdeeds
   Troubles the billow:
   "Whip po' Will—Will, oh!
   Whip po' Will—Will, oh!
Whip po' Will, Whip po' Will, Whip po' Will—Will, oh!"

And where is he of whom they speak?
Is he just playing hide and seek
Among the thickets up the creek,
Or is he resting from his play
In some cool grotto, far away,
Where lullaby-crooning zephyrs stray,
   Smoothing his pillow?
   "Whip po' Will—Will, oh!
   Whip po' Will—Will, oh!
Whip po' Will, Whip po' Will, Whip po' Will—Will, oh!"

## Richard Lewis Free

R. L. FREE was born September 17, 1874, near Damascus, Early County, Georgia. Graduated from Mercer University in 1901, B.S. Degree. Taught school 1901-5. Naval stores operator, 1905-10. In banking business Doerun, Georgia, as officer and stockholder, 1909-27. Also farming during this time.

Baptist, Democrat, Mason, Woodman, Elk. Councilman, City of Doerun, Georgia, 1909-15. Member of Board of Education, Doerun, 1915-30.

R. L. Free was child of Lewis Manly Free, who was born September 25, 1839, in Edgefield County, South Carolina, married February 4, 1868, in Miller County, Georgia, and

## RICHARD LEWIS FREE

died on November 4, 1911, at Damascus, Georgia. He served four years in the Civil War, being a member of Stonewall Jackson's corps in the army of Northern Virginia, surrendered under Lee at Appomattox. Baptist and successful farmer.

Mother of R. L. Free was Julia Alice Hardy, born on May 14, 1850, in Edgefield County, South Carolina, and died on August 12, 1924, at Arlington, Georgia. Active member of the Baptist Church. Educated in advance of her time, she did real pioneer work in the church, organizing and carrying forward Sunday School work. Having studied medicine, she gave freely of her time to the relief of suffering in the community in which she spent her life. Richard Hardy Free was the paternal grandfather of R. L. Free, and was born on February 11, 1815, in Edgefield County, South Carolina, and died in Decatur County, Georgia. He served with distinction as captain during the Civil War, was a Baptist and a large planter in Decatur County.

Maiden name of maternal grandmother of R. L. Free was Julia Ann Lanier, born December 20, 1818, in Edgefield County, South Carolina, and died in December, 1912, in Miller County, Georgia.

R. L. Free married Stella Pickren, on October 19, 1910, in Savannah, Georgia. She was born on October 14, 1885, in Coffee County, Georgia. Graduated from Andrew Female College, Cuthbert, Georgia, in class of 1906, with A.B. degree. Taught school a number of years. Methodist, Democrat.

Father-in-law of R. L. Free was Thomas Levett Pickren, born June 16, 1862, in Coffee County, Georgia, married October 9, 1884, in Coffee County, Georgia, and died on June 27, 1936, at Folkston, Georgia. School teacher and a merchant at first, later for forty years prominent naval stores operator of Southeast Georgia. Representative of Charlton

County, Georgia, several terms in the General Assembly of Georgia. State Senator, 1925-6. Judge of the County Court of Charlton County for a number of years. Mayor of Folkston. Member City and County Board of Education. Methodist, Mason, Shriner, K. of P., Odd-fellow.

Maiden name of mother-in-law of R. L. Free was Kathleen Georgia Wilcox, born September 22, 1863, Coffee County, Georgia, died on May 24, 1896, at McRae, Georgia. Daughter of Rev. J. M. Wilcox, Methodist minister, who was a member of the Georgia legislature, both as Representative and Senator from Coffee County. Democrat, scholar, Civil War veteran, planter of means. Died at a ripe old age in 1897.

Children of R. L. Free and Stella Pickren Free are: Louise Free, born July 22, 1911; Alice Free, born August 15, 1914; R. L. Free, born August 4, 1915; Mary Ellen Free, born January 22, 1925; Gene Lovett Free, born May 3, 1926; Virginia Free, born May 1, 1913, died August 3, 1913.

## Jacob Hunter Hires

THIS CITIZEN of Colquitt was born in 1853, at Isom, Brooks County, Ga. He was educated in the common schools of Brooks County and was a student of current affairs all his life. He was admitted to the Bar about 1889, having read law in the office of Henry G. Turner, the celebrated statesman, in Quitman. He practiced law in Brooks and surrounding counties, finally moving to Moultrie, where he formed a partnership for the practice of law with John C. Chason, at Moultrie. He was a Baptist, a Democrat, and a Mason. He participated in the Spanish-American War, being a corporal in the U. S. Army in Cuba.

He represented Colquitt County in the House of Representatives of the General Assembly of Georgia in 1911-12.

## JACOB HUNTER HIRES

Jacob Hunter Hires was the son of Philip Hires, a native of North Carolina, born there in 1812, and was married in Brooks County, Ga., in 1835 to Pollie Alderman, a native of Brooks County, Ga. Both Philip Hires and his wife, Pollie Alderman Hires, have departed this life and are buried in Brooks County.

J. H. Hires married in 1874 in Brooks County, Ga. The maiden name of his wife was Sarah Strickland, who was born in 1852, and died in December, 1919, in Colquitt County, Ga. She was educated in the common schools of Brooks County, and was a member of the Baptist Church. She was the daughter of John Strickland, who was born in 1846, in Brooks County, Ga., and who was married in Brooks County, Ga., and who died in 1887 in the same county. John Strickland was a farmer, and a member of the Primitive Baptist Church. The maiden name of the wife of John Strickland, who was the mother-in-law of J. H. Hires, was Jencie Alderman, also a native of Brooks County.

The names of the children of J. H. Hires and Sarah Strickland Hires, his wife, are as follows:

James Hires, born 1874, married and a resident of Tampa, Fla.
Lula Hires, born in 1876, died in October, 1926.
Plenny Hires, born in 1877, now living in Colquitt County, Ga.
Gussie Hires, born in 1879 (Mrs. E. H. Hall), Miami, Fla.
Irvin Hires, born 1881, died in 1908.
Sarah Hires, born in 1883, a school teacher.
Willie Hires, born in 1885 (Mrs C. F. Chitty), Colquitt County.
Eunice Hires, born in 1887 (single, with Moultrie Tel. Co. for 15 years).

Harry Livingston Hires, born 1891, Tax collector, Colquitt County, Ga., 1937.

Thomas Watson Hires, born 1894, Supt. H. H. Myers Packing Co., Cincinnati, Ohio.

Ruby Elizabeth Hires, born 1896 (Mrs. E. N. Gail), Ft. Pierce, Fla.

## George B. Hunt

THIS CITIZEN OF COLQUITT COUNTY was born at Pineboro, Colquitt County, Ga., August 26, 1881. Educated in the common schools of Colquitt County. Profession is fireman. Entered service of Moultrie Fire Department on July 1, 1914. On November 14, 1915, became Chief, and has held this position continuously since. Methodist. Democrat. Mason.

G. B. Hunt was a son of Wm. Jefferson Hunt, who was born April 3, 1861, and died October 14, 1912. He was born in Columbia County, Ala., and spent most of his life in Colquitt County, where he died. He was ordained Methodist minister, and was postmaster at Silar, Ga., from 1897 to 1902. Mother of G. B. Hunt was Dicy Ruth Baker, born January 8, 1859, in Colquitt County, Ga., and died in the same county on October 4, 1935.

Paternal grandfather, Cardy Hunt, was born in 1811, in Ireland, and died in 1904 in Colquitt County, Ga. Emigrated to the United States about 1816, and became by profession a farmer and a slave-owner. He married Amie Stokes, who was born in Ireland about 1816, and died in November, 1899. Cardy Hunt was killed in battle, in 1864, somewhere in Virginia, having volunteered as a private from Colquitt. He married in Charleston, S. C., about 1834.

Maternal grandfather of C. B. Hunt was Burrell Baker, born about 1830 in Colquitt County, Ga., and died on one of the battlefields of the Confederate War in 1864, having gone out with the first Colquitt Volunteers.

Maternal grandmother of G. B. Hunt was Ruth Norman, a daughter of Jas. Mitchell Norman and Ruth Tillman Norman, being born about 1830 in Colquitt County. She died

# HISTORY OF COLQUITT COUNTY 255

in 1859 in Colquitt County. She married, in 1857, Burrell Baker.

G. B. Hunt was married on November 3, 1907, in Moultrie, Ga., to Miss Tommie Jane Hall, who was born March 26, 1882, in Colquitt County. She was a daughter of Lawrence A. Hall, who was born in Thomas County, Ga., and died in Colquitt County. Private in the Confederate Army, being wounded once. He taught school in Colquitt and surrounding counties for many years. He was carrying the mail on a star route when he died. His wife was Narsises Turner, a daughter of Amos Turner, who was once a Clerk of the Superior Court of Colquitt County, and who was the first State Senator of Colquitt in the General Assembly of Georgia.

G. B. Hunt and his wife, Tommie Jane Hunt, have one child in life, namely: Arthur B. Hunt, born November 8, 1908.

Before his connection with Moultrie's fire department, G. B. Hunt worked with Huber-Norman Lumber Co., at Moultrie, in 1907-8. Carried U. S. mail on star route in 1900-01. Worked as a carpenter in Colquitt County from November, 1909 to 1914.

## Cliff Jenkins

THIS CITIZEN of Colquitt is a native of Bartow County, Ga., having been born there in the year 1896. His parents were Davis Jenkins, also a native of Bartow County, and ...... Jenkins, who was also a native of Bartow County, and both of whom now reside in Colquitt County, Ga.

Cliff Jenkins is a Democrat and a Mason, and for some while has been a member of the Board of County Commissioners of Colquitt County. He was elected chairman of this board at their January, 1937, meeting for a term of twelve months. Mr. Jenkins is a farmer and a saw-mill owner and operator.

## Chas. H. Johnson

MENTION HAS BEEN MADE hereinbefore of Chas. H. Johnson, shown by the 1860 census to have been the wealthiest citizen of Colquitt County at that date. Since this was written, we have come into some additional information as to Mr. Johnson, through the courtesy of Mr. Lewis Perry, who married a granddaughter of Mr. Johnson, and who now resides on the old Johnson plantation:

(a) It is definitely known that Chas. H. Johnson died in 1886, and was buried in the Johnson family burial plot on the plantation. As we know from the 1860 census that Mr. Johnson was born in 1790, it results that he reached the great age of 96. So far as we know, this entitles him to a record age for a man, in Colquitt; a record that seems to have been equaled by only one woman, Sally Hawkins, found in 1860 by Census Marshal Wing. As Mr. Johnson was a contemporary of the author of "Two Years Before the Mast," he must have been a most interesting character. We are able to present elsewhere a cut of this old sea rover and land pioneer, made from a photograph taken about the year Colquitt was organized.

## W. W. King

THIS CITIZEN of Colquitt was born March 29, 1893, on a farm four miles southwest of Doerun, Ga., near Sinai Missionary Baptist Church, being a son of H. C. King, who was born in Putnam County, Ga.

His maternal grandmother was born in Colquitt County. His maternal grandfather was born in Coweta County, Ga.

George Tucker, great grandfather on mother's side, was a son of Elder H. Crawford Tucker, pioneer in Colquitt County. Another great-grandfather, pioneer in Colquitt County, was John Nelson Phillips, born in South Carolina.

W. W. King was married on December 31, 1916, to Lollie Dell Morton, of Colquitt County, Ga. Mary Tucker, daughter of George Tucker, was his maternal grandmother. The maiden name of the mother of W. W. King was Martha Jane Phillips.

The children of W. W. King and Lollie Dell Morton King are: Elsie Mae King, 1924; Nannie Ruth King, 1926; and W. C. King, 1930.

W. W. King is by profession a farmer. He is a member of Mount Sinai Baptist Church. He is a member of the present Board of County Commissioners of Colquitt County, in which position he succeeded his father, who held this office himself for many years.

## John Elzie Ladson

Mr. J. E. Ladson was born January 12, 1885, in Montgomery County, Ga. His education was obtained in the common schools of Georgia and in the Georgia-Alabama Business College, from which he was graduated in 1904.

He is a member of the First Missionary Baptist Church, at Moultrie, as are the other members of his family. In politics, Mr. Ladson is a Democrat; and he is a Knight of Pythias. He has served on the Aldermanic Board of the City of Moultrie, and is a past-president of the Moultrie Chamber of Commerce.

John Elzie Ladson is a son of Isaac Ladson, who was born on December 16, 1852, in Montgomery County, Ga., who married Pinkie Connell on July 2, 1874, and he now resides with his son, the subject of this sketch, at Moultrie, Ga. Pinkie Connell Ladson died on June 22, 1916, and is buried in Hamilton Cemetery, in Montgomery County, Ga.

Isaac Ladson is the son of John Conaway Ladson, who was born on December 25, 1813, in Barnwell County, S. C., and who died in 1894 in Montgomery County, Ga. He was a farmer by profession, and was a Confederate soldier. The founder of the Ladson family was John Ladson, a native of Northamptonshire, England, who settled St. John's Island, Charleston, S. C. "Ladson Street," in Charleston, derives its name from these people; and they erected the Ladson residence, on Meeting Street, in that city.

The wife of John Conaway Ladson, being the grandmother of John Elzie Ladson, was Mary Ann Calhoun, who was born in 1816, in Barnwell County, S. C. She died on August 2, 1872, in Montgomery County, Ga. She was a daughter of James I. Calhoun, of Barnwell, S. C.

John Elzie Ladson married Miss Annie Laurie Rhodes on March 8, 1910, in Moultrie, Ga. She was born February 22, 1888, in Berrien County, Ga. She was educated in the Tifton Public Schools; and was a daughter of Aaron Rhodes, who was born in 1845, in Richmond County, Ga., and died in August, 1905, in Tifton, Ga. He was a Confederate veteran, and by profession a farmer. He is buried at Bethesda Cemetery, at Brookfield, Tift County, Ga.

The mother-in-law of J. E. Ladson was Anna Elizabeth Coursey, born March 27, 1851, in Richmond County, Ga. She died November 13, 1931, in Colquitt County, Ga. She was a daughter of John B. Coursey and Mary Johnson Coursey. The Rhodes family was one of the first settlers of

Richmond County, Ga., and from the first were active in its development.

Mrs. John E. Ladson is a member of the John Benning Chapter of the Daughters of the American Revolution, and of the Moultrie Chapter of the Worth While Club. She is a member of the First Baptist Church, and is active in its church and social work.

John Elzie Ladson came to Moultrie in the year 1910, and engaged in the wholesale lumber business, which he carried to instant success. He still "knows his lumber" and carries on at Moultrie. As if this success were not enough, he commenced some twenty years or more ago buying an occasional Colquitt farm; and has kept it up till, at present, he operates 140 plows, this placing him easily in the first place among the farmers of this wonderful county. And, what is greatly to his credit, he deals justly with his tenants, whether white or colored.

As a climax to the life work of this successful couple, it is stated that there are in life, at present, children, the issue of the marriage of John Elzie Ladson and Annie Laurie Rhodes Ladson, four children, as follows:

John Elzie Ladson, Jr., born September, 1912.
Wm. Francis Ladson, born October 9, 1916.
Caroline Ladson, born February 19, 1920.
Mary Ladson, born October 11, 1923.

All these are popular social favorites with the people among whom they move, and for the reason that they are all fine children. John Elzie Ladson, Jr., was graduated from the Moultrie Public Schools and from Furman University, and both Wm. Francis Ladson and Caroline Ladson are alumnae of the Moultrie Public Schools.

## Matthew Lawrence Lee

M. L. LEE was born August 31, 1885, in Crawford County, Georgia. He was graduated from R. E. Lee Institute, Thomaston, Georgia, in 1902. Collection Clerk and Bookkeeper with Upson Banking and Trust Company, Thomaston, Georgia, 1902-5. Bookkeeper with Moultrie Banking Company, 1905-6. Assistant Cashier Moultrie Banking Company, 1906-16. Cashier Moultrie Banking Company, 1916-36.

Methodist, Democrat, W. O. W. He was the son of Benjamin Franklin Lee and Mary Cassandra Sandwich Lee. B. F. Lee was born January 17, 1845; married April 6, 1869; and died October 28, 1929. He lived on a farm at Zenith, Crawford County, Georgia, until 1889, when he moved to Thomaston, Georgia, where he taught school and did various clerical work. Mary C. S. Lee was born October 11, 1846, in Upson County, Georgia, and died on January 8, 1933, in Thomaston, Georgia. She was the daughter of Matthew Hale Sandwich.

M. L. Lee married on May 15, 1907, Mary Alma Hicks, who was born July 20, 1885, in Johnson County, Georgia, being daughter of Dr. William J. Hicks and Samantha Kent Hicks. Dr. W. J. Hicks practiced medicine in Macon County, Georgia, till 1902, and from 1902 to the date of his death in Moultrie, Georgia. Samantha Kent Hicks was born in Johnson County, and died in Moultrie, Georgia. One child of M. L. Lee and Mary Alma Lee is named Mary Lenelle Lee, and was born in Moultrie, Georgia, December 10, 1910.

M. L. Lee joined the Methodist Church at Thomaston, Georgia, in 1895. Secretary Methodist Sunday School, Thomaston, 1902-5. Superintendent Methodist Sunday School, Moultrie, 1906-26. Steward Moultrie Methodist Church, 1906-1936.

## Paul DeWitt Leverett

The subject of this sketch was born April 28, 1895, at Weston, Webster County, Ga. He was graduated from the Doerun High School in 1911. He attended Mercer University Law School and graduated in 1916. Since that date he has been continuously in the practice of law, first at Albany and for several years past at Moultrie, Ga.

He is a Presbyterian, a Democrat, a Mason, a W. O. W., and a member of the American Legion.

He has been Solicitor of the City Court of Colquitt County since August 1, 1931.

He is the son of M. Lafayette Leverett, who was a native of Webster County, Ga., and who married in Webster County in 1893, and died December 7, 1932, in Doerun, Ga. He was first a farmer, then a merchant, and for the twenty-five years before his death he was a rural letter carrier out of Doerun.

The maiden name of the mother of Paul D. Leverett was Mary Fannie Holloman, a native of Webster County, Ga., who died November 10, 1912, in Doerun, Ga.

Maiden name of paternal grandmother of Paul D. Leverett was Eliz. Foreman, born 1850 in State of Virginia, and died in 1930, in Webster County.

Name of maternal grandfather of Paul D. Leverett was John Holloman, a native of Webster County, Ga. His wife was Frances Shivers, being the maternal grandmother of Paul D. Leverett. She also was a native of Webster County.

Paul D. Leverett married on December 23, 1925, Cordia Ray McLeod, born December 27, 1897, in Worth County, Ga., and who still lives with her husband at Moultrie, Ga.

She was a graduate of Poulan High School and Tifton A. and M., and Freeman's Business College. For five years prior to marriage, she was Secretary-Treasurer of the Farmer's Land Loan and Title Co., of Albany, Ga. She was the daughter of Daniel J. McLeod, a native of Robeson County, N. C., who died in 1900 in Worth County, Ga. He came to Georgia while a young man, and was a successful turpentine man and farmer.

The maiden name of the mother-in-law of Paul D. Leverett was Frances Ann Conoly, born in Robeson County, N. C., and died on November 5, 1935, in Colquitt County. As widow of Daniel J. McLeod, she reared successfully their three daughters.

There is in life a child, the issue of the marriage of Paul D. Leverett and Cordia Ray McLeod Leverett, whose name is Paul D. Leverett, Jr.

## Richard Jonathan Lewis

THE SUBJECT OF THIS SKETCH was born on October 17, 1887, at McIntyre, in the County of Wilkinson, in the State of Georgia. He received a high school education at Norman Institute, Norman Park, Ga., from 1906 to 1909. He taught school in Colquitt County, Ga., in the years 1909 and 1910, was a farmer practically continuously until 1929. He practiced law in Moultrie, Ga., in 1916-1924. From 1924 to this date (1936), he has held the position of Deputy Clerk of the Superior Court of Colquitt County. For five years past, he has been a minister in the Missionary Baptist Church, and at present serves three churches in Georgia and one in Florida.

R. J. Lewis is a Democrat, Woodman of the World, and a member of the Royal Arcanum. He was a member of the

House of Representatives of the General Assembly of Georgia in 1921-2 and 1924-5.

R. J. Lewis was the son of Richard Joel Lewis and Exa Ann Ethridge Lewis. Richard Joel Lewis was born on August 31, 1842, in Wilkinson County, Ga.; by profession he was a school teacher and a farmer. Member of Company "F," Third Ga. Regiment, Longstreet's Brigade, and served from the beginning of the War Between the States until he was wounded at Gettysburg. Mother of Richard Jonathan Lewis was also born in 1842 (October 1), in Wilkinson County, Ga., and died on August 15, 1910, in Omega, Tift County, Ga.

James R. Lewis and Sarah Ann Rivers Lewis were the paternal grandparents of Richard Jonathan Lewis, both born in Wilkinson County, Ga. Lewis Ethridge was his maternal grandfather, and he was a native of Wilkinson County, Ga. His maternal grandmother was named Lucinda.

Richard Jonathan Lewis married on December 18, 1910, in Colquitt County, Miss Lenora May Newton, who was born on February 10, 1888, in Colquitt County, Ga. She was the daughter of George F. Newton and Julia Elvina Norman. George F. Newton was born on September 21, 1841, in Brooks County, Ga., married in Colquitt County, Ga., and died in Colquitt County, Ga., on February 7, 1922. He was a farmer by profession, and during his life held the offices of both Tax Receiver and Tax Collector of Colquitt County; and was a member of the Georgia House of Representatives for two terms. He was a member of Lee's Army, and left an arm at Gettysburg, being wounded in the same section of that battlefield as Richard Joel Lewis.

Julia Elvina Norman was born on May 31, in Colquitt County, Ga., and died on September 26, 1918. She was the daughter of Jeremiah Bryant Norman, Sr., a pioneer leader of Colquitt County, otherwise referred to in this history, and of his wife, Sarah Ann Elizabeth, also referred to herein.

The following are the children of the marriage of Richard Jonathan and Lenora May Lewis:

Jonathan Wilburn Lewis, born October 21st, 1911.
Gordon Felton Lewis, born September 3rd, 1914.
Julia Inez Lewis.
Mable Claire Lewis.
James Richard Lewis.

As will be seen from other pages of this history, the children of R. J. Lewis are as well born as any in the entire County of Colquitt. This historian thinks there is not in the County of Colquitt a more useful citizen than Mr. Lewis.

## William Frank McCall

THIS CITIZEN of Colquitt County was born on March 18, 1894, at Quincy, Fla. He was graduated from the Gadsden County High School, being a member of the Class of 1911. He was also graduated from Massey's Business College of Jacksonville, Fla., in 1912. He has been an active merchant of Moultrie, since 1921. He is a member of the M. E. Church, South, and has always affiliated with the Democratic Party as a political organization.

He was President of the Moultrie Kiwanis Club in 1925, and is at present an active member of that organization. His father, Wm. S. McCall, was born in Decatur County, Ga., and died on November 4, 1912, in Quincy, Fla. The mother of W. F. McCall was, before her marriage, Mary Emily Smith. She was also born in Gadsden County, Fla., and died in Quincy, county-site of said county, on December 11, 1911.

W. F. McCall married Miss Susie Clark on January 6, 1915, in Albany, Ga. She was born May 12, 1896, in

Dougherty County, Ga., and was a graduate of Albany High School. Susie Clark was the daughter of John S. Clark, a native of Buckingham County, Va., and for twelve years before his death was Clerk of the Superior Court of Dougherty County. Previous to that time he was railway accountant for the Central of Georgia Railway. The mother-in-law of W. F. McCall was Susan Dodson.

There are at present in life, issue of the marriage of W. F. McCall and Susie Clark, his wife, children as follows:

William F. McCall, Jr., born April 14, 1916.
John Clark McCall, born October 31, 1919.
William Sherrod McCall, born December 28, 1922.
Sarah Clark McCall, born August 11, 1925.
Susan Clark McCall, born January 6, 1930.

William Frank McCall, Sr., the subject of this sketch, was a charter member of the Moultrie Kiwanis Club; he is a member of the City School Board of Moultrie; a member of the Board of Directors of the Y. M. C. A. of the city; member of the Board of Directors of the Moultrie Chamber of Commerce; member of the Court of Honour of the Boy Scouts; member of the Board of Stewards of the First M. E. Church, Moultrie; Superintendent Sunday School, M. E. Church.

Mr. McCall is at the head of one of the most flourishing retail grocery businesses in Moultrie.

## Claude Early McLendon

THIS CITIZEN AND RESIDENT of Colquitt County was born on September 28, 1884, in Greenville, Meriwether County, Ga. He was educated in the common schools of Meriwether County, and is by occupation a farmer. He is a Methodist and a Democrat. He has been a Justice of the Peace in and for Colquitt County for several years. He is at present

Chairman of the Democratic Executive Committee of Colquitt County, and is also Chairman of the Board of County Registrars.

He is a son of W. E. McLendon, a native of Meriwether County, who was born in 1851, and who died on June 10, 1892, in Meriwether County. He was a Chief of Police of Greenville, Ga., for some years. W. E. McLendon married Zubie Johnson in 1883. She was born in 1862 in Meriwether County, Ga., and is yet alive in Colquitt County. Maternal grandfather of Claude McLendon was Rufus Johnson and his maternal grandmother was Mary Elizabeth Thrash.

C. E. McLendon was married in 1908, in Colquitt County, Ga., to Miss Lillian Manning, who was born February 26, 1884, in Milton County, Ga. She is still alive and a resident of Funston, in Colquitt County. She is a daughter of W. N. Manning, who was born in 1848, in Cherokee County, Ga., and died on November 29, 1929, in Colquitt County. He was once Clerk of the Superior Court of Milton County, Ga. His only wife was Nancy Jane Rucker, born in 1854 in Milton County, Ga., and she still lives at Funston. The Ruckers have been for several generations leaders in the County of Milton and surrounding territory. W. N. Manning and his said wife were married December 21, 1876.

The children of C. E. McLendon and his said wife now in life are as follows:

Marion, born in 1901.
Elizabeth, born in 1911.
Terrell, born in 1912 (died in infancy).
Hiram Warner, born in 1914.
Dora, born in 1916 (died in infancy).
Caroline, born in 1919.
C. E., Jr., born in 1920.

Marion McLendon married Lillian Singleterry, and they have a girl child named Bettie, 17 months old.

## William Jefferson Matthews

W. J. MATTHEWS was born on February 8, 1856, at Pineville, in Marion County, Georgia. He was educated at the country schools around Pineville, and finished at Collinsworth Institute, at Talbotton, Georgia.

He worked on a farm during a part of 1874. Left the farm and clerked for Harrell Johnson and Company, Merchants and Warehousemen, at Americus, Georgia.

W. J. and ELLA SHAW MATTHEWS

W. J. Matthews is a Methodist, a Democrat, and a Mason. He was the son of Benjamin Franklin Matthews and Mary Elizabeth Wright Matthews. B. F. Matthews was born October 21, 1828, in Wilkerson County, Georgia, married on February 20, 1855, in Macon County, Alabama, and died on August 19, 1899, in Americus, Georgia. Mary Elizabeth Matthews died in September, 1914, in Americus, Georgia.

B. F. Matthews was the child of William Matthews and Elizabeth Hall Matthews. William Matthews was born in 1797, in Wilkerson County, Georgia, married in Wilkerson County, Georgia, and died in 1859 in Marion County, Georgia. Elizabeth Hall Matthews died in 1869 in Marion County, Georgia, and married in Wilkerson County, Georgia.

The mother of Mary Elizabeth Wright Matthews was Elizabeth Wilmot, who was born March 12, 1797, in Columbia County, Georgia, and died in 1867 in Macon County, Alabama.

W. J. Matthews married on February 12, 1878, Ella Shaw in Cusseta, Georgia. Ella Shaw was born on February 12, 1860, in Stewart County, Georgia, and died on May 5, 1932, in Moultrie, Georgia. She was the daughter of David J. Shaw and Margaret Wardlaw Shaw. David J. Shaw was born in Sumter County, Georgia, married in Chattahoochee County, Georgia, in 1859, and died in 1913, in Columbus, Georgia. Margaret Wardlaw Shaw was born in Stewart County, Georgia, and died in Columbus, Georgia.

Children of W. J. Matthews and Ella Shaw Matthews are: Shaw Hall Matthews, 1878; Maud Matthews Tharpe, 1880; Willabell Matthews Turnbull, 1883; Margaret Elizabeth Wink, 1887. Mr. W. J. Matthews, still alive and active at Moultrie, Georgia, he has conducted a mercantile business, at the same time successfully operating his extensive farming interests.

While he has never been a candidate for public office, he has at all times maintained an intelligent interest in public affairs; and the number of his personal friends is remarkably large, wherever he has lived.

Mr. Matthews was at one time in his life extensively connected with the railroad development of South Georgia. Commencing in 1882, in connection with Major Hawkins, of Americus, Ga., he commenced building short lines and extensions both to the east and the west of Americus; and by 1897 they had completed a line of railroad extending from Savannah, through Americus to Montgomery, Ala. The "SAM Road," it was called; and is now a part of the Seaboard System. Mr. Matthews was at one time General Superintendent of the "S. A. M."

## Zachary Thomas Millsap

THIS COLQUITT COUNTY CITIZEN was born May 1, 1891, at Thomasville, Ga., and was educated in the Moultrie Public School. He is a son of Zachary Taylor Millsap, who was born on January 1, 1856, in Robeson County, N. C.; married in January, 1874, in Ashpole, N. C.; and died November 1, 1891, in Ashpole, N. C.

Mother of Z. T. Millsap was Mary Eliza McHargue, who was born on April 16, 1860, in Robeson County, N. C., and died April 5, 1892, in Moultrie, Ga.

Paternal grandfather of Z. T. Millsap was Richard James Millsap, born in Iredell County, N. C., in 1824, married in 1843, and died in Robeson County, N. C., in 1893. Paternal grandmother of Z. T. Millsap was Mary Ann McLean, born April 27, 1825, in Robeson County, N. C.

Maternal grandfather of Z. T. Millsap was James McHargue, born April 2, 1825, in Iredell County, N. C., and died on April 29, 1900. He was a soldier in the Civil War. Maiden name of maternal grandmother of Z. T. Millsap was Mary Pope, born and died in Robeson County, N. C.

Z. T. Millsap married on June 17, 1917, in Liddington, La.; married Mary Mina Chesnutt, who was born on February 19, 1893, in Lufkin, Angelina County, Texas. She was a daughter of Wm. Lott Chesnutt, who was born December 7, 1850, in Clinton, N. C., and of his wife, Mary Lydia Shofner Chesnutt, who was born January 17, 1861, in Angelina County, Texas, and died on November 28, 1911, in Port Arthur, Texas. William Lott Chesnutt died on April 21, 1930, in Weed, California.

Children of Z. T. Millsap and Mary Mina Millsap are:

Zachary Thomas Millsap, Jr., born March 13, 1922.

Mina Chestnutt Millsap, born August 18, 1923.

Zachary Thomas Millsap, Sr., has been Superintendent of the Municipal Water and Light Plant in Doerun, Ga., continuously during the past 18 years. In politics, he is a Democrat.

## Lammie Lamar Moore

THIS RESIDENT OF COLQUITT COUNTY was born in Elbert County, Ga., on November 22, 1880; and was educated in the common schools of that county, and studied law at Mercer University, Macon, Ga., receiving its degree of LL.B. By profession, he is a practicing attorney-at-law, having begun the practice at Moultrie, Ga., in September, 1904. Baptist. Democrat. W. O. W. Kiwanian. Knight of Pythias. He was Sargent Moultrie Rifles, 1904, 1905 and 1906.

He was City Attorney of Moultrie, Ga., 1913-1918. Member House of Representatives of Georgia, 1927-1928, 1929-1930. Member Georgia State Senate, 1931-1932. At present is Judge City Court of Colquitt County.

The father of L. L. Moore was John Henry Moore, born August 5, 1852, in Elbert County, Ga.; married on December 3, 1879, in Elbert County, Ga., and died August 20, 1930, in Elbert County, Ga. He was a farmer, and for

## LAMMIE LAMAR MOORE

many years was a Justice of the Peace in and for the 202 District, G. M., Elbert County, Ga. (Webbsboro District). Maiden name of the mother of L. L. Moore was Mary Campbell, born March 24, 1862, in Elbert County, Ga., and is still living, having reared ten children, of whom L. L. Moore is the oldest.

Name of paternal grandfather of L. L. Moore was Joel W. Moore, born October 13, 1821, in Elbert County; married about 1848, in Elbert County, Ga., and died in 1913, in Elbert County, Ga. He was a farmer, and reared five sons and a daughter. Maiden name of paternal grandmother was Sarah Hewell, born about 1825, in Wilkes County, Ga., and died about 1890 in Elbert County, Ga.

Name of maternal grandfather of L. L. Moore was James C. Campbell; born about 1820, in Elbert County Ga.; married about 1845; and died about 1907, in Madison County, Ga. He was a farmer, and reared ten children. Maiden name of maternal grandmother was Jerusha Higgenbotham, who was born about 1825, in Elbert County, Ga., and died about 1917, in Madison County, Ga.

L. L. Moore married on April 29, 1914, in Moultrie, Ga., Miss Pearl Scarboro, who was born June 13, 1889, in Bulloch County, Ga. She was educated in the public schools and at Brenau College, at Gainesville, Ga.

Name of father-in-law of L. L. Moore was Jas. H. Scarboro, who was born February 14, 1860, in Bulloch County, Ga.; married in Bulloch County, Ga., and died in Colquitt County, Ga. He lived in Bulloch County, Ga., until about 1900, when he moved to Colquitt County, where he operated a farm for a while, and finally moved to Moultrie, where he held the office of City Clerk for more than 20 years. Name of the mother-in-law of L. L. Moore was Sallie Daughtry, who was born on August 9, 1865, in Bulloch County. She is still living.

As issue of the marriage of L. L. Moore and Pearl Scarboro Moore, there are in life children, as follows:

Russell Lamar Moore, born March 18, 1918.

Barbara Moore, born February 16, 1924.

James Henry Moore, born February 9, 1926.

"Double L," as he is affectionately called, grew up on a farm before the days of good roads and adequate schools. While still in his teens he wrote articles to the *Elberton Star*, in such topics, especially schools. Being without money or property, in the beginnings of his life, he early in life developed a sympathy for all working people, which he has never lost, and hopes never to lose. He wants to see an economical structure that will bring about absolute equality of opportunity to all the children of Georgia, and is willing to work at bringing it to pass.

## George William Newton

THIS CITIZEN OF COLQUITT COUNTY was born in 1867, and was the oldest child of G. F. Newton and his wife, Julia Norman Newton. He was educated in the early public schools of Colquitt County. He is a Democrat and a member of the Missionary Baptist Church, as are all the members of his family. The history of the ancestry of G. W. Newton is fully set forth elsewhere in this chapter in the sketches of George F. Newton and his wife, Julia Norman Newton. By reference to these it will be seen that on his mother's side Mr. G. W. Newton is descended from the Tillmans and the Normans, the earliest pioneers of Colquitt County. His father, Mr. George F. Newton, was born in Brooks County, being the son of G. W. Newton, Sr., for whom the subject of this sketch was named. The Newtons were originally a numerous pioneer family of North Carolina. George F.

## GEORGE WILLIAM NEWTON

Newton was a Confederate soldier and a veteran of Gettysburg Battle, where he left an arm. He also served Colquitt as her representative in the House of Representatives of Georgia. For several terms he was Tax Collector and Tax Receiver of Colquitt County.

G. W. Newton, the subject of this sketch, has also served Colquitt as representative in the Georgia Legislature; and for many years has held the position of County Administrator of Colquitt County. He also served one term as Sheriff of the county.

He married in 1889, Miss Elizabeth A. Barber, daughter of Rev. John D. Barber, natives of Colquitt County. The children of this union who are now in life are as follows:

Elvana Newton (Mrs. J. E. Gordon).
John Thomas Newton, Colquitt farmer.
Willie Newton, Colquitt farmer.
Esther Newton (Mrs. P. H. Croy).
Ethel Newton (Mrs. J. B. Pope).
Alice Newton (Mrs. Foster).
Dora Newton (Mrs. Bordon Manley).
David Lanier Newton, Colquitt farmer.

All of these children are sterling citizens of Colquitt County. Mr. Newton and his wife have for fifty years enjoyed the cordial respect of the whole population of the county, as do their children.

## Jeremiah Bryant Norman, Sr.

J. B. Norman, Sr., was the oldest child of James Mitchell Norman and Ruth Tillman Norman, a pioneer couple. He was born in Liberty County, Georgia, in 1821, came to Irwin County, Ga., with his parents, when he was an infant in arms. He spent the first few years of his life with his parents, near Nashville, Georgia; and later removed with them to the territory that was later incorporated with Colquitt County. He was looked upon as a leader of the pioneers of the section that is now Colquitt, during the most of his life; and he lost that leadership only when the torch dropped from his aging hands, to be lifted and borne along by his son, Jeremiah Bryant Norman, Jr.

This writer called on this good man, in his ripe old age. He lived with his youngest son, V. F. Norman, and his wife. His wife had been dead for some time. He was uncultured in a way; but he presented a dignified appearance. Like a Roman Senator of the era of the Republic. Surrounded, he was by his numerous descendants who continued so long as he lived to be "ordered around" by "Pappy." Not a one of them ever even thought of crossing him. Not even "Wheeler."

"Pappy," or "Bryant," as his contemporary relatives called him was on the whole a conservative in his ways and thoughts. Kept his membership at Pleasant Grove Primitive Baptist Church, as long as he lived; and, when he died, his children laid him to "sleep thegither at the foot" with his wife, "Aunt Sally Ann," in the graveyard, at that church.

Said he to Wheeler, when he was talking up his "Institute," at Norman Park,

"Yes; and when all the children are going to your dern school, who's going to do the work, in this county?"

J. B. NORMAN, JR.

## Jeremiah Bryant Norman, Jr.

THE SUBJECT of this sketch was born in 1853, being the fifth child and the second son of Jeremiah Bryant Norman, Sr., and his wife Sarah Ann Norman. J. B. Norman, Sr., was the oldest child of James Mitchell Norman and Ruth Tillman Norman, pioneer settlers in the Colquitt territory, before the county was created. As will appear from a review of the biographical sketch of J. B. Norman, Sr., appearing in this history, J. B. Norman, Sr., was a family and a county leader during nearly the whole of his life; and it is a fact that when the mantle of leadership gradually passed from his aging hand, it was taken up by his son and namesake, J. B. Norman, Jr., who possessed all the pushing qualities of leadership of his father, and had the advantage of exercising these talents in a far larger field.

By the time J. B. Norman, Jr., was forty years old he had extensive naval stores manufacturing interests, which rapidly became prolific sources of income. A little later, he was successful in interesting outside capitalists in Colquitt's resources, and induced them to join him in developing the lumber business on the eastern side of the county, among them D. C. Bacon, of Savannah, Ga., and Martin F. Amorous, a young industrialist of Atlanta. These two men and Mr. Norman organized the "Pinopolis Saw Mill Company," at Bayboro, in the eastern part of the county, buying up extensive timber, and constructing a tramroad from Sparks on the Georgia Southern and Florida Railroad to their mills at Bayboro, and westward to Moultrie, which was reached a little after the Georgia Northern Railway line reached it, as it was pressing on towards Albany. About 1900, this concern was merged with the Union Lumber Co., a big concern organized to cut the extensive holdings of W. W. Ashburn, lying generally to the south of Moultrie. The merger was incorporated under the name and style of "Union Pinopolis Saw Mill Company." What had happened was that Messrs. Bacon, Amorous and Norman had bought the holdings of the Union Lumber Company. What matters in this writing is that Mr. Norman was increasing his holdings, which he held until the timber of the Union Pinopolis Corporation's holdings were entirely cut over.

When there was an end of the timber of the Union Pinopolis Company, Mr. Norman's associates turned over several thousand acres of cut-over pine lands to Mr. Norman, on very easy terms; and he proceeded to offer them for settlement at very low prices. He sold nothing with the idea that he might get it returned to him, plus the improvements; but fixed such prices on these lands that the purchaser could manage to make his payments and retain possession and title to them.

During the last fifteen years of Mr. Norman's life, he was constantly in the market for rent-yielding property in Moultrie—especially brick buildings located centrally. Such was his desire to purchase such property that he simply bought it when ever offered, and without any haggling over prices. Of course, the event has justified Mr. Norman's judgment, since there has been a steady increase in the demand for such property, and its rental value, at all times during the past thirty-five years; and the prospects seem good for a further enhancement in such values.

Mr. Norman was a man of tireless energy—so much so that his father called him "Wheeler"—a nickname that came to be applied to him by his relatives and friends throughout the county, and far beyond. He was first a "wheel-horse;" and this was shortened into "Wheeler." Martin F. Amorous, personal friend and intimate business associate of Mr. Norman for a quarter of a century, once said, "Wheeler Norman was the greatest executive I have ever known."

Like John Tucker, Wheeler Norman came into the world with his hands wide open. He "stood for" more men, and indorsed more paper of Colquitt citizens than any five men that ever lived here. Hundreds of his neighbors took advantage of his perpetual desire to be of help; and, as was once said of a French Prince, "When a favor was asked of him it was he that appeared obliged." But he dismissed this trait with a laugh, claiming that he got pleasure out of it, since a man who asked him for a favor was paying tribute to him. And, to a remarkable degree the persons whose obligations he indorsed paid up. He lost practically nothing.

Mr. Norman was catholic in his ministrations. He would help a youth pay his expenses at Emory as quickly as one who wanted to go to Mercer. When he was a youth of 17 years, he subscribed fifty dollars towards a fund for the erection of the first Methodist Church building in Moultrie. It was perhaps the heaviest contribution of all. This he told this writer. "And I paid it, too. I killed deer, and sold the hides and the smoked venison, and got the money, and paid every cent of it."

He was deeply sentimental and deeply emotional. Miles Monk, Sr., who married his sister, "Sookey," once told this writer that, when his mother died, he would wake up of nights, and sob and cry till dawn; and this for a long time. They were afraid he would lose his mind, Mr. Monk said.

He passed under another and heavier dispensation of an afflictive providence, when he was an old man comparatively. His oldest son was killed in Florida. For this he never ceased to grieve, so long as he lived.

He was deeply religious; and often resorted to prayer. He gave more than half of the cost of the fine Baptist Church building at Norman Park. For some years he maintained a missionary school in China.

## JEREMIAH BRYANT NORMAN, JR.

While he was a sentimental mystic, as we have said; at all that he was eminently practical. He believed that the best way to help people—especially young folks was to put them in the way of earning their own keep. He early reached the conclusion that education cost too much. Also, he easily saw that the idea of sending a boy or girl away from their parents was not only expensive; but that it was a very dangerous thing to do. So he decided that he would bring the education so close to the youth of Colquitt that they could spend their week-ends, at least, at home. The result was "Norman Institute," which is now "Norman Junior College."

Of course, Mr. Norman was too canny and resourceful a canvasser to let any of his business acquaintances off from making a helping contribution; even at that, his contribution explained more than half of the total, amounting to more than $80,000.00 originally; and he continued to work at this charity till the end of his life. This contribution to human welfare entitles Mr. Norman to high rank among the philanthropists of all time; and constitutes his claim for immortality. He geared his resources and his life into forces that range into eternity.

In early life, Mr. Norman was married to Miss Lovedian Permelia Livingston. From this union there were children as follows:

Missouri Elizabeth (Mrs. K. W. Horne), deceased.
Lovedian Permelia (Mrs. J. H. Hall).
Georgia (Mrs. Sam Harrell).
John Hansell (died unmarried).
Matthew Bryant.
Nancy Annie (Mrs. Charley Beall).
James Franklin.
Turner Davis (died in infancy).
Joseph Kiser (died in young manhood).

All these live in Colquitt, except, of course, the deceased ones. The wife and children of J. Kiser Norman live at Norman Park, in Colquitt County.

J. B. Norman, Jr., held the office of sheriff of Colquitt County two terms; he represented Colquitt County four years as a member of the House of Representatives of the General Assembly of Georgia and he represented this county four years as a member of the Georgia State Senate.

## Lindsey Monterville Potts

THIS CITIZEN OF COLQUITT COUNTY was born on April 14, 1864, in Cherokee County, Ga., and had his education in the common schools of that county. He was the son of Monterville Potts, who was born in Cherokee County, in 1843. The parents of Monterville Potts were Henry Potts and Clara Jane Potts, natives of South Carolina. The mother of L. M. Potts was Martha Jane Wetherby, also a native of Cherokee County. L. M. Potts married in December, 1882, Miss Lula Cagle, a native of Cherokee County, Ga., who was the daughter of James Cagle and his wife, Jane Sumner Cagle, both natives of South Carolina. James Cagle was a son of George Cagle, Sr., who lived at one time in Hall County, Ga.

L. M. Potts, in his young manhood, moved to Bartow County, Ga., where he remained eighteen years, engaged in farming and the management of a country store near Pine Log, Ga. In 1909 he removed to Colquitt County, Ga., and bought property a few miles north of Moultrie, which he successfully developed.

The children now in life, being the issue of the marriage of L. M. Potts and Martha Jane Wetherby Potts, are as follows:

## HISTORY OF COLQUITT COUNTY

Lela Potts (Mrs. Hope Dooley).
Dillard Potts, Automobile Business, Atlanta, Ga.
Clifford Potts, Swift and Co. Employee, Moultrie, Ga.
Emma Potts (Mrs. George Tucker), Moultrie, Ga.
Curran Potts, Atlanta, Ga.
Mayo Potts, Moultrie, Ga.
Eugenia Potts (Mrs. Lester Thompson), Moultrie, Ga.
Zuma Potts, Moultrie, Ga.
Bobbie Grace Potts, Moultrie, Ga.
L. M. Potts, Jr., Moultrie, Ga.
Myrtle Potts (Mrs. Herbert Conger), Worth County, Ga.

In addition to these is Verner Potts, accidentally killed at Tampa, Fla., in young manhood, and two girl children, Lindsay Jane and Bertha, both of whom died in infancy.

Mr. L. M. Potts is a Democrat, and a member of the Baptist Church. He has been all his life a hard-working farmer, and a shrewd business man; and is now very nicely situated on his large farm near Moultrie, upon which he has lived since coming to Colquitt County. He is a trustee of the Okapilco Consolidated School, and is looked upon by his neighbors and acquaintances as a sterling good citizen of the county, being interested in social enterprises of all kinds.

## Emanuel William Rhoden

THIS CITIZEN OF COLQUITT COUNTY is a native of the county, having been born here on November 16, 1885. He was educated in the Moultrie Public Schools, having been graduated from them in 1906. His diploma is the first ever to be issued to a male student in Colquitt County.

By profession Mr. Rhoden is a printer, commencing work in this profession in Moultrie in 1898. He was proprietor of the Moultrie Printing Company in 1907, and is present proprietor of Rhoden's Stationery and Printing Company, and has been such since 1922.

He is a Missionary Baptist and a Democrat. He was Sergeant in Company "B" of the National Guard ("Moultrie Rifles"). He was elected First Lieutenant, but the organization was disbanded before his commission was received.

Mr. Rhoden was the son of Emanuel Rasberry Rhoden, a native of the State of Georgia, and a Primitive Baptist preacher. The mother of Mr. E. W. Rhoden was Martha Patten, a native of Berrien County, Ga. She was the daughter of James Patten and Kizzie Drawdy.

E. W. Rhoden married Cora Lee Daniel on February 13, 1911, at that time a resident of Moultrie, Ga. She was born on August 23, 1889, in Ware County, Ga. She was graduated from Moultrie Public Schools. She was president of the Adult Baptist Training Union of the First Baptist Church of Moultrie, Ga. She is President of the Ladies Bible Class of the First Baptist Church now. Her father was William James Daniel, who was born July 11, 1852, in Brooks County, Ga.; married his wife in Ware County, Ga., and died in April, 1915, in Colquitt County, Ga. His wife, the mother-in-law of E. W. Rhoden, was Nancy James, born July 9, 1871, in Ware County, Ga., and died in 1914 in Colquitt County, Ga. Mr. E. W. Rhoden has been Clerk of Colquitt County Baptist Association since 1934. He is Past Illustrious Master of the Moultrie Council R. and S. M. (Masons). He has been High Priest of Moultrie Chapter Royal Arch Masons from 1935 to 1936. He has been Worthy Patron Moultrie Chapter No. 139 Order of the Eastern Star from 1936 to 1937. Senior Warden Moultrie Lodge No. 391 Free and Accepted Masons. Prelate in Bethlehem Commandery Knights Templars, 1935-1937. He is Intermediate Leader, Baptist Training Unions, Colquitt County Association of the Missionary Baptist Church; Adult

Leader Sunday Schools, Colquitt County Association. He is Adult Superintendent Sunday School, First Missionary Baptist Church, Moultrie, Ga. He is Senior Deacon, Colquitt County Masonic Convention. He has been a member of the Woodmen of the World for twenty years.

Children in life, being the issue of the marriage between Emanuel William Rhoden and Cora Lee Daniel Rhoden, are as follows:

Emanuel William Rhoden, Jr., born January 10, 1911.
Martha Neta Rhoden, born June 16, 1912.
Helen Vivian (Jackie) Rhoden, born September 24, 1914.
James Lee Rhoden, born September 2, 1919.

All these children are graduates of the Moultrie High School. The girls, Martha Neta Rhoden and Helen Vivian Rhoden, are both graduates of the Georgia State College for Women at Milledgeville, Ga., and are now engaged in the profession of teaching.

## William Henry Rhodes

This citizen of Colquitt County, and who lives near Moultrie, Ga., was born on May 21, 1890, at Moultrie, Ga., and obtained his education in the Moultrie Public Schools. Since his graduation from the Moultrie High School, he has taught some in the common schools of Colquitt County, and is now operating extensive farming interests near Moultrie.

He is a Methodist, a Democrat, a Mason, an Odd Fellow, and a W. O. W.

He participated in the World War. Was stationed at Fort Oglethorpe as a private of the first class, and served in General Hospital 14. Trustee of Okapilco Consolidated School, 1936, 1937, 1938.

Name of father was William Joseph Rhodes, born October 31, 1858, in Dougherty County, Ga.; married on December 30, 1888, in Colquitt County, Ga., and died on September 21, 1921, in Moultrie, Ga. U. S. Postmaster at Maple Ford and Justice of the Peace in Colquitt County. By profession he was a merchant and a farmer. Maiden name of the mother of W. H. Rhodes was Leila Jackson McCollum, born March, 1871, in Mitchell County. Leila M. E. Church, South, situated in the northeast part of Colquitt County, was named for her. She still survives, living at Moultrie, Ga.

Name of paternal grandfather of W. H. Rhodes was John A. Rhodes, born October 13, 1834, in Dooly County, Ga., and died April 17, 1918. Confederate veteran and farmer. Name of paternal grandmother was Mary Thorn Calhoun, born January 12, 1836, in Calhoun County, Ga. Name of maternal grandfather was Moses A. McCollum, born March 26, 1847, in Monroe County, N. C., married January 6, 1868, in Colquitt County, Ga., and died July 17, 1906, in Colquitt County, Ga. He was a local Methodist minister and a farmer. Maiden name of maternal grandmother of W. H. Rhodes was Arra P. Hayes, born January 28, 1846, in Camden County, S. C., and died on April 16, 1918, in Colquitt County,

W. H. Rhodes married on November 26, 1922, in Moultrie, Ga. The maiden name of his wife was Nellie Clyde McFather, and she was born on October 9, 1897, in Worth County, Ga. Her father was Wm. D. McFather, who was born August 11, 1871, in Randolph County, Ga., and died on January 3, 1933, at Tarpon Springs, Fla. He was a farmer. The mother of Nellie Clyde McFather Rhodes was Jessie Rogers Cosby, who was born March 15, 1875, in Randolph County, Ga., and who died on March 31, 1910, in Colquitt County, Ga. She was a teacher in the common schools of Randolph County, Ga., before her marriage.

One child, Edgar Olin Rhodes, the issue of the marriage of W. H. Rhodes and Nellie Clyde McFather Rhodes lives with his parents near Moultrie, Ga., and was born February 3, 1924.

William Henry Rhodes is at present Commander of Thomas S. Teabeaut Post 41.

## George Alexander Shaver

G. A. SHAVER was born on the 29th day of April, 1881, at Plano, Cherokee County, Ala. His education consisted of attendance in the common schools of Cherokee County, Ala., and two years at the Normal School at Jacksonville, Ala. Occupations of G. A. Shaver have been farmer, school teacher, bank clerk and bank cashier. Since October, 1921, he has been Clerk of the City of Moultrie, Ga., continuously. Member of the Church of Christ. Democrat. Mason. W. O. W.

Parents of G. A. Shaver were John Reed Shaver, born September 1, 1851, in Cherokee County, Ala., and died September 23, 1931, at Piedmont, Ala., and Mary Amanda Crews, who was born on March 23, 1864, in Cherokee County, Ala., and who is still living. Parents were married on December 25, 1879. Parents just good, clean people, much interested in each other and in their children and grandchildren.

Paternal grandfather of G. A. Shaver was George Shaver and his paternal grandmother was Nancy May. They were both natives of North Carolina, where they were married. George Shaver was drowned in a stream in Cherokee County, Ala., known as "Terrapin Creek," in 1875. The place is still known as "Shaver's Ford," about 15 miles from Piedmont, Ala. With him were two of his sons. Paternal grandmother was born April 12, 1812, in North Carolina, and died in 1896, at Pope, Ala.

Paternal grandparents of G. A. Shaver were Alex Ellenburg and Mary Crews, both of whom were natives of South Carolina, and both of whom died in Cherokee County, Ala. Grandfather Ellenburg was a noted rifle shot, and much interested in relics and antiques.

G. A. Shaver was married on January 4, 1910, in Cartersville, Ga., to Miss Ella May Bradley. She was a daughter of Joe Bradley and Catherine Matilda Miles. Her maternal side came from the Sluders of Asheville, N. C. She and her husband, Joe Bradley, were reared in the same home from childhood, being brought together by marriage of a widower and a widow, each of whom had a bunch of children which were reared together, and these two intermarried.

The children of the marriage of G. A. Shiver and Ella May Bradley are:

John Bradley Shaver, May 13, 1912.
Geo. Alexander Shaver, Jr., July 10, 1914.
Mary Catherine Shaver, March 7, 1924.
Mina Margurite Shaver, February 9, 1927.

John Bradley Shaver married Florrie Mitchell of Morrow, Ga., on June 26, 1932. They have a child, Barbara Anne Shaver, born October 3, 1933.

## John Suber

JOHN SUBER was born in Colquitt County, Ga., on October 15, 1892. His parents were James F. Suber, a native of Macon County, Ga., and Susie Eleanor Tucker. John Suber was a son of George Suber, a native of South Carolina, who was born in 1825. The wife of George Suber was Sarah Ann

Truluck. James F. Suber was born in 1857, and still lives on his farm in Colquitt County, being a prosperous and respected citizen. Sarah Ann Truluck Suber was born in Georgia in 1828.

Susie Eleanor Tucker Suber was a daughter of Richard Tucker and Civil America Hancock. Richard Tucker was a son of Elder Henry Crawford Tucker, frequently referred to in this History as a pioneer settler in Colquitt County, Ga. His wife, Civil America Hancock Tucker, was a member of a pioneer family of Colquitt County. Richard Tucker was at one time sheriff of Colquitt County, Ga.

As will be seen from the above sketch, every drop of the blood in the veins of John Suber came out of the veins of the pioneers; and Mr. Suber is properly proud of this fact.

John Suber is a W. O. W. and a Democrat. He is a member of the County Executive Committee of that party. He is at present an efficient member of the Board of Commissioners of Roads and Revenues of Colquitt County. He has never married.

## William Tillman

WILLIAM TILLMAN was born on October 20, 1879, in Colquitt County, Georgia. He obtained such education as the common schools of the time afforded and has resided in Colquitt all his life. He was the child of John A. Tillman, who was a farmer, living in Colquitt all his life. William Tillman is also a farmer.

The mother of William Tillman was Harriet Baker, a daughter of Absalom Baker, a representative of a distinguished pioneer family of Colquitt. The wife of Absalom Baker was Zilpha Tillman.

288    HISTORY OF COLQUITT COUNTY

Speaking of big families among the Colquitt pioneers, here is a "bunch of children" got up by Mr. and Mrs. W. M. Tillman, since the beginning of the present century. One thing that characterizes the big families of Colquitt is that they are generally "raised" to adulthood. Take a look, ye generations to come, at these fourteen children of Mr. and Mrs. Bill Tillman. Also take a look at Mrs. Tillman. And oh well, take notice of Mr. Tillman pere. Names of this little army, from right to left, may be found in family sketch of Mr. W. M. Tillman in the chapter devoted to such matters, hereinafter.

William Tillman married Ollie Doris, a daughter of Jesse Doris of Thomas County, Ga., in the year 1898. The maiden name of the mother-in-law of William Tillman was Lela Gandy.

The children being the issue of the marriage of Wm. Tillman and Ollie Doris Tillman are as follows:

Ed. Tillman, employee of the City of Moultrie, married Ruby Mock.

Frank Tillman, mechanic, living in Tampa, Fla., married Ruby Lindsey.

Lester C. Tillman, employee Swift & Co., married Ray Livingston.

Samuel Tillman, employee of Colquitt County, married Gladys Wilks.

Rosie Lee Tillman, married .......... Strickland of Colquitt County.

Hattie Tillman, married Elbert Dorminy of Colquitt County.

Charley Tillman, resident Colquitt County.

## WILLIAM TILLMAN

Robert Lee Tillman, electrician, resident of Moultrie.
Alice T. Weeks.
Paul Tillman, U. S. Navy.
Dixie Tillman, child, living with parents.
Margie Tillman, living with parents.
Russell, living with parents.
Jessie, schoolboy, living with parents.

The group picture appended here shows Mr. and Mrs. Wm. Tillman seated and their fourteen children standing. The names of these children may be ascertained by commencing on the right with Ed. Tillman, No. 1, and proceeding to the right in order of their ages, ending with Jessie Tillman, on the extreme left. We believe such an attractive family is rarely seen. There are no twins and not a single blemish in the family.

Here is a picture of John Tillman and Fariba Mercer Tillman, grandparents of Wm. Tillman. John Tillman was a Georgia State Senator in 1859-60. He was born in 1800, and his wife was born in 1805. They are buried in the cemetery at Hopewell Missionary Baptist Church, a few miles out of Moultrie, near the Moultrie and Quitman paved highway. The 1860 census of Colquitt shows Fariba Mercer resided at the home of John Tillman. She was ninety years old, and died, later in the year.

JOHN and FARIBA MERCER TILLMAN

## W. R. Tucker

This citizen of Colquitt is a resident of Moultrie, and was born October 4, 1898, in Colquitt County, Ga., and was educated in the common schools of Colquitt County. Reared on his father's farm, he has been a meat cutter for twenty years, and operates a meat market at this time in Moultrie. He is a Missionary Baptist, a Democrat, a Mason, an Odd Fellow, Knight of Pythias, Modern Woodman, and a member of the Royal Arcanum. He was a volunteer seaman in the World War.

He was a child of John C. Tucker, born in Colquitt County, where he still lives, and Sallie Newton Tucker, born in Colquitt, in 1868, who died in Colquitt County in August, 1934. His paternal grandparents were John Tucker, born March 24, 1833, and died in Colquitt in 1919, and Susan A. Stephenson Tucker, born in Raleigh, N. C., in 1835, and died in Colquitt County, Ga., in September, 1917. John Tucker was a son of Elder Henry Crawford Tucker, born in 1803, and died in 1881, who is buried in Bridge Creek Church cemetery, in Colquitt County.

His maternal grandparents were Geo. F. Newton, born in North Carolina, who went to the Civil War from Brooks County, Ga., and Julia Norman, who was born in Colquitt County, Ga., being a daughter of Jeremiah Bryant Norman and Sarah Ann Elizabeth Norman, who are buried side by side in the Pleasant Grove Primitive Baptist Church cemetery in Colquitt County. Jeremiah Bryant Norman, Sr., was the oldest child of James Mitchell Norman, a native of Liberty County, Ga., and Ruth Tillman Norman. Reference is here made to the family sketches of these pioneers to be found in this chapter.

W. R. Tucker was married to Vera Page, born February 3, 1901, in Colquitt County, and who is still living in Colquitt County. She is Missionary Baptist, and is a child of W. A. Page, native of Randolph County, now resident in Colquitt County, and Mattie White Page, born in 1877 in Randolph County, and now living in Colquitt County with her said husband.

W. R. Tucker and his wife, Vera Page Tucker, have the following children all in life, in their home, in Moultrie:

Raiford, Jr., born in 1920.
Lamar, born in 1922.
Linwood, born in 1924.
Lanelle, born in 1926.
Ronald, born in 1929.
Louise, born in 1932.

## Samuel P. Turnbull

This resident of Moultrie, in Colquitt County, Ga., was born April 29, 1876, at Monticello, Fla., and educated at Jefferson Collegiate Institute, at Monticello, Fla. His parents were Samuel J. Turnbull, a native of South Carolina, and Virginia Finlayson ........ Turnbull, a native of the State of Virginia. One of his grandfathers was John Turnbull, a native of South Carolina.

Samuel P. Turnbull was married to Miss Willie Belle Matthews at Moultrie, Ga., on .............. She is a daughter of William Jefferson Matthews, a resident of Moultrie, and reference is hereby made to his biographical sketch appearing in this chapter for further details as to her family history.

Two children are in life, the issue of the marriage of S. P. Turnbull and Willie Belle Matthews Turnbull, namely:

Mildred, Assistant to Dean, G. S. W. C., Valdosta.
Eleanor, Moultrie High School student.

292   HISTORY OF COLQUITT COUNTY

S. P. Turnbull is a direct descendant of John C. Calhoun, the wonderful political philosopher of South Carolina. He is a charter member of Moultrie Chamber of Commerce. Second to oldest member of W. A. Covington's Bible Class of Moultrie. A member of the Building Committee which had direction of the construction of the First M. E. Church, South, of Moultrie. Had part in the building of the First Baptist and the First Presbyterian churches, in Moultrie. Connected substantially with the origin of Moultrie Y. M. C. A., Moultrie Packing Plant, and Hotel Colquitt. Had direction of the fight to secure proper freight rates for Moultrie, appearing before the Railroad Commission of Georgia and the Interstate Commerce Committee at Washington.

## William Coachman Vereen

ON ONE SEPTEMBER DAY IN 1864, a man in uniform met a five-year-old boy who was taking a walk in the care of his nurse. He tapped him on the head and somewhat affectionately called him "a little Rebel." It was on a sidewalk in Cheraw, S. C. The military man was General William Tecumseh Sherman, and the boy was William Coachman Vereen. And the boy was of rebel stock all right, and belonged to the Southern aristocracy which General Sherman had admired since he left West Point.

On his father's side the boy could trace his ancestry straight back to the Huguenots whose beginnings in French history dated from Henry of Navarre, a rebel prince of the latter part of the Sixteenth Century. In 1680, Louis XIV repealed the Edict of Nantes and kindled the fires of persecution in France. The result was that the Huguenots left France in hundreds of thousands to settle in many foreign lands. Great numbers settled in Pennsylvania, Delaware, Maryland, and South Carolina. Since the ranks of the

WILLIAM COACHMAN VEREEN

Huguenots were made up of the aristocracy and middle classes of France, it resulted that wherever they settled, they immediately became moral and political leaders. Witness, for instance, the Bayards and the Duponts of Delaware, the Delanos of New York, the Lamars of Georgia, and the Vereens of South Carolina.

By his mother, Eugenia McNair, he acquired more rebel background. The McNairs and other "Macks" in this branch of his family were descended from Scotch immigrants who got their religion and their politics from John Knox and his covenanting associates. It is too easily forgotten that on one fearful occasion, when the fires of political liberty had been put out in all lands save Scotland, the Scottish ministry alone held up the torch and from their pulpits fed its flickering flame. The debt of democracy to Mr. Knox and his confreres is immeasurable.

It is a good thing to be closely related in time to the pioneers—men who from the days of Abraham have given direction to the currents of history. And with such a background, one would be surprised had W. C. Vereen spent all the voyage of his life in shallows and in misery. And the reader will not be surprised when he hears how that early in life he demonstrated that his soul was of the stuff of heroes —men capable of making immense sacrifices.

At 18, he was an employee of a New York wholesale hat firm, for a short while; and then he worked briefly at a few other things. On October 13, 1880, he married Miss Mary McNeill, a representative of a prominent South Carolina family, being a daughter of Major Neill McK. McNeill.

In 1885, with his wife and child, he moved to Montgomery County, Ga., where he engaged in the manufacture of naval stores for two years. He then removed to Coffee County, Ga., where he engaged in the same business for some three years.

He came to Colquitt County in 1890, where Major McNeill and sons were established in the naval stores business toward the southwest corner of the county. After looking over the situation, he leased timber and commenced naval stores operations towards the northwest corner of the county, erecting two turpentine stills—the first one a matter of one-half mile west of the Giles old mill site, and a second one near the present site of Doerun. He moved his family into a double-pen log house, erected by John Tucker, and there with his devoted wife put in six years of pure unremitting application to his business. The John Tucker house was at the site of the first still.

Since the Pidcock family had extended, in 1893, their timber road to Moultrie, Mr. Vereen had been wagoning his products to Moultrie. In 1896, in the midst of the so-called Cleveland Panic, he moved his residence to Moultrie, into a two-story frame building on the site of his present elaborate brick residence. The first campaign had been brought to a victorious conclusion. From that time until the present, Mr. Vereen has been identified with the marvelous industrial development of Colquitt County. Looking back over it, he could well adopt the language of Father Aeneas to Queen Dido, and say, "All of which I saw and a great part of it I have been." Some of the high points of Mr. Vereen's business career are:

1. The Moultrie Banking Co., which was established in 1896 by Mr. Vereen, Mr. W. W. Ashburn, and Mr. Z. H. Clark. Mr. Vereen was made active vice-president and held that position until the death of President Ashburn. He has been president of this bank from that date until now; so that for forty years he has never missed his duties of overseeing the daily business of this bank.

2. In 1901, we find him leading his associates in establishing a unit of the textile industry in Moultrie. He thus

became the president of the Moultrie Cotton Mills at a time when the textile industry was in its pioneer stage in the South, and when the impression was general that our climate was not favorable to the spinning of cotton yarns. At the moment this is being written, Mr. Vereen is in charge of extensive reconditioning of the equipment of this plant.

3. In 1914, in the midst of the ravages of the boll weevil, Mr. Vereen and a few "Old Guard" associates, like Jim Corbett, W. J. Matthews and W. H. Barber, projected the establishment of a meat-packing plant at Moultrie. This, despite the fact that the farm papers of the South were united in disparaging the establishment of such plants, saying to the farmers with apparently convincing logic, "You do not produce the necessary live stock for the maintenance of such plants." But these men went ahead and erected the plant at a time when there was not another one in the South, from Richmond to Fort Worth. This has turned out to be the most important industrial movement for Colquitt and surrounding territory since the Seminoles gave up possession, more than a century ago.

4. Coincident with the coming of the Swifts was the work of Moultrie's industrialists for providing a market for diversification of crops. Mr. Vereen was in the forefront of the battle for diversification, putting his bank and his personal fortune behind the intelligent farmers. This in itself is mainly responsible for the fact that Colquitt is the leading agricultural county in the United States.

There is space here for mention of only the high spots of Mr. Vereen's business achievements. Enough has been written, however, to render it certain that regardless of its nature he would have made a success of any profession or business to which he might have addressed himself.

Nor has he been completely absorbed by his business undertakings. While a very modest man, he has never rejected a call for social service. At one time, for instance, he was induced to take charge of a Bible class for men in the Moultrie Presbyterian Church; and built its membership to over 200. Recently, in looking over the records of this church, we found that in the 258 sessions during the first 25 years after its organization Mr. Vereen attended 249. The same records show that he never missed a communion service except when he was unavoidably absent from town. He spent more than half the time of his residence in Moultrie as a trustee of the Moultrie Public Schools. He is at present a trustee of Agnes Scott College. He was Mayor of Moultrie, at 52; President Moultrie Packing Co., at 55; President of Downing Co., at 67; a member of the Democratic Delegation to the Baltimore Convention of 1912; and was appointed by Governor Hardman a member of Georgia's State Highway Board, in which his work was a credit to him and of great benefit to the State.

This historian once attended a meeting of his neighbors called at Moultrie to consider a State-wide request that he consent to the use of his name as a candidate for Governor of Georgia. When there seemed no doubt that he could have been elected he refused because of his relations to his business associates, his children and his Sunday school class. He loved them and did not want to move away from them, so he said.

It will perhaps hearten the generations to come to know that Mr. Vereen has never indulged in vulgar or profane language. He does not indulge in intoxicants, and attends to no business of a secular nature on Sunday. At all that he has a fine sense of humor; and has always found interest in the great men and women of the country and of the world. Such great men as Dr. Joseph R. Wilson, the father of Woodrow Wilson, were frequent house guests at the home of W. J. Vereen, the father of W. C. Vereen, in Cheraw. This, in connection with his cultured forbears, is accountable for his cultivated tastes.

As has been said herein before, Mr. Vereen married Miss Mary McNeill on October 13, 1880. Children, the issue of this marriage, are as follows:

Jessie (Mrs. J. H. Smithwick).
Jennie (Mrs. R. C. Bell).
William J.
Eugene M.

All these are in life and residents of Moultrie except Mrs. Bell, who lives at Cairo and in Atlanta. Three other children of this couple died after reaching maturity, as follows:

Pearl (Mrs. M. H. Stewart).
Thomas W.
John M.

The mother of all these children died in 1898; and in 1899 Mr. Vereen married her sister, Miss Ellen McNeill, who also died on the 23rd of June, 1934. Both these women were exemplary wives and mothers, and in addition manifested constant interest in the people of Colquitt County.

## Eugene Michael Vereen

THIS RESIDENT of Colquitt County all his life, was born on February 5, 1893, near Moultrie, in Colquitt County, Ga. He was educated in the Moultrie Public Schools, at Riverside Military Academy, Gainesville, Ga., and at Davidson College, Davidson, N. C.

He is now Executive Vice-President of Moultrie Banking Company, Vice-President and Treasurer of Moultrie Grocery

Company, and President and Treasurer of Colquitt County Tobacco Warehouse Company.

He is a Presbyterian and a Democrat.

He was a member of the U. S. Marine Naval Reserve Corps, stationed at U. S. Naval Air Station, at Pensacola,

EUGENE MICHAEL VEREEN

Fla., during the participation of the United States during the World War.

He was a member of the Moultrie City Council four years, during which he served as Mayor pro-tem.

300  HISTORY OF COLQUITT COUNTY

His father is Mr. William C. Vereen, who was born at Cheraw, S. C., on August 5, 1859, and who was first married on October 13, 1880, in Cheraw, S. C., and who still lives at Moultrie, Ga. His mother was Miss Mary McNeil, who was born July 1, 1861, in............County, N. C., who married W. C. Vereen, as stated above, and who died at Moultrie, Ga., on the 1st day of August, 1898.

Paternal grandfather of E. M. Vereen was William J. Vereen, who was born May 9, 1829, in Marion County, S. C., and died on May 29, 1877, at Cheraw, S. C. The maiden name of paternal grandmother of E. M. Vereen was Uegenia McNair, who was born on June 25, 1825, and died in Moultrie, Ga., on the 10th day of February, 1905.

The maternal grandfather of E. M. Vereen was Neil McKay McNeil, born June 10, 1825, in North Carolina, and who died on December 29, 1902. Major McNeil was a soldier in the army of Northern Virginia, and for years carried on a successful business near Moultrie, Ga. The Moultrie-McNeil Chapter of the United Daughters of the Confederacy was named for him.

The name of the maternal grandmother of E. M. Vereen was Jane Johnson Pegrue, born December 3, 1835, in Chesterfield County, S. C., and died March 20, 1900, in Colquitt County.

E. M. Vereen was married on May 31, 1917, in Edison, Ga., to Miss Wyolene Nance, who was born August 26, 1898, in Arlington, Early County, Ga. She was a daughter of Samuel Thomas Nance, who was born September 13, 1868, in Harris County, Ga., and married on August 19, 1890, in Sumter County, at Americus, Ga. He died on August 4, 1925, in Arlington, Ga., in Early County. Maiden name of mother-in-law of E. M. Vereen was Minnie Easterlin, born May 6, 1872, at Americus, Ga.

One child, the issue of the marriage of E. M. Vereen and Wyolene Nance, was born on August 9, 1920, and resides with his parents at Moultrie, Ga.

## William Jerome Vereen

W. J. (Will) Vereen was born on the 11th day of June, 1885, in Montgomery (now Wheeler) County, Ga., and was the child of William Coachman Vereen and Mary McNeill Vereen. His paternal grandfather was W. J. Vereen, for whom he was named, and who was a native of South Carolina, as was W. C. Vereen, his father. The grandfather was born on May 9, 1829, in Marion County, S. C., and W. C. Vereen, his father, was born on August 5, 1859, in Cheraw, S. C.

The name of the paternal grandmother of W. J. Vereen was Eugenia McNair, who was born June 25, 1835, in Cheraw, S. C., Chesterfield County. The name of the maternal grandfather of W. J. Vereen was Neill McKay McNeill, who was born June 20, 1825, and died on December 29, 1902, in Moultrie, Ga. The maiden name of the maternal grandmother of W. J. Vereen was Jane Johnson Pegues, born December 3, 1835, in Chesterfield County, S. C., and died on March 20, 1900, in Colquitt County, Ga.

W. J. Vereen, the subject of this sketch, married on December 29, 1908, in Thomaston, Ga. The maiden name of his wife was Miss Lottie Thompson, who was born on September 2, 1888. The name of the father of Mrs. Lottie Thompson Vereen was Isaac Cheney Thompson, of Thomaston, Ga. The maiden name of the wife of Isaac Cheney Thompson was Alice Jordan, and she was born in Midway, Ala. The maternal grandparents of Lottie Thompson Vereen were Ira Jordan and Mary Temperance Feagan Jordan. The paternal grandparents of Lottie Thompson Vereen were Dr. John Thompson and Elizabeth Anne Cheney Thompson.

W. J. Vereen was educated in the Moultrie Public Schools, and at Georgia Military Academy, College Park, Ga. He is a member of the Presbyterian Church, as are all the members of his family. He was Mayor of the City of Moultrie at the

WILLIAM JEROME VEREEN

age of thirty, in 1915-1916. In politics, he is a Democrat, having been, during the years 1920-1921, the Chairman of the Executive Committee of that organization in Georgia; and

HISTORY OF COLQUITT COUNTY 303

he could have had the nomination of his party—equivalent to an election— to the highest civil offices in Georgia, at any time during the past twenty years, had he manifested any desire for such honors.

In 1919, he was President of the Cotton Manufacturers Association of Georgia. During the years 1925-1926, he was President of the American Cotton Manufacturers Association and is still on its Board of Directors.

W. J. Vereen is at present President and Treasurer of the Riverside Manufacturing Company of Moultrie, Ga.; Vice-President of the Moultrie Banking Company, and Vice-President and Treasurer of the Moultrie Cotton Mills. Besides these high points of financial position, he has been connected with numerous smaller enterprises in Colquitt County.

Mrs. W. J. Vereen is a charter member of the John Benning Chapter of the Daughters of the American Revolution, and is also a member of the Colonial Dames.

There are at present in life, being the issue of the marriage of W. J. Vereen and Lottie Thompson Vereen, children as follows:

Mary Vereen (Mrs. Thomas A. Huguenin), Charleston, S. C.
Rosalind Vereen (Mrs. George H. Lanier, Jr.), New York City.
William C. Vereen, Jr., Moultrie, Ga.
Thomas Jerome Vereen, now a student at Darlington School at Rome, Ga.

## Aaron Vick, Jr.

THIS CITIZEN of Colquitt County is a son of Aaron Vick, Sr., and his wife, Sarah Luke Vick. He was educated in the common schools of Colquitt County, and was reared on the farm, and for some years past has resided in Moultrie, where he has been an automobile salesman, and deputy sheriff. His paternal grandfather was Wm. Vick, born in 1825 in South Georgia, and died in the Eighth Land District of what was then Thomas County, and which is now Colquitt County, about the year that Colquitt County was organized. The wife of Wm. Vick, the paternal grandmother of Aaron Vick, Jr., was Nancy Alderman, born near what is now Pavo, Ga., in the year 1827. At the beginning of her widowhood, Nancy Vick had children as follows: Aaron Vick, Sr., born about 1848; James Vick, born about 1846; Missouri Vick, born 1849; Timothy Vick, born 1851; John H. Vick, born 1852; Ezekiel Vick, born 1855. Nancy Vick must have been a remarkable woman; she reared the above children— every one of them into good citizens—and died at the great age of 93 in Colquitt County. James Vick was a representative from Colquitt in the House of Representatives, going as a Democrat, and following the era of reconstruction.

He died not long ago in Thomas County, Ga., leaving two or three generations of good citizens. Aaron Vick, Sr., during his whole life, was a highly respected citizen of West Colquitt. Aaron Vick, Jr., was born on March 15, 1890, married Amzie Smith in the year 1919, she being the daughter of C. J. Smith, who died at Hartsfield in 1930.

Aaron Vick, Jr., was a member of the American Expeditionary Forces in the World War, serving more than a year as a member of the 47th Engineers. He and his cousin, Aubrey Vick, grandson of James Vick, served in the front lines in the Argonne Wood, where Aubrey Vick died a soldier's death.

The children of Aaron Vick, Jr., and Amzie Smith Vick are as follows: Walter Eugene Vick, 13; Leroy Vick, 11; and Aaron Vick, III, $2\frac{1}{2}$ months.

Aaron Vick, Jr., served fifteen years as deputy sheriff of Colquitt County under Sheriff Beard.

## The Weeks Family

THE FIRST CENSUS of Colquitt County, which was taken in 1860, shows Michael Weeks to have been a citizen of Colquitt County at that date (July 5, 1860), and that he was born in South Carolina, in 1785. This man was the progenitor of all the Weeks who have ever lived in Colquitt County. All trace their lineage back to Michael Weeks, and Judy Ann Weeks, his wife.

This couple moved to the neighborhood of what is now Ellenton, about one hundred years ago, settling on a ninety-acre tract of land. They raised nine children, six of whom were sons, who reached maturity. The boys were named Benjamin, Charles, Thomas, David, James, and Seaborn. The girls were named Ann, Betsy, and Sally. There were no railroads, and consequently, no express service and no mail. Also, there were no books, no newspapers, and practically no schooling.

Eight of the children of Michael and Judy Ann Weeks established families and settled around their parents. They formed a kind of clan, which came together often, and established several cooperative enterprises—such as schools, a church, cooperative marketing and buying, and cooperative shoe making and clothes making.

The oldest son of pioneer Michael Weeks was Benjamin. He was born in 1819, in South Carolina, and was eight years old when his parents moved from South Carolina to this section. He was married to Sarah Harrell.

Benjamin Weeks, or Ben Weeks, as he was always called by his intimates and familiars, would have been a remarkable man, at any time or place. His home, where David Weeks now lives, was a community center. He had a large family of his own, consisting of himself, his wife, two elderly single sisters, and nine children; and when his brother died and left a family of nine orphans, Benjamin and his wife took them in. So that at one time, he had in his home eighteen children, two unmarried sisters, his wife and his brother's widow, making twenty-three in all. They still tell of two or three beeves killed per week at patriarch Benjamin's house.

Tradition has it that Benjamin Weeks was inducted into the Christian Church by Flournoy Clark, a local Methodist preacher, and a friend and neighbor. These men were largely responsible for the establishment of "Weeks' Chapel," thought to be the first church of the Methodist denomination ever erected in Colquitt County. This was erected soon after the creation of Colquitt County.

The home of Benjamin Weeks was quite a manufacturing center, as well as a social and religious center. He had vats for tanning leather, and kept on hand an assortment of shoe lasts, being the individual lasts of his relatives and neighbors. These, of course, were used in shoe making, as the necessities of the case demanded. Also under shelter, he had cotton cards, old-fashioned spinning wheels, weaving looms, coloring vats, etc., for making clothing. Practically all the family clothing for his own set-up, as well as those of his neighbors was from cloth turned out by machinery in the Weeks establishment, and from cotton and wool produced on the farms of the relatives and neighbors.

He was an ardent advocate of universal education, and patronized at all times such schools as were accessible. It is said that at one time as many as thirteen pupils attended a single school from his home—that is, from his children and his nephews and nieces.

Among the children of Ben Weeks were Joe S., Sarah Ann, Judy Ann, Michael, Samson, Ben. C., Wesley, Elizabeth, P. P., T. J., F. C., James H., and Sidney.

## THE WEEKS FAMILY

Other children of Michael and Judy Ann Weeks were: Charles, who married Phebe Harrell, this couple had children as follows: William C., Jane, Jim, Mike, Phebe, Martha, Betty, John, and Joe. The third son of Michael and Judy Ann Weeks was Thomas, who married Phoebe Robinson.

The fourth son of David Weeks married Frances Dawdry. To this couple were born the following children: Rosa, Seaborn, Jr., Daniel, Jane, David, and Benjamin.

The fifth son of Michael Weeks, was Seaborn Weeks, who married Nancy Harrell. Of this union there were the following children: Jane, John Taylor, F. M., Martha, Euphemia, Seaborn, and Laura.

Among the present generation of the Weeks family are the following well-known heads of families: Jim Weeks, John Weeks, Henry Weeks, David Weeks, Malley Weeks, Spenser Weeks, Montgomery Weeks, Wesley Weeks, John B. Weeks, Charley Weeks, Alex Weeks, John Weeks, Joe Weeks, Bob Weeks, Hardy Weeks, General Weeks, William Weeks, Stonewall Weeks, Grady Weeks, and D. C. Weeks. All these are mostly great-grandsons and great-great-grandsons of Michael Weeks. The Harrell clan were neighbors of the Weeks for two generations, and five of the Weeks men married Harrells, while at least one Harrell married a Weeks girl.

## Colquitt County Board of Education

| Name | Date of Comm'n |
|---|---|
| B. E. Watkins | May 5, 1871 |
| Henry Daniel | May 5, 1871 |
| John W. Luke, Sr. | May 5, 1871 |
| James J. Willis | May 5, 1871 |

                                Date of Election or Appointment

Henry Gay..............................May term, 1872 (for 4 yrs.)
Jared J. Gandy......................May term, 1872 (for 4 yrs.)
Samuel C. Gregory..............May term, 1872 (for 2 yrs.)
                (Died before qualifying)
James H. Daniels..................May term, 1872 (for 2 yrs.)
Henry G. Scott.......................May term, 1872 (for 2 yrs.)
John R. M. Linsey................May term, 1874 (for 4 yrs.)
John A. Alderman................May term, 1874 (for 4 yrs.)
Darlin Creed..........................May term, 1874 (for 4 yrs.)
       (Removed from county—S. P. Coon, successor)
S. P. Coon..............................................................March, 1875
                 (Removed from county)
John Tucker .........................Sept. term, 1876 (for 4 yrs.)
                  (Successor to Gay)
Miles Monk............................Sept. term, 1876 (for 4 yrs.)
                (Successor to Gandy)
Charles Hiers........................Sept. term, 1876 (for 4 yrs.)
                (Successor to Coon)

John Rhodes
William Branch
E. H. Bryan
Joshua S. Bryan
William McMullin

## COLQUITT COUNTY BOARD OF EDUCATION

|  | Date of Comm'n | Term Expired |
|---|---|---|
| Franklin Nelson | Apr. 14, 1885 | May, 1888 |
| M. M. Blanton | Apr. 14, 1885 | May, 1888 |
| E. H. Bryan | May 4, 1886 | May, 1890 |
| Joshua S. Bryan | Oct. 12, 1887 | May, 1890 |
| J. T. Hammond | Dec. 17, 1887 | May, 1890 |
| G. C. Laney | Feb. 8, 1889 | Next session of Grand Jury |
| M. M. Blanton | May 2, 1889 | May, 1892 |
| S. G. Gregory | Oct. 21, 1889 | (Declined) |
| H. T. Russ | Oct. 21, 1889 | May, 1894 |
| W. W. Robinson | Oct. 21, 1889 | May, 1894 |
| G. S. Nelson | Apr. 17, 1890 | May, 1894 |
| E. H. Bryan | Apr. 17, 1890 | May, 1892 |
| M. M. Blanton | May 2, 1893 | May, 1896 |
| James L. Hartsfield | May 2, 1893 | May, 1896 |
| G. S. Nelson | Apr. 11, 1894 | May, 1898 |
| J. A. Millsap | Apr. 11, 1894 | May, 1898 |
| J. J. Calhoun | Apr. 11, 1894 | May, 1898 (Resigned) |
| James W. Walters | July 30, 1896 | May, 1900 |
| James H. Scarboro | July 30, 1896 | May, 1900 (Resigned Dec. 4, 1900) |
| G. F. Clark | June 29, 1897 | May, 1898 |
| G. S. Nelson | Apr. 20, 1899 | May, 1902 |
| G. F. Clark | Apr. 20, 1899 | May, 1902 |
| W. G. Stovall | Apr. 20, 1899 | May, 1902 |
| Sam Gay | July 6, 1901 | June 4, 1904 (Declined) |
| James W. Walters | July 6, 1901 | May, 1904 |
| G. S. Nelson | Sept. 20, 1902 | May, 1906 |
| G. F. Clark | Sept. 20, 1902 | May, 1906 |

310  HISTORY OF COLQUITT COUNTY

|  | Date of Comm'n | Term Expired |
|---|---|---|
| C. B. Harrell | Sept. 20, 1902 | May, 1906 |
| Sam Gay | Apr. 17, 1909 | |
| John G. Norman | Apr. 17, 1909 | |
| Isaac Newton | Apr. 24, 1909 | |
| M. E. NeSmith | Apr. 18, 1910 | |
| D. S. Smith | Apr. 18, 1910 | |
| T. W. A. Womble | Apr. 18, 1910 | |
| Joseph A. Williams | May 9, 1913 | |
| W. T. Cooper | May 9, 1913 | |
| M. E. NeSmith | Feb. 17, 1914 | |
| David S. Smith | Feb. 17, 1914 | |
| Geo. W. Wilks | 1917 | |
| W. P. Sloan | 1919 | |
| John G. Norman | 1921 | |
| J. A. Summerlin | 1924 | |
| W. M. Turner | 1924 | |
| G. W. Newton | 1925 | |
| C. M. Edge | 1925 | |
| B. F. Folsom | 1926 | |
| E. E. Simmons | 1930 | |
| T. A. Dekle | 1932 | |
| T. W. Coleman | 1936 | |

## HISTORY OF COLQUITT COUNTY

## County School Commissioners

| NAME | DATE OF ELECTION |
|---|---|
| Dr. B. E. Watkins | Sept. 16, 1872 |
| Henry Gay | Dec. 16, 1876 |

| NAME | DATE OF COMMISSION | DATE OF EXPIRATION OF TERM |
|---|---|---|
| Henry Gay | Oct. 20, 1884 | June 4, 1888 |
| N. N. Marchant | Oct. 8, 1888 | June 4, 1892 |
| N. N. Marchant | June 1, 1892 | June 4, 1896 |
| N. N. Marchant | May 29, 1896 | June 4, 1900 |
| N. N. Marchant | March 30, 1900 | June 4, 1904 |
| J. H. Smithwick | July 1, 1904 | Nov. 22, 1904 |
| J. E. Howell | May 12, 1908 | |
| Lee S. Dismuke | Dec. 16, 1910 | |
| Mrs. Lee S. Dismuke | May, 1918 | July, 1918 |
| O. A. Thaxton | July, 1918 | Sept., 1920 |
| L. O. Rogers | Sept., 1920 | Jan., 1925 |
| F. G. Clark | Jan., 1925 | Jan., 1933 |
| L. O. Rogers | Jan., 1933 | |

## Congressional Representation of Colquitt County

### Congressional Districts

1st  Feb. 25, 1856-Mch. 23, 1861—(Acts 1855-56, p. 108).

2d  Mch. 23, 1861-Oct. 26, 1865—(Confederate Records I, p. 732; Code 1860, p. 12).

1st  Oct. 26, 1865-July 30, 1872—(Confederate Records IV, p. 146).

2d  July 30, 1872-date—(Acts 1872, p. 12).

### Members of Congress
#### U. S. A.

| District | Term of Service | Name | Post Office |
|---|---|---|---|
| 1st | Feb. 25, 1856-Mch. 3, 1857 | James L. Seward | Thomasville |
| 1st | Mch. 4, 1857-Mch. 3, 1859 | James L. Seward | Thomasville |
| 1st | Mch. 4, 1859-Jan. 23, 1861 | *Peter E. Love | Thomasville |

#### C. S. A. Provisional

| | | | |
|---|---|---|---|
| 1st | Feb. 4, 1861-Mch. 23, 1861 | Francis S. Bartow | Savannah |
| 2d | Mch. 23, 1861-Feb. 18, 1862 | Martin J. Crawford | Columbus |

#### C. S. A. Permanent

| | | | |
|---|---|---|---|
| 2d | Feb 18, 1862-Feb. 18, 1864 | Charles J. Munnerlyn | Bainbridge |
| 2d | Feb. 18, 1864-Overthrow | William E. Smith | Albany |

#### U. S. A.

| | | | |
|---|---|---|---|
| 1st | Dec. 15, 1865-Mch. 3, 1867 | †Solomon Cohen | Savannah |
| 1st | July 25, 1868-Mch. 3, 1869 | ‡Joseph W. Clift | Savannah |
| 1st | Jan. 23, 1871-Mch. 3, 1871 | ‡William W. Paine | Savannah |
| 1st | Mch. 4, 1871-July 30, 1872 | Archibald T. MacIntyre | Thomasville |
| 2d | July 30, 1872-Mch. 3, 1873 | Richard H. Whiteley | Bainbridge |
| 2d | Mch. 4, 1873-Mch. 3, 1875 | Richard H. Whiteley | Bainbridge |
| 2d | Mch. 4, 1875-Mch. 3, 1877 | William E. Smith | Albany |
| 2d | Mch. 4, 1877-Mch. 3, 1879 | William E. Smith | Albany |
| 2d | Mch. 4, 1879-Mch. 3, 1881 | William E. Smith | Albany |
| 2d | Mch. 4, 1881-Mch. 3, 1883 | Henry G. Turner | Quitman |
| 2d | Mch. 4, 1883-Mch. 3, 1885 | Henry G. Turner | Quitman |

## HISTORY OF COLQUITT COUNTY

| District | Term of Service | Name | Post Office |
|---|---|---|---|
| 2d | Mch. 4, 1885-Mch. 3, 1887 | Henry G. Turner | Quitman |
| 2d | Mch. 4, 1887-Mch. 3, 1889 | Henry G. Turner | Quitman |
| 2d | Mch. 4, 1889-Mch. 3, 1891 | Henry G. Turner | Quitman |
| 2d | Mch. 4, 1891-Mch. 3, 1893 | Henry G. Turner | Quitman |
| 2d | Mch. 4, 1893-Mch. 3, 1895 | Benjamin E. Russell | Bainbridge |
| 2d | Mch. 4, 1895-Mch. 3, 1897 | Benjamin E. Russell | Bainbridge |
| 2d | Mch. 4, 1897-Mch. 3, 1899 | James M. Griggs | Dawson |
| 2d | Mch. 4- 1899-Mch. 3, 1901 | James M. Griggs | Dawson |
| 2d | Mch. 4, 1901-Mch. 3, 1903 | James M. Griggs | Dawson |
| 2d | Mch. 4, 1903-Mch. 3, 1905 | James M. Griggs | Dawson |
| 2d | Mch. 4, 1905-Mch. 3, 1907 | James M. Griggs | Dawson |
| 2d | Mch. 4, 1907-Mch. 3, 1909 | James M. Griggs | Dawson |
| 2d | Mch. 4, 1909-Jan. 5, 1910 | **James M. Griggs | Dawson |
| 2d | Feb. 28, 1910-Mch. 3, 1911 | Seaborn A. Roddenbery | Thomasville |
| 2d | Mch. 4, 1911-Mch. 3, 1913 | Seaborn A. Roddenbery | Thomasville |
| 2d | Mch. 4, 1913-Sep. 25, 1913 | **Seaborn A. Roddenbery | Thomasville |
| 2d | Nov. 20, 1913-Mch. 3, 1915 | Frank Park | Sylvester |
| 2d | Mch. 4, 1915-Mch. 3, 1917 | Frank Park | Sylvester |
| 2d | Mch. 4, 1917-Mch. 3, 1919 | Frank Park | Sylvester |
| 2d | Mch. 4, 1919-Mch. 3, 1921 | Frank Park | Sylvester |
| 2d | Mch. 4, 1921-Mch. 3, 1923 | Frank Park | Sylvester |
| 2d | Mch. 4, 1923-Mch. 3, 1925 | Frank Park | Sylvester |
| 2d | Mch. 4, 1925-Mch. 3, 1927 | Edward Eugene Cox | Camilla |
| 2d | Mch. 4, 1927-Mch. 3, 1929 | Edward Eugene Cox | Camilla |
| 2d | Mch. 4, 1929-Mch. 3, 1931 | Edward Eugene Cox | Camilla |
| 2d | Mch. 4, 1931-Mch. 3, 1933 | Edward Eugene Cox | Camilla |
| 2d | Mch. 4, 1933-Jan. 3, 1935 | Edward Eugene Cox | Camilla |
| 2d | Jan. 3, 1935- | Edward Eugene Cox | Camilla |

*Withdrew.
**Died.
†Commissioned; not seated.
‡Took his seat.

### Roster of Colquitt County's Representatives in the House of Representatives of Georgia

1857- 8-   —Henry Gay.
1859-60-   —Henry Gay.
1861- 2- 3—Ex. Henry Gay.

314    HISTORY OF COLQUITT COUNTY

1863- 4- 5—Ex. J. W. Wells.
1865- 6- 7—Willis W. Watkins.
1868- 9-70—Ex. Willis W. Watkins.
1871- 2- 3—Adj. Isaac Carlton.
1873- 4- —John Tucker.
1875- 6- —J. B. Norman, Sr.
1877- —James Vick.
1879- —Adj. James Vick.
1880- 1- —Adj. M. B. McClellan.
1882- 3- —Ex. Ann. Adj. John Tucker.
1884- 5- —Adj. A. D. Watkins.
1886- 7- —Adj. George F. Newton.
1888- 9- —Adj. John A. Alderman.
1890- 1- —Adj. J. M. Odom.
1892- 3- —J. B. Norman, Jr.
1894- 5- —George F. Newton.
1896- 7- —Adj. G. G. Henderson.
1898- 9- —Sam Gay.
1900- 1- —Robt. L. Shipp.
1902- 3- 4—George W. Newton.
1905- 6- —William A. Covington.
1907- 8- —Ex. William A. Covington.
1909-10- —J. M. Walters.
1911-12- —Ex. J. H. Hiers.
1913-14- —John A. Carlton.
1915-16-17—Ex. Robert L. Shipp.
1917-18- —M. E. NeSmith.
1919-20- —William A. Covington.
1921-22- —Richard J. Lewis, R. G. Clark. (Aug. 31, 1912.)
1923-24- —Ex. Robert L. Norman, William A. Covington.
1925-26- —Richard J. Lewis, Hoyt H. Whelchel.
1927-28- —R. L. Moore, J. L. Dowling.
1929-30- —L. L. Moore, John C. Parker.
1931-32- —T. W. Mattox, W. A. Sutton.
1933-34- —John C. Parker, W. A. Sutton.
1935-36- —John C. Parker, Jason Shirah.
1937-38- —John C. Parker, John Barlow.

# HISTORY OF COLQUITT COUNTY

## State Senators---Colquitt County

COLQUITT COUNTY has been in the following Senatorial Districts:

.Feb. 25, 1856-July 2, 1861—Colquitt County.
July 2, 1861-Nov. 5, 1918—7th District.
Nov. 5, 1918-Date—47th District.

### COLQUITT COUNTY
### Created Feb. 25, 1856

| | |
|---|---|
| 1857-58 | Amos Turner |
| 1859-60 | John Tillman |

### SEVENTH DISTRICT

| | |
|---|---|
| 1861-62-63 Ex. | James L. Seward |
| 1863-64 Ex.-64-65 Ex. | C. E. Groover |
| 1865-66-66 | Benning B. Moore |
| 1868 Ex.-69-70 Ex. | M. C. Smith (Rev.) |
| 1871-72-72 Adj. | William L. Clark |
| 1873-74 | William L. Clark |
| 1875-76 | James McDonald |
| 1877 | James McDonald |
| 1878-79 Adj. | James Pate Turner |
| 1880-81 Adj. | Elijah Peck Smith Denmark |
| 1882-83 Ex.-83 Ann. Adj. | Jeremiah Bryant Norman |
| 1884-85 Adj. | Robert Goodwin Mitchell, I |
| 1886-87 Adj. | Thomas J. Livingston |
| 1888-89 Adj. | James Vick |
| 1890-91 Adj. | Robert Goodwin Mitchell, I |
| 1892-93 | W. S. Humphries |
| 1894-95 | J. B. Norman, Jr. |
| 1896-97 Adj.-97 | Henry William Hopkins |
| 1898-99 | W. S. Humphries |
| 1900-01 | J. B. Norman |
| 1902-03-04 | Henry William Hopkins |
| 1905-06 | Stanley S. Bennet |
| 1907-08-08 Ex. | J. A. Wilkes |

1909..................................................Jesse S. Ward, Jr. (died 3/8/10)
1910..................................................R. S. Burch
1911-12 Ex.-12.................................L. C. Graham
1913-14..............................................S. Morton Turner
1915-15 Ex.-16-17 Ex.....................John A. Carlton
1917-18..............................................Henry William Hopkins

### Forty-Seventh District
Created Aug. 17, 1918 (Constitutional Amendment)

1919..................................................T. H. Parker (died)
1920..................................................M. M. Kendall
1921-22..............................................Robert Cothran Ellis
1923-23 Ex.-24.................................John Henry Adams
1925-26 Ex.-26 2d Ex.....................Robert L. Norman
1927..................................................E. P. Bowen
1929-31 Ex.........................................Reason Paulk
1931..................................................Lammie Lamar Moore
1933..................................................Mrs. Susan T. Moore
1935..................................................C. Z. Harden
1937..................................................W. H. Sutton

## CLERKS OF THE SUPERIOR COURT

| Name | Date of Commission |
|---|---|
| William McLeod | March 28, 1856 |
| William McLeod | Jan. 13, 1858 |
| Amos Turner | Jan. 10, 1860 |
| Amos Turner | Jan. 24, 1862 |
| Amos Turner | Feb. 16, 1864 |
| Amos Turner | Jan. 22, 1866 |
| Elkanah Johnson | May 10, 1866 |
| C. W. Haynes | Feb. 7, 1871 |
| A. Turner | Jan. 24, 1873 |
| A. D. Patterson | Jan. 15, 1875 |
| A. D. Patterson | Jan. 20, 1877 |
| A. D. Patterson | Jan. 10, 1879 |

| Name | Date of Commission |
|---|---|
| A. D. Patterson | Jan. 12, 1881 |
| A. D. Patterson | Jan. 15, 1883 |
| E. H. Bryan | Jan. 13, 1885 |
| E. H. Bryan | Jan. 11, 1887 |
| E. H. Bryan | Jan. 8, 1889 |
| E. H. Bryan | Jan. 13, 1891 |
| G. W. Newton | Jan. 10, 1893 |
| G. W. Newton | Jan. 9, 1895 |
| G. W. Newton | Oct. 14, 1896 |
| G. G. Henderson | Oct. 20, 1898 |
| R. G. Clark, | Qualified Nov. 27, 1900; date of commission not given. |
| R. G. Clark | Oct. 10, 1902 |
| R. G. Clark | Oct. 17, 1904 |
| R. G. Clark | Nov. 1, 1906 |
| R. G. Clark | Nov. 3, 1908 |
| R. G. Clark | Nov. 5, 1910 |
| R. G. Clark | Oct. 19, 1912 |
| R. G. Clark | Nov. 30, 1914 |
| R. G. Clark | Dec. 4, 1916 |
| Ashley NeSmith | Dec. 9, 1920 |
| Joe N. Horne | Dec. 4, 1924 |
| Joe N. Horne | Dec. 5, 1928 |
| Joe N. Horne | Dec. 1, 1932 |

## CORONERS

| Name | Date of Commission |
|---|---|
| Elijah Tillman | March 28, 1856 |
| Wright Flowers | Jan. 13, 1858 |
| Joseph Castleberry | Jan. 24, 1862 |
| S. Mercer | Feb. 16, 1864 |
| Hardy Carlton | Jan. 22, 1866 |

## HISTORY OF COLQUITT COUNTY

| Name | Date of Commission |
|---|---|
| Hardy Carlton | Aug. 22, 1868 |
| Hardy Carlton | Feb. 7, 1871 |
| Hardy Carlton | Jan. 24, 1873 |
| Hardy Carlton (Resigned April 8, 1876) | Jan. 15, 1875 |
| James W. Pyles (Appointed by ordinary) | June 10, 1876 |
| J. D. Roberson (Declined) | Jan. 20, 1877 |
| John J. Scott | Jan. 10, 1879 |
| E. Gregory | Jan. 12, 1881 |
| E. Gregory | Jan. 15, 1883 |
| B. F. Marchant | Jan. 13, 1885 |
| M. C. Norman | Jan. 11, 1887 |
| Moses Norman | Jan. 8, 1889 |
| A. J. Twitty | Jan. 13, 1891 |
| William R. Key | Jan. 10, 1893 |
| P. J. Poppell | Jan. 9, 1895 |
| E. L. Akins | Oct. 14, 1896 |
| E. L. Akins | Oct. 20, 1898 |
| J. A. Barber, | Qualified Dec. 23, 1900; date of commission not given. |
| J. A. Barber | Oct. 10, 1902 |
| John Barber | Oct. 17, 1904 |
| J. E. Holland | Nov. 1, 1906 |
| W. E. Dyke | Nov. 3, 1908 |
| W. E. Dyke | Nov. 5, 1910 |
| W. E. Dyke | Oct. 14, 1912 |
| W. E. Dyke | Nov. 30, 1914 |
| J. A. Barber | Dec. 4, 1916 |
| J. A. Barber | Dec. 9, 1920 |
| J. A. Barber | 1924 |
| J. A. Barber | 1928 |
| J. A. Barber | 1932 |
| F. A. White (Appointed) | Mar. 2, 1935 |

# Colquitt County
(Created Feb. 25, 1856)

## JUSTICES OF THE INFERIOR COURT
(Four-Year Terms)

| | |
|---|---|
| Abraham Strickland | March 28, 1856-Jan. 12, 1857 |
| Philip Hiers | March 28, 1856-1856 |
| John Gregory | March 28, 1856-Jan. 12, 1857 |
| Nathaniel Giles | March 28, 1856-Jan. 12, 1857 |
| James W. Getty | March 28, 1856-Jan. 12, 1857 |
| Daniel O. Saffold | Aug. 13, 1856-Jan. 12, 1857 |
| Abraham Strickland | Jan. 12, 1857-1858 |
| James W. Getty | Jan. 12, 1857-1859 |
| Nathaniel Giles | Jan. 12, 1857-Jan. 10, 1861 |
| Daniel O. Saffold | Jan. 12, 1857-Jan. 10, 1861 |
| James M. Norman | Jan. 12, 1857-1860 |
| Linton Carlton | May 5, 1858-Jan. 10, 1861 |
| Henry Scott | Aug. 8, 1859-Jan. 10, 1861 |
| George W. Tucker | April 9, 1860-Jan. 10, 1861 |
| John G. Coleman | Jan. 10, 1861-1862 |
| Jeremiah Bryant Norman | Jan. 10, 1861-Jan. 23, 1865 |
| Linton Carlton | Jan. 10, 1861-1862 |
| Henry Gay | Jan. 10, 1861-Jan. 23, 1865 |
| James Robinson | Jan. 10, 1861-Jan. 23, 1865 |
| James Douglass | Jan. 25, 1862-1863 |
| Thomas F. Hampton | Feb. 7, 1862-1864 |
| George W. Tucker | March 11, 1863-Jan. 23, 1865 |
| Elijah Tillman | March 4, 1864-1864 |
| James Murphy | March 26, 1864-Jan. 23, 1865 |
| Jeremiah Bryant Norman | Jan. 23, 1865-1868 |
| Elijah Tillman | Jan. 23, 1865-1868 |
| James Murphy | Jan. 23, 1865-1868 |
| George W. Tucker | Jan. 23, 1865-1868 |
| Absalom Baker | Jan. 23, 1865-1868 |

Office abolished by Constitution of 1868.

## ORDINARIES

| Name | Date of Commission |
|---|---|
| Hardy Chastain | March 28, 1856 |
| Peter O. Wing | May 5, 1858 |
| Peter O. Wing | Jan. 10, 1860 |
| J. Carlton | Feb. 16, 1864 |
| James T. J. Cooper | Feb. 14, 1872 |
| Job Turner, | |
| (Ex. Dept. series gives date as Jan. 24, 1873) | Jan. 18, 1873 |
| Henry Gay | Jan. 20, 1877 |
| Henry Gay | Jan. 12, 1881 |
| Henry Gay | Jan. 13, 1885 |
| Henry Gay | Jan. 8, 1889 |
| S. G. Gregory, | |
| (Ex. Dept. series gives date as Jan. 28, 1890) | Feb. 19, 1890 |
| S. G. Gregory | Jan. 10, 1893 |
| S. G. Gregory | Oct. 14, 1896 |
| S. G. Gregory, | |
| Qualified April 1, 1900; date of commission not given. | |
| T. H. Parker | Oct. 17, 1904 |
| T. H. Parker | Nov. 10, 1908 |
| A. B. Buxton | Oct. 19, 1912 |
| A. B. Buxton | Dec. 4, 1916 |
| R. A. Cooper | Oct. 24, 1917 |
| R. A. Cooper | Dec. 9, 1920 |
| T. E. Lewis | Dec. 29, 1932 |

## SHERIFFS

| Name | Date of Commission |
|---|---|
| Jacob F. Reichert | March 28, 1856 |
| Darlin Creed | Feb. 10, 1858 |
| Jacob F. Reichert | Jan. 10, 1860 |
| Hiram Gay | March 16, 1861 |
| John Selph | Jan. 24, 1862 |
| John Sloan | Feb. 16, 1864 |

## SHERIFFS

| Name | Date of Commission |
|---|---|
| John Sloan | Jan. 22, 1866 |
| Richard Tucker | May 10, 1866 |
| R. J. Norman | Aug. 22, 1868 |
| Thomas R. Foyster | Feb. 7, 1871 |
| J. T. Register (Declined) | Jan. 24, 1873 |
| W. T. Robinson (Resigned) | May 2, 1873 |
| John Sloan | Dec. 5, 1873 |
| John Sloan | Jan. 15, 1875 |
| J. B. Norman | Jan. 20, 1877 |
| J. B. Norman | Jan. 10, 1879 |
| J. K. Frasier | Jan. 12, 1881 |
| J. T. Register | Jan. 15, 1883 |
| J. T. Register (Removed Dec. 18, 1885) | Jan. 13, 1885 |
| D. T. English | Jan. 8, 1886 |
| Sam Gay | Jan. 11, 1887 |
| Franklin Wilson (Resigned Nov. 21, 1890) | Jan. 8, 1889 |
| G. W. Newton | Jan. 13, 1891 |
| T. B. Sharp | Jan. 10, 1893 |
| J. S. Fisher | Jan. 9, 1895 |
| J. S. Fisher | Oct. 14, 1896 |
| J. S. Fisher (Resigned Oct. 2, 1900) | Oct. 20, 1898 |
| David or Daniel Murphy, Sr., | |
| Qualified Dec. 31, 1900; date of commission not given. | |
| David Murphey | Oct. 10, 1902 |
| J. A. Campbell | Oct. 17, 1904 |
| J. A. Collier | Nov. 1, 1906 |
| W. W. Boyd | Nov. 3, 1908 |
| W. W. Boyd | Nov. 5, 1910 |
| W. W. Boyd | Oct. 12, 1912 |
| W. W. Boyd | Nov. 30, 1914 |
| W. W. Boyd | Dec. 4, 1916 |
| T. V. Beard | Dec. 9, 1920 |

## HISTORY OF COLQUITT COUNTY

| NAME | DATE OF COMMISSION |
|---|---|
| T. V. Beard | Dec. 9, 1924 |
| T. V. Beard | Dec. 4, 1928 |
| T. V. Beard | Dec. 1, 1932 |

### SURVEYORS

| | |
|---|---|
| Amos Turner | March 28, 1856 |
| Robert N. McLin | Jan. 13, 1858 |
| Samuel C. Gregory | Jan. 10, 1860 |
| Samuel C. Gregory | Jan. 24, 1862 |
| H. Gay | Feb. 16, 1864 |
| P. B. Monk | Jan. 22, 1866 |
| Samuel C. Gregory | May 10, 1866 |
| Samuel C. Gregory | Aug. 22, 1868 |
| W. Costin | (Declined) Feb. 7, 1871 |
| John S. Harrell | Jan. 24, 1873 |
| P. U. Sineath | Jan. 15, 1875 |
| Mathew Tucker | Jan. 20, 1877 |
| Mathew Tucker | Jan. 10, 1879 |
| Mathew Tucker | Jan. 12, 1881 |
| Mathew Tucker | Jan. 15, 1883 |
| Mathew Tucker | Jan. 13, 1885 |
| Mathew Tucker | Jan. 11, 1887 |
| Mathew Tucker | Jan. 8, 1889 |
| W. W. Roberson | Jan. 13, 1891 |
| Mathew Tucker | Jan. 10, 1893 |
| Mathew Tucker | Jan. 9, 1895 |
| Mathew Tucker | Oct. 14, 1896 |
| Mathew Tucker | Oct. 20, 1898 |

Mathew Tucker,
    Qualified Dec. 27, 1900; date of commission not given.

| | |
|---|---|
| Mathew Tucker | Oct. 10, 1902 |
| J. S. Robinson | Oct. 17, 1904 |
| J. S. Robinson | Nov. 1, 1906 |

HISTORY OF COLQUITT COUNTY 323

| Name | Date of Commission |
|---|---|
| J. S. Robinson | Nov. 3, 1908 |
| J. S. Turner | Nov. 5, 1910 |
| J. S. Turner | Oct. 14, 1912 |
| O. H. Long | Nov. 30, 1914 |
| O. H. Long | Dec. 4, 1916 |
| John M. Norman | Dec. 9, 1920 |

## TAX COLLECTORS

| | |
|---|---|
| Job Turner | March 28, 1856 |
| Job Turner | Jan. 12, 1857 |
| Job Turner | Jan. 13, 1858 |
| Solomon P. Mims | Jan. 10, 1859 |
| Darlin Creed | Jan. 10, 1860 |
| Darlin Creed | Jan. 10, 1861 |
| Darlin Creed | March 1, 1862 |
| Darlin Creed | Feb. 16, 1864 |
| William H. H. Norman | March 8, 1866 |
| W. H. H. Norman | Aug. 22, 1868 |
| S. C. Gregory | Feb. 7, 1871 |
| S. C. Gregory (Ousted) | Jan. 24, 1873 |
| C. C. Walters | Jan. 15, 1875 |
| W. H. H. Norman | Jan. 20, 1877 |
| George F. Newton | Jan. 10, 1879 |
| G. T. Newton | Jan. 12, 1881 |
| G. F. Newton | Jan. 15, 1883 |
| G. F. Newton (Resigned Sept. 23, 1886) | Jan. 13, 1885 |
| W. Croft | Jan. 11, 1887 |
| William N. Croft | Jan. 8, 1889 |
| M. S. Cheshire | Jan. 20, 1891 |
| J. G. Truluck | Jan. 10, 1893 |
| G. G. Truluck | Jan. 9, 1895 |
| J. C. May | Oct. 14, 1896 |
| J. L. Hartsfield | Oct. 20, 1898 |

## HISTORY OF COLQUITT COUNTY

NAME | DATE OF COMMISSION

J. L. Hartsfield,
    Qualified Dec. 31, 1900; date of commission not given.
J. L. Hartsfield..................................................Oct. 10, 1902
P. F. Hutchinson................................................Oct. 17, 1904
W. H. Gibson.....................................................Nov. 1, 1906
W. H. Gibson.....................................................Nov. 3, 1908
W. H. Gibson.....................................................Nov. 5, 1910
W. H. Gibson..........................................(Died) Oct. 18, 1912
Henry Murphy....................................................Jan. 19, 1914
W. H. Murphy...................................................Nov. 16, 1914
W. H. Murphy....................................................Dec. 4, 1916
W. H. Murphy....................................................Dec. 9, 1920
W. H. Murphy....................................................Dec. 6, 1924
W. H. Murphy....................................................Dec. 1, 1928
W. H. Murphy....................................................Dec. 1, 1932

## TAX RECEIVERS

John A. Alderman..........................................March 28, 1856
John A. Alderman...........................................Jan. 12, 1857
John A. Alderman...........................................Jan. 13, 1858
John A. Alderman...........................................Jan. 10, 1859
John Tucker.....................................................Jan. 10, 1860
John Tucker.....................................................Jan. 10, 1861
Darlin Creed...................................................March 1, 1862
J. J. Norman....................................................Feb. 16, 1864
John Tucker...................................................March 8, 1866
John Sloan......................................................Aug. 22, 1868
R. Tucker.........................................................Feb. 7, 1871
R. Tucker.........................................................Jan. 24, 1873
J. A. Alderman................................................Jan. 15, 1875
John Owens.....................................................Jan. 20, 1877
George F. Newton............................................Jan. 10, 1879
Daniel Cooper.................................................Jan. 12, 1881
Daniel S. Cooper.............................................Jan. 15, 1883

## HISTORY OF COLQUITT COUNTY

| Name | Date of Commission |
|---|---|
| Daniel Cooper | Jan. 13, 1885 |
| D. S. Cooper | Jan. 11, 1887 |
| D. S. Cooper | Jan. 8, 1889 |
| G. F. Clark | Jan. 13, 1891 |
| G. F. Clark | Jan. 10, 1893 |
| J. C. Curles | Jan. 9, 1895 |
| J. C. Curles | Oct. 14, 1896 |
| J. A. Wilkes | Oct. 20, 1898 |
| J. J. Wilkes......Qualified Jan. 1, 1900; date of commission not given. | |
| M. E. NeSmith | Oct. 10, 1902 |
| G. W. Rhodes | Oct. 17, 1904 |
| G. W. Rhodes | Nov. 1, 1906 |
| J. S. Simmons | Nov. 3, 1908 |
| W. J. Perry | Nov. 5, 1910 |
| W. J. Perry | Oct. 17, 1912 |
| J. R. O. Lindsey | Nov. 16, 1914 |
| J. R. O. Lindsey | Dec. 4, 1916 |
| Shelton Sharp | Dec. 9, 1920 |

## TREASURERS

| | |
|---|---|
| Mathew Tucker | May 10, 1866 |
| Mathew Tucker | Feb. 7, 1871 |
| Mathew C. Dukes | Jan. 24, 1873 |
| Mathew Tucker | Jan. 15, 1875 |
| R. Bearden | Jan. 20, 1877 |
| Richard J. Norman | Jan. 10, 1879 |
| R. J. Norman | Jan. 12, 1881 |
| E. H. Bryan | Jan. 15, 1883 |
| M. M. Blanton | Jan. 13, 1885 |
| J. D. Barber | Jan. 11, 1887 |
| L. H. Hall | June 6, 1888 |
| M. M. Blanton | Jan. 8, 1889 |
| M. M. Blanton | Jan. 13, 1891 |
| John A. Tillman | Jan. 10, 1893 |

| Name | Date of Commission |
|---|---|
| John A. Tillman, Sr. | Jan. 9, 1895 |
| J. G. Culpepper | Oct. 14, 1896 |
| J. G. Culpepper | Oct. 20, 1898 |
| J. G. Culpepper, Qualified Nov. 24, 1900; date of commission not given. | |
| J. A. Milsap | Oct. 10, 1902 |
| J. G. Culpepper | Dec. 10, 1903 |
| Miles Monk, Jr. | Oct. 17, 1904 |
| John A. Barber | Nov. 1, 1906 |
| John A. Barber | Nov. 3, 1908 |
| Wright Murphy | Nov. 5, 1910 |
| Wright Murphy | Oct. 16, 1912 |
| Wright Murphy | Nov. 30, 1914 |
| Wright Murphy | Dec. 4, 1916 |
| Ward Murphy | Dec. 17, 1918 |
| W. E. Dyke | Dec. 9, 1920 |

## MAYORS AND CLERKS OF THE CITY OF MOULTRIE FROM 1893 TO 1937

| | |
|---|---|
| 1893- | —M. M. Blanton, Mayor; W. W. Robinson, Clerk. |
| 1894- 5- | —R. L. Shipp, Mayor; W. H. Cooper, Clerk. |
| 1895- | —B. P. Crenshaw, Mayor; W. H. Spivey, Clerk. |
| 1897- | —B. P. Crenshaw, Mayor; S. L. Lyles, Clerk. |
| 1898- | —J. G. Culpepper, Mayor; I. M. Autrey, Clerk. |
| 1899- | —C. E. Holmes, Mayor; J. F. Monk, Clerk. |
| 1900- | —C. E. Holmes, Mayor; J. F. Monk, Clerk. |
| 1901- | —B. P. Crenshaw, Mayor; C. L. Austin, Clerk. |
| 1902- | —B. P. Crenshaw, Mayor; C. L. Austin, Clerk. |
| 1903- | —P. B. Allen, Mayor; C. L. Austin, Clerk. |
| 1904- 5- | —J. F. Monk, Mayor; J. H. Scarborough, Clerk. |
| 1906- | —W. D. Scott, Mayor; H. E. Parrish, Clerk. |
| 1907- | —J. F. Monk, Mayor; J. H. Scarborough, Clerk. |
| 1908- 9- | —W. D. Scott, Mayor; J. H. Scarborough, Clerk. |
| 1910-11- | —C. E. Holmes, Mayor; J. H. Scarborough, Clerk. |
| 1912-13- | —W. C. Vereen, Mayor; J. H. Scarborough, Clerk. |
| 1913-14- | —George R. Kline, Mayor; J. H. Scarborough, Clerk. |

HISTORY OF COLQUITT COUNTY

1915-16- —W. J. Vereen, Mayor; J. H. Scarborough, Clerk.
1917-18- —W. A. Covington, Mayor; J. H. Scarborough, Clerk.
1919-20-21—J. S. Johnson, Mayor; J. H. Scarborough, Clerk.
1921-22-23—W. A. Covington, Mayor; G. A. Shaver, Clerk.
1923-25- —Howard Ashburn, Mayor Unexpired Term W. A. Covington; G. A. Shaver, Clerk.
1926-27- —P. Q. Bryan, Mayor; G. A. Shaver, Clerk.
1928-29- —P. Q. Bryan, Mayor; G. A. Shaver, Clerk.
1930-31- —C. G. Watson, Mayor; G. A. Shaver, Clerk.
1932-33- —C. G. Watson, Mayor; G. A. Shaver, Clerk.
1934-35- —J. Frank Norman, Mayor; G. A. Shaver, Clerk.
1936-37- —J. F. Norman, Mayor; G. A. Shaver, Clerk.

## Professional Men of Colquitt County

### Attorneys

L. L. Moore, Waldo DeLoache, P. Q. Bryan, Hoyt Whelchel, John T. Coyle, Philip Covington, Robert Humphreys, James Humphreys, W. A. Covington, John T. Parker, Robert Cranford, W. B. Withers, P. D. Hartsfield, Emmet Edwards, William Riddlespurger, R. E. Cheshire, Jr., M. L. Bivins, Hugh Aderhold, T. W. Maddox.

### Dentists

T. P. Tison, W. S. Pierce, W. G. Hitchcock, R. E. L. Pattillo, R. H. Rogers, J. H. Killibrew, W. F. Blasingame.

### Physicians

Everett Daniel, C. C. Fletcher, J. E. Lanier, C. M. Hitchcock, C. C. Brannen, H. T. Edmundson, C. L. Bennett, E. L. Lawson, T. H. Chestnut, James R. Paulk, A. G. Funderburk, R. M. Joiner, W. R. McGinty, S. M. Withers, C. B. Slocumb, J. C. Stone, H. M. Megee, H. H. Trimble (Osteopath), C. L. Dean (Chiropractor), Lynwood Riddlespurger (Chiropractor), J. B. Woodall.

## HISTORY OF COLQUITT COUNTY

### Justices of the Peace

| Name | Dist. | Date of Com'n | Date Succeeded |
|---|---|---|---|
| Richard B. Gregory | 799 | May 20, 1856 | Jan. 27, 1857 |
| Josiah Johnson | 799 | May 20, 1856 | Jan. 27, 1857 |
| James Robinson | 1020 | June 28, 1856 | Jan. 27, 1857 |
| Flournoy Clark | 1020 | June 28, 1856 | Jan. 27, 1857 |
| James M. Norman | 1151 | Aug. 2, 1856 | Jan. 27, 1857 |
| James NeSmith | 1151 | Aug. 2, 1856 | Jan. 27, 1857 |
| Harman Matthis | 1151 | Jan. 27, 1857 | Mch. 22, 1858 |
| Henry F. Mabbett | 1151 | Jan. 27, 1857 | Feb. 20, 1860 |
| Hardin Hancock | 799 | Jan. 27, 1857 | Jan. 21, 1858 |
| John Sloan Seigner | 799 | Jan. 27, 1857 | Jan. 21, 1858 |
| Flournoy Clark | 1020 | Jan. 27, 1857 | |
| James Robinson | 1020 | Jan. 27, 1857 | |
| James R. Alger | 799 | Jan. 21, 1858 | Feb. 4, 1860 |
| John Tucker | 799 | Jan. 21, 1858 | Feb. 4, 1860 |
| John W. Fulwood | 1151 | Mch. 22, 1858 | Mch. 11, 1859 |
| Seaborn Weekes | 1184 | Dec. 21, 1858 | |
| Durham Handcock | 1020 | Jan. 1, 1859 | |
| Jonathan M. Dukes | 1151 | Mch. 11, 1859 | Sept. 22, 1859 |
| James M. Savage | 1151 | Sept. 22, 1859 | Feb. 20, 1860 |
| James R. Alger | 799 | Feb. 4, 1860 | |
| Daniel Bustle | 799 | Feb. 4, 1860 | |
| James M. Norman | 1151 | Feb. 20, 1860 | |
| Mathew Tucker | 1151 | Feb. 20, 1860 | |
| J. M. Norman | 1151 | Jan. 16, 1861 | Jan. 28, 1865 |
| James Brown | 1151 | Jan. 16, 1861 | Mch. 15, 1862 |
| Hardin Hancock, Sr. | 799 | Jan. 16, 1861 | Jan. 27, 1862 |
| A. P. Hutchison | 799 | Jan. 16, 1861 | Jan. 27, 1862 |
| J. A. Alderman | 1020 | Jan. 16, 1861 | Mch. 28, 1863 |
| J. W. Wells | 1020 | Jan. 16, 1861 | Mch. 28, 1863 |
| Flournoy Clark | 1184 | Mch. 21, 1861 | Jan. 28, 1865 |
| Seaborn Weekes | 1184 | Mch. 21, 1861 | Jan. 28, 1865 |
| James B. Hancock | 799 | Jan. 27, 1862 | Nov. 11, 1862 |
| James R. Alger | 799 | Jan. 27, 1862 | Nov. 11, 1862 |
| R. J. (S.) Marlow | 1151 | Mch. 15, 1862 | Jan. 28, 1865 |
| John Tucker | 799 | Nov. 11, 1862 | Jan. 28, 1865 |
| Wiley N. Holland | 799 | Nov. 11, 1862 | Jan. 28, 1865 |
| Charles H. Johnson | 1020 | Mch. 28, 1863 | May 4, 1864 |
| William Russell | 1020 | Mch. 28, 1863 | Jan. 28, 1865 |

## HISTORY OF COLQUITT COUNTY 329

### JUSTICES OF THE PEACE

| Name | Dist. | Date of Com'n | Date Succeeded |
|---|---|---|---|
| John Robinson | 1020 | May 4, 1864 | Jan. 28, 1865 |
| Robert Bearden | 1151 | Jan. 28, 1865 | |
| W. J. Alderman | 1020 | Jan. 28, 1865 | Mch. 20, 1866 |
| J. W. Giles | 1151 | Jan. 28, 1865 | |
| C. A. Hiers | 1020 | Jan. 28, 1865 | Mch. 20, 1866 |
| Hardin Hancock | 799 | Jan. 28, 1865 | |
| John Tucker | 799 | Jan. 28, 1865 | June 20, 1866 |
| Seaborn Weekes | 1184 | Jan. 28, 1865 | |
| Flournoy Clark | 1184 | Jan. 28, 1865 | |
| James Robinson | 1020 | Mch. 20, 1866 | |
| William W. Burgess | 1020 | Mch. 20, 1866 | |
| Josiah Johnson | 799 | June 20 1866 | |
| Daniel F. Luke | 799 | May 1, 1869 | (Resigned Sept. 1870) |
| James Gay | 1151 | May 1, 1869 | |
| Worthy Martin | 1020 | Feb. 15, 1871 | |
| Joe Ruchtey | 799 | Feb. 15, 1871 | |
| John S. Harrell | 1184 | May 9, 1872 | |
| J. Richter | 799 | Jan. 22, 1873 | (Resigned May 8 1875) |
| Owen Gregory | 1151 | Jan. 22, 1873 | |
| G. F. Cooper | 1020 | Jan. 22, 1873 | |
| Absalom Baker | 1184 | June 2, 1873 | (Resigned Mch. 8 1875) |
| Franklin J. Walker | 1020 | July 20, 1874 | (Declined) |
| George W. Hooker | 1020 | Oct. 16, 1874 | |
| Henry L. Pollock | 1184 | Mch 15, 1875 | (Removed Dec. 1, 1875) |
| R. Tucker | 799 | Aug. 31, 1875 | |
| Seaborn Weekes | 1184 | Dec. 27, 1875 | |
| George W. Hooker | 1020 | Jan. 30, 1877 | |
| Randal N. Folsom | 1184 | Jan. 30, 1877 | |
| Richard Tucker | 799 | Jan. 30, 1877 | |
| Owen Gregory | 1151 | Jan. 30, 1877 | |
| G. W. Hooker | 1020 | Jan. 24, 1881 | |
| J. F. Cooper | 1151 | Jan. 29, 1881 | |
| Seaborn Weekes | 1184 | Mch. 2, 1881 | |
| Richard Tucker | 799 | Mch. 2, 1881 | |
| Eli Clark | 1373 | May 17, 1884 | |
| H. B. Lawson | 1374 | May 26 1884 | |
| A. J. Strickland | 1151 | Jan. 22 1885 | |
| M. J. Horn, Sr. | 1373 | Jan. 22, 1885 | |

## Justices of the Peace

| Name | Dist. | Date of Com'n | Date Succeeded |
|---|---|---|---|
| William T. Robinson | 1020 | Jan. 22, 1885 | |
| W. W. Hawkins | 1374 | Jan. 22, 1885 | (Resigned Apr. 7, 1885) |
| James J. Willis | 1374 | Feb. 17, 1886 | |
| W. T. Robinson | 1020 | Jan. 23, 1889 | |
| W. R. Stallings | 1151 | Jan. 23, 1889 | |
| M. J. Horn | 1373 | Jan. 23, 1889 | (Resigned Mch. 14, 1891) |
| R. Tucker | 799 | Jan. 23, 1889 | |
| J. J. Keigans | 1184 | Jan. 23, 1889 | |
| G. F. Clark | 1374 | Jan. 26, 1889 | (Resigned Jan. 23, 1891) |
| G. W. Hooker | 1020 | May 8, 1890 | |
| J. J. Wilkes | 1445 | July 3, 1891 | |
| T. G. (J.) Lindsey | 1374 | July 3, 1891 | |
| D. A. Mashburn | 1393 | July 6, 1891 | |
| Jacob Shiver | 1482 | Mch. 18, 1892 | |
| T. B. Sharp | 1184 | Apr. 18, 1892 | |
| J. C. Curles | 1020 | July 28, 1892 | |
| G. W. Rolan | 799 | Jan. 25, 1893 | |
| Daniel Burney | 1020 | Jan. 25, 1893 | |
| J. W. Strickland | 1151 | Jan. 25, 1893 | |
| Isaac Horn | 1373 | Jan. 25, 1893 | |
| J. J. Wilkes | 1445 | Jan. 25, 1893 | |
| Jacob Shiver | 1482 | Jan. 25, 1893 | |
| J. D. Hartsfield | 1510 | Nov. 4, 1893 | |
| W. W. Baker | 1374 | Jan. 16, 1894 | |
| G. W. Hooker | 1151 | Feb. 4, 1895 | |
| J. E. Crawford | 1184 | Feb. 4, 1895 | |
| J. W. Taylor | 1538 | July 6, 1896 | (Resigned Nov. 4, 1897) |
| G. W. Hooker | 1151 | Jan. 12, 1897 | |
| W. J. Rhodes | 1549 | Jan. 12, 1897 | |
| J. H. Young | 1184 | Jan. 12, 1897 | |
| F. J. Walker | 1020 | Jan. 12, 1897 | (Resigned Jan. 19, 1899) |
| J. S. Robinson | 1373 | Jan. 12, 1897 | |
| Jacob Shiver | 1482 | Jan. 12, 1897 | |
| Richard Tucker | 799 | Jan. 12, 1897 | |
| J. T. Monroe | 1510 | Jan. 12, 1897 | |
| J. J. Wilkes | 1445 | Jan. 12, 1897 | (Resigned Oct. 17, 1898) |
| W. W. Baker | 1374 | Jan. 12, 1897 | |
| G. W. Hammond | 1445 | Jan. 13, 1899 | |

## HISTORY OF COLQUITT COUNTY

### Justices of the Peace

| Name | Dist. | Date of Com'n | Date Succeeded |
|---|---|---|---|
| W. T. Cooper | 1020 | Apr. 4, 1899 | |
| A. B. Lay | 1582 | Sept. 1, 1900 | |
| J. D. Calhoun | 1374 | Dec. 18, 1900 | (Resigned Dec. 16, 1902) |
| Jacob Shiver | 1482 | Dec. 18, 1900 | |
| M. G. Scarboro | 1373 | Dec. 18, 1900 | |
| J. B. Sheppeard | 1582 | Dec. 18, 1900 | (Resigned Aug. 5, 1901) |
| G. W. Hooker | 1151 | Dec. 18, 1900 | |
| Daniel Burney | 1020 | Dec. 18, 1900 | |
| Richard Tucker | 799 | Dec. 18, 1900 | |
| W. J. Rhodes | 1549 | Dec. 18, 1900 | (Resigned Mch. 24, 1902) |
| G. W. Hammond | 1445 | Dec. 18, 1900 | (Resigned July 21, 1904) |
| J. G. Smith | 1510 | Dec. 18, 1900 | |
| D. F. Luke | 1538 | Dec. 18, 1900 | |
| J. T. Monroe | 1582 | Dec. 15, 1904 | |
| John M. Walters | 1510 | Dec. 15, 1904 | (Resigned) |
| G. W. Hooker | 1151 | Dec. 15, 1904 | |
| R. P. Hening | 1482 | Dec. 15, 1904 | (Removed) |
| G. W. West | 1445 | Feb. 7, 1905 | |
| W. T. Cooper | 1020 | Feb. 7, 1905 | |
| A. J. Smith | 1373 | Mch. 16, 1905 | |
| J. D. Hansford | 1617 | July 6, 1905 | (Resigned) |
| J. D. Hartsfield | 1510 | July 6, 1905 | |
| T. J. Adams | 1538 | Mch. 2, 1907 | |
| W. J. Ross | 1617 | Mch. 16, 1907 | |
| D. J. Newton | 1549 | Dec. 14, 1907 | |
| J. S. Simmons | 1665 | Dec. 14, 1907 | (Resigned Dec. 30, 1908) |
| A. J. Smith | 1373 | Dec. 19, 1908 | |
| W. T. Bell | 1482 | Dec. 19, 1908 | |
| W. T. Cooper | 1020 | Dec. 19, 1908 | |
| Richard Tucker | 799 | Dec. 19, 1908 | |
| J. M. Pope | 1665 | Dec. 19, 1908 | |
| J. D. Hartsfield | 1510 | Dec. 19, 1908 | |
| T. J. Adams | 1538 | Dec. 19, 1908 | |
| G. W. Handley | 1549 | Dec. 19, 1908 | (Resigned Dec. 12, 1910) |
| G. W. Hooker | 1151 | Dec. 19, 1908 | |
| J. T. Monroe | 1582 | Jan. 11, 1909 | |
| J. J. Sorrell | 1684 | Aug. 17, 1909 | (Term began) |
| D. L. Griffin | 1374 | Oct. 11, 1910 | |

## History of Colquitt County

### Justices of the Peace

| Name | Dist. | Date of Com'n | Date Succeeded |
|---|---|---|---|
| J. T. Monroe | 1582 | Dec. 18, 1912 | |
| J. T. Dunlap | 1445 | Dec. 18, 1912 | (Declined) |
| J. D. Calhoun | 1617 | Dec. 18, 1912 | |
| J. D. Hartsfield | 1510 | Dec. 18, 1912 | |
| G. W. Hooker | 1151 | Dec. 18, 1912 | (Resigned Feb. 21, 1914) |
| J. J. Sorrell | 1684 | Dec. 18, 1912 | |
| W. F. Walters | 1538 | Dec. 18, 1912 | |
| W. W. Baker | 1374 | Dec. 18, 1912 | |
| J. M. Pope | 1665 | Dec. 18, 1912 | |
| M. W. Schwall | 1549 | Dec. 18, 1912 | |
| W. T. Bell | 1482 | Dec. 18, 1912 | |
| C. E. McLendon | 799 | Dec. 18, 1912 | |
| W. T. Cooper | 1020 | Jan. 2 1913 | |
| S. W. Scott | 1373 | Jan. 2, 1913 | |
| W. B. Ingram | 1184 | Feb. 6 1913 | |
| J. O. Gibson | 1151 | June 11, 1914 | |
| W. L. Greene | 1374 | Oct. 1, 1914 | |
| J. T. Walters | 1582 | July 1, 1915 | |
| J. J. Strickland | 799 | Dec. 21 1916 | |
| J. J. Sorrell | 1020 | Dec. 21, 1916 | |
| R. C. Norman | 1151 | Dec. 21, 1916 | |
| E. E. Simmons | 1184 | Dec. 21, 1916 | |
| G. T. Tucker | 1373 | Dec. 21, 1916 | (Resigned Dec. 17, 1917) |
| J. H. Sumner | 1374 | Dec. 21, 1916 | |
| W. T. Bell | 1482 | Dec. 21, 1916 | |
| J. G. Smith | 1510 | Dec. 21, 1916 | (Resigned Aug. 6, 1918) |
| A. G. Jones | 1538 | Dec. 21, 1916 | |
| M. W. Schwall | 1549 | Dec. 21, 1916 | |
| J. T. Walters | 1582 | Dec. 21, 1916 | |
| L. W. Cone | 1617 | Dec. 21 1916 | |
| J. M. Pope | 1665 | Dec. 21, 1916 | |
| J. B. Tillman | 1684 | Dec. 21, 1916 | |
| J. O. Gibson | 1151 | Dec. 21, 1916 | (Resigned Oct. 5, 1917) |
| C. E. McLendon | 1759 | Oct. 10, 1917 | |
| Arthur Chambers | 1020 | Oct. 26, 1917 | |
| L. F. Maire, Jr. | 1151 | Nov. 9, 1917 | |
| S. S. Luke | 1510 | Dec. 12, 1918 | |
| W. H. Hatchet | 1020 | Nov. 4, 1919 | |

## HISTORY OF COLQUITT COUNTY

### Justices of the Peace

| Name | Dist. | Date of Com'n | Date Succeeded |
|---|---|---|---|
| J. E. Brantley | 1769 | Oct. 28, 1919 | |
| W. W. Rhodes | 1510 | Jan. 1, 1921 | (Resigned Apr. 19, 1921) |
| Louis F. Maire, Jr. | 1151 | Jan. 1, 1921 | (Resigned Jan. 17, 1923) |
| L. W. Cone | 1617 | Jan. 1, 1921 | |
| J. T. Walters | 1582 | Jan. 1, 1921 | |
| J. E. Bradley | 1769 | Jan. 1, 1921 | |
| W. H. Folsom | 1184 | Jan. 1, 1921 | |
| J. A. Green | 1549 | Jan. 1, 1921 | (Resigned Oct. 31, 1922) |
| M. C. Snipes | 1759 | Jan. 1, 1921 | |
| W. H. Hatchet | 1020 | Jan. 1, 1921 | |
| C. H. Baker | 1374 | Jan. 1, 1921 | |
| J. M. Pope | 1665 | Feb. 23, 1921 | |
| W. T. Bell | 1482 | Feb. 23, 1921 | |
| Joe A. Bannister | 1538 | May 30, 1921 | |
| J. W. Harvey | 799 | Nov. 21, 1921 | |
| L. G. Gregory | 1510 | Sept. 21, 1922 | |
| John T. Coyle | 1151 | Aug. 13, 1923 | |
| J. W. Walters | 1582 | Dec. 15, 1920 | |
| J. W. Walters | 1582 | Dec. 20, 1925 | |
| W. C. Snipes | 1759 | Dec. 15, 1920 | |
| J. J. Chambers | 1759 | Dec. 20, 1924 | |
| Joe A. Bannister | 1538 | April 23, 1921 | |
| Joe A. Bannister | 1538 | Jan. 1, 1929 | |
| J. G. Smith | 1510 | Dec. 20, 1924 | |
| J. G. Smith | 1510 | Dec. 20, 1928 | |
| L. G. Norman | 1684 | Mch. 9, 1925 | |
| J. F. Mashburn | 1373 | Dec. 20, 1924 | |
| J. G. Coyle | 1151 | Aug. 30, 1923 | |
| J. G. Coyle | 1151 | Dec. 20, 1924 | |
| J. R. Green | 1549 | Dec. 15, 1920 | |
| A. C. Cannon | 1549 | Dec. 20, 1924 | |
| J. E. Bradley | 1769 | Dec. 20, 1924 | |
| J. M. Pope | 1665 | Dec. 13, 1921 | |
| J. M. Pope | 1665 | Dec. 20, 1924 | |
| W. H. Hatchet | 1020 | Dec. 25, 1920 | |
| W. T. Bell | 1482 | Feb. 12, 1921 | |
| G. C. Monroe | 1482 | Dec. 20, 1924 | |
| C. H. Baker | 1374 | Dec. 15, 1920 | |

## History of Colquitt County

### Justices of the Peace

| Name | Dist. | Date of Com'n | Date Succeeded |
|---|---|---|---|
| D. R. Powell | 1374 | Jan. 31, 1935 | |
| W. H. Folsom | 1184 | Dec. 15, 1920 | |
| J. M. Folsom | 1184 | Dec. 15, 1924 | |
| Perry Tucker | 799 | Dec. 20, 1928 | |
| J. F. Cogland | 1617 | Dec. 20, 1928 | |
| J. T. Walters | 1582 | Dec. 20, 1928 | |
| J. J. Chambers | 1759 | Dec. 20, 1928 | |
| H. M. Allegood | 1538 | Dec. 20, 1928 | |
| R. D. Goolsby | 1510 | May 2, 1932 | |
| J. T. Mashburn | 1373 | July 23 1929 | |
| J. T. Cagle | 1151 | Dec. 20, 1928 | |
| J. T. Green | 1549 | Dec. 20, 1928 | |
| J. E. Bradley | 1769 | July 23 1929 | |
| J. M. Pope | 1665 | Dec. 20 1928 | |
| H. R. Foreman | 1665 | Dec. 11, 1930 | |
| W. H. Hatchet | 1020 | Dec. 20, 1928 | |
| G. C. Monroe | 1482 | Dec. 20, 1928 | |
| D. R. Powell | 1374 | Dec. 20, 1928 | |
| I. M. Folsom | 1184 | Dec. 20, 1928 | |
| W. O. Baldy | 1184 | Dec. 13, 1929 | |
| Perry Tucker | 799 | Dec. 20, 1928 | |
| J. W. Stafford | 1617 | Jan. 17, 1933 | |
| J. T. Walters | 1582 | Jan. 9, 1933 | |
| J. J. Chambers | 1759 | Jan. 4, 1933 | |
| H. M. Allegood | 1538 | Dec. 1 1932 | |
| R. D. Goolsby | 1510 | Jan. 4, 1933 | |
| Henry T. Baker | 1684 | Jan. 1, 1933 | |
| J. F. Mashburn | 1373 | Dec. 31, 1932 | |
| J. T. Coyle | 1151 | Dec. 1, 1932 | |
| J. T. Green | 1549 | Jan. 18, 1933 | |
| H. R. Foreman | 1665 | Dec. 1, 1932 | |
| J. M. Odom | 1020 | Dec. 1, 1932 | |
| G. C. Norman | 1482 | Jan. 17, 1933 | |
| D. R. Powell | 1374 | Dec. 20, 1932 | |
| W. O. Baldy | 1184 | Dec. 31, 1932 | |

## World War Veterans

Adams, Ed (colored)...............Moultrie
Adams, Thomas F. (colored)...............Doerun
Adams, William L...............Moultrie
Akridge, Jesse F...............Doerun
Akins, Clifford F...............Autreyville
Aldridge, William O...............Moultrie
Alexander, Charles H. (colored)...............Moultrie
Alderman, William I...............Moultrie
Allegood, James Linton, R. R. 1...............Moultrie
Allegood, David W...............Moultrie
Allen, Daniel (colored), 621 2nd St...............Moultrie
Alton, Charles L...............Ellenton
Ammons, George W...............Moultrie
Anderson, Earl J...............Moultrie
Arnett, Grover, R. R. 1...............Moultrie
Arnold, Humble (colored), 610 2nd St. N. E...............Moultrie
Asbell, James F., R. R. 2...............Moultrie
Asbell, Noah J., 4 West St...............Moultrie
Avera, Arnold L...............Berlin
Baker, Asa, R. R. 1...............Norman Park
Baker, David Martin...............Ellenton
Baker, Frank...............Ellenton
Baker, Ivey...............Moultrie
Baker, Jerry I...............Moultrie
Baker, Jobe J., R. R. 1...............Moultrie
Baker, Moses T...............Moultrie
Banister, Levi A...............Meigs
Barlow, Charlie D., R. R. 4...............Moultrie
Barlow, John T., R. R. 4...............Moultrie
Barnett, George W. (colored), 618 3rd St. N. W...............Moultrie
Barrow, Henry H...............Meigs
Beal, Courtney (colored)...............Moultrie

## HISTORY OF COLQUITT COUNTY

Beard, Thomas V., Box 284..................................................Moultrie
Beard, William P.................................................................Doerun
Belcher, Gordon L................................................................Moultrie
Belcher, Jesse O., R. R. 2..................................................Norman Park
Bell, Fred (colored), R. R. 1, Box 83................................Omega
Bell, Joseph Matthew..........................................................Moultrie
Bellamy, Josh (colored).....................................................Moultrie
Beverly, Harry B., N. Main St............................................Moultrie
Blackburn, Daniel W...........................................................Doerun
Blacke, John F. (colored)...................................................Moultrie
Blalock, Herman (colored)................................................Moultrie
Blassingame, Walter A.......................................................Moultrie
Bobo, Carter T....................................................................Autreyville
Bobo, Idus..........................................................................Autreyville
*Borders, Ellis, R. R. 4......................................................Moultrie
Boykin, John (colored)......................................................Norman Park
Bozeman, John W..............................................................Norman Park
Bozeman, Patrick G. W......................................................Norman Park
Bragg, Olin F.....................................................................Funston
Brazel, Lonnie, R. R. 4.......................................................Doerun
Brimley, Robert (colored).................................................Norman Park
Brice, Albert......................................................................Moultrie
Brooks, Howard Orville, 305 5th Ave..............................Moultrie
Brown, Cleveland (colored), R. R. 3................................Doerun
Brown, Joshua B. (colored), 609 3rd St..........................Moultrie
Brown, Ossie (colored), 310 Northeast 5th St.................Moultrie
Brown, Olga R....................................................................Moultrie
Brown, Toler (colored)......................................................Moultrie
Brownlee, Stonewall, R. R. 1............................................Doerun
Bruce, Vernon L.................................................................Crosland
Bryant, Ernest A................................................................Hartsfield
Bryan, Michael J., 519 1st Ave. N. E................................Moultrie
Bryan, Murray, R. R. 3.......................................................Moultrie
Bryan, T. M., 519 1st St....................................................Moultrie
Bryan, William G., R. R.....................................................Hartsfield

## WORLD WAR VETERANS

Bryant, Obie (colored)..................................................Autreyville
Bullock, Grady (colored) Northeast 5th Ave......................Moultrie
Burgess, Walter L., R. R. 1, Box 45.................................Berlin
Burk, Alonza (colored)..................................................Berlin
Burt, John (colored), R. R. 5........................................Moultrie
Burton, Robert A.........................................................Moultrie
Butler, Dennis (colored)...............................................Moultrie
Butler, Geo. Jr. (colored), R. R. 4, Box 65......................Moultrie
Butler, Harry (colored), R. R. 4....................................Moultrie
Butler, Hoyt B., Box 75................................................Norman Park
Butts, Eugene (colored)...............................................Moultrie
Bynum, Andrew H., R. R. 1..........................................Hartsfield
Byrd, James H.............................................................Crosland
Caesar, Julius (colored)................................................Moultrie
*Cain, Mack B. (colored), 310 2nd Ave...........................Moultrie
Calhaun, Joseph B.......................................................Moultrie
Callon, Richard...........................................................Moultrie
Cannon, Jesse (colored), R. R. 3...................................Moultrie
Carlisle, Spurgeon (colored).........................................Moultrie
Carlton, Charlie T., 5th Ave.........................................Moultrie
Carter, James H...........................................................Berlin
Carter, Samuel M. (colored).........................................Crosland
Carver, Rowan P.........................................................Moultrie
Carver, William A.......................................................Doerun
Castleberry, William J.................................................Omega
Chafin, Allen R., R. R. 1.............................................Norman Park
Chalkley, Willard A....................................................Doerun
Chapman, Adair P., R. R. 3.........................................Berlin
Chatham, John G., R. R. 5..........................................Berlin
Cheney, George W.......................................................Berlin
Clark, Franklin G., R. R. 2..........................................Crosland
Clark, James F., R. R. 2..............................................Crosland
Clark, James H., R. R. 4.............................................Moultrie
Clark, Thomas H.........................................................Doerun
Clark, William R., R. R. 1, Box 120..............................Autreyville

HISTORY OF COLQUITT COUNTY

Cleveland, Evans O. S. (colored), 311 4th St.....................Moultrie
Colbert, John H. (colored).......................................................Doerun
Cole, Eugene (colored), 7th St................................................Moultrie
*Coleman, Walter W..................................................................Berlin
Collier, Wade C........................................................................Moultrie
Cooper, Luther B......................................................................Moultrie
Commander, Paul P., R. R. 2..................................................Doerun
Conger, Bengman D..........................................................Norman Park
Connard, Clifford (colored)...................................................Moultrie
Cooper, Carlos G.....................................................................Moultrie
Cooper, Eldred...........................................................................Berlin
Cooper, Fred (colored).....................................................Norman Park
Cooper, Luther B......................................................................Moultrie
Covington, Andrew (colored)...................................................Funston
Covington, John (colored).......................................................Moultrie
Covington, Sidney S., 606 3rd St. S. E................................Moultrie
Crawford, James W..................................................................Moultrie
Crawford, Thomas C...............................................................Moultrie
Croft, Chester L., R. R. 1....................................................Autreyville
Croft, George L., R. R. 2................................................................Pavo
Croft, Harmon H........................................................................Berlin
Croft, Ruford..............................................................................Berlin
Crosby, Daniel E.......................................................................Ellenton
Crosby, Henry, R. R. 1................................................................Doerun
Crosby, Nelson Washington, R. R. 1..............................Norman Park
Crosby, Rogers..................................................................Norman Park
Crosby, William R....................................................................Moultrie
Cross, Fred (colored)..............................................................Moultrie
Curls, John M..............................................................................Berlin
Curls, Lee F.................................................................................Berlin
Curles, James H..........................................................................Berlin
Daniels, Rufus (colored), 214 7th St....................................Moultrie
Davidson, James T., R. R. 5...................................................Moultrie
Davis, Carvey G..........................................................................Doerun
Davis, Doll (colored), 302 2nd St. N. W............................Moultrie

## WORLD WAR VETERANS

Davis, Felix (colored), R. R. 2..................................................Murphy
Davis, George T..............................................................Hartsfield
Davis, Julius (colored)....................................................Norman Park
Davis, John A. (colored)......................................................Moultrie
Davis, Olin M.................................................................Moultrie
Davis, Perry L., R. R. 1........................................................Doerun
Davis, Thomas (colored).......................................................Moultrie
*Davis, Van (colored)............................................................Berlin
Davis, Walker...............................................................Hartsfield
Davis, William H................................................................Doerun
Delaney, Thomas C., R. R. 3...................................................Moultrie
Dill, John T., R. R. 2........................................................Moultrie
Dillard, James C..............................................................Moultrie
Dillard, Jeptha, R. R. 4......................................................Moultrie
Dismuke, Marcellous.............................................................Doerun
Dismuke, Zadock M...............................................................Doerun
Dodson, Custis T..............................................................Crosland
Dowling, James L., 703 1st Ave................................................Moultrie
Duke, Melvin M., R. R. 4........................................................Doerun
Dukes, Alonzo H. (colored), 500 2nd Ave. N. W.................................Moultrie
Dunn, Clarence H..............................................................Moultrie
Edwards, Joe (colored)........................................................Moultrie
Elder, James H. (colored), 417 2nd St. N. W...................................Moultrie
Elder, Ollie (colored), R. R. 1...............................................Moultrie
Enoch, Henry (colored).....................................................Norman Park
Eubanks, William T............................................................Moultrie
Evers, John H.................................................................Moultrie
Evans, Floyd E................................................................Moultrie
Everett, John (colored).......................................................Moultrie
Exum, Jess.......................................................................Berlin
Faircloth, Byron B., R. R. 4....................................................Doerun
Faircloth, Jaddie.............................................................Moultrie
Farris, Cleve (colored), R. R. 3................................................Doerun
Fellis, Joe (colored).........................................................Moultrie
Fenn, Fred A..................................................................Moultrie

Fender, Frank..................................................Ellenton
Felts, Edward L..............................................Ellenton
Fletcher, Roy Steven........................................Moultrie
Fletcher, Wiley M...........................................Moultrie
Flewellen, Cliff W. (colored)...............................Doerun
Floyd, Leonard I............................................Moultrie
Folsom, Ellis....................................................Berlin
Foreman, Charlie Will.................................Norman Park
Forrester, Joe (colored)...................................Moultrie
Foster, Lester................................................Moultrie
Frazier, Harvey (colored)...............................Moultrie
Frederick, Charlie J. (colored), 517 3rd St. S. W............Moultrie
Fryer, John (colored)..................................Norman Park
Fussell, Homer D., R. R. 3................................Moultrie
Fussell, John B..............................................Moultrie
Gaines, Clyde R..............................................Doerun
Gancy, Walter C................................................Berlin
Garland, Pierce (colored), R. R. 3, Box 33.................Doerun
Garris, James W..............................................Crosland
Gautier, David P............................................Funston
Gay, David H., R. R. 1................................Norman Park
Gay, Hiram......................................................Doerun
Gay, John Cary, R. R. 3, Box 48............................Moultrie
Gay, Perry....................................................Moultrie
Gay, Robert H., R. R. 4.....................................Moultrie
Gay, Warren..................................................Moultrie
Gibson, Robert L.............................................Moultrie
Giddens, Carl T..............................................Moultrie
Giles, John W., R. R. 1.....................................Hartsfield
Giles, Joseph D.......................................Norman Park
Giles, Lacey, R. R. 2........................................Moultrie
Godwin, Theodore R..........................................Moultrie
Goff, James M................................................Moultrie
Going, Clinton Field..........................................Doerun
Goings, Merrell E., R. R. 3................................Moultrie

WORLD WAR VETERANS 341

Goolsby, Devon Jefferson......................................................Moultrie
Gordon, Harrison (colored)....................................................Moultrie
Gordon, Robert (colored)......................................................Moultrie
Gordon, Roy (colored)..........................................................Moultrie
Graddy, John Richard (colored), R. R. 4, Box 44..............Moultrie
Graham, Prince (colored).................................................Norman Park
Grant, James J., R. R. 2.......................................................Hartsfield
Grant, John A., R. R. 2........................................................Hartsfield
Grayer, Elbert (colored), R. R. 2............................................Doerun
Gray, Alvin, R. R. 2..............................................................Moultrie
Gray, George, R. R. 2...........................................................Moultrie
Gray, Kendrick.....................................................................Moultrie
Gray, Wiley, R. R. 2..............................................................Moultrie
Green, Calvin D...................................................................Moultrie
Green, Walter L...................................................................Moultrie
Hall, Alexander....................................................................Moultrie
Hall, Colonel (colored).........................................................Ellenton
Hall, Earl, R. R. 2..................................................................Doerun
Hall, Hosea M., R. R. 3.........................................................Doerun
*Hall, Lewis (colored).........................................................Doerun
Hall, Ottie L....................................................................Norman Park
Hall, Robin A......................................................................Moultrie
Hall, William T., Gen. Del................................................Norman Park
Hall, Willie C. (colored), 7th St..........................................Moultrie
Hallis, Charlie (colored), R. R. 3...........................................Doerun
Haman, Warren..............................................................Norman Park
Hammack, Hubert A..............................................................Doerun
Hancock, Leonard Hugh, R. R. 2..........................................Doerun
Hancock, Tom, R. R. 4.........................................................Moultrie
Harden, Earley M................................................................Moultrie
Harrell, Edwin C...................................................................Doerun
Harrell, Wade H...................................................................Doerun
Harrington, Sam (colored)....................................................Moultrie
Harris, Acie (colored), R. R. 2, Box 62..................................Doerun
*Harris, Elmer H...................................................................Moultrie

*Harris, Jim (colored), R. R. 4................Doerun
Harris, Will (colored)................Crosland
Harrod, John H. Jr., R. R. 2................Moultrie
Hasty, Allen H., R. R. 1................Funston
Hawkins, Charles W., 315 2nd St. N. W................Moultrie
Hay, John, R. R. 1................Moultrie
Hendricks, Samuel P................Norman Park
Hendrix, James K................Moultrie
Henry, Elbert (colored)................Moultrie
Herring, Arthur (colored)................Moultrie
Herring, Grover C................Moultrie
Harrington, Drew (colored)................Moultrie
Hester, Jesse L................Berlin
Hester, Thoe (colored)................Moultrie
Hester, Willie J................Berlin
Hires, Dock, R. R. 1................Moultrie
Hobgood, William H................Hartsfield
Hodges, Silas (colored)................Moultrie
Holder, Wesley R................Moultrie
Holland, David T................Ellenton
Holland, Edward, R. R. 1................Moultrie
Holland, Elmo H................Hartsfield
Holland, Enos R., R. R. 1................Hartsfield
Hollis, Monroe (colored), R. R. 1................Moultrie
Hollis, Will (colored)................Moultrie
Holt, W(alter) E................Berlin
Holton, Simp................Moultrie
Horkoer, Jack D., 519 East Ave................Moultrie
Horne, George H., R. R. 4................Moultrie
Horn, James R., R. R. 2................Doerun
Horne, Macjah R................Moultrie
Horne, Macajah R., R. R. 4................Moultrie
Horne, Marion B., R. R. 4................Moultrie
Houser, Jim (colored)................Moultrie
Howard, Carl................Moultrie

## WORLD WAR VETERANS 343

Howell, Irvy P..................................................................Moultrie
Huff, Robert L., R. R. 4..................................................Doerun
Hurley, Bill (colored)....................................................Moultrie
Hurley, Jeff (colored)....................................................Moultrie
Hyatt, Charlie (colored)................................................Moultrie
Irving, Willie (colored), R. R. 1....................................Funston
Isom, Don Russell..........................................................Moultrie
Jackson, Andrew (colored), R. R. 5, Box 9.................Moultrie
Jackson, Boss (colored)................................................Moultrie
Jackson, Fred (colored)..............................................Norman Park
Jackson, Joe (colored), 616 E. 2nd St..........................Moultrie
Jackson, Scolly (colored)..............................................Moultrie
Jacobson, Morris............................................................Moultrie
James, Arthur (colored), R. R. 3..................................Moultrie
Jarman, Claud Foy........................................................Moultrie
Jeffords, Jerry................................................................Doerun
Jefferson, Madison (colored)......................................Moultrie
Jenkins, Joseph T(homas) (colored)..........................Moultrie
Jenkins, Paul, R. R. 2....................................................Doerun
Jennings, Charlie (colored)..........................................Moultrie
Johnson, James P., R. R. 1............................................Funston
Johnson, Johnny (colored)..........................................Moultrie
Johnson, Murry S., R. R. 2............................................Moultrie
Johnson, Oliver J., Jr....................................................Moultrie
Johnson, Ross, R. R. 3..................................................Doerun
Johnson, Roy W., 906 Main St....................................Moultrie
Johnston, Pearry............................................................Moultrie
Jones, Charlie L. (colored)..........................................Moultrie
Jones, Charlie (colored), Gen. Del..............................Moultrie
Jones, Earnest (colored)..............................................Moultrie
Jones, George, R. R. 2..................................................Hartsfield
Jones, George (colored), R. R. 3................................Ellenton
Jones, Lester (colored)................................................Moultrie
Jones, Orange (colored)..............................................Funston
Jordon, Alonzo (colored), 502 2nd St. N. E..............Moultrie

Jordan, Charles W..................................................................Moultrie
Jordan, James L....................................................................Moultrie
Jordan, Jason R., R. R. 2.....................................................Moultrie
Jordan, Wade G....................................................................Moultrie
Keigans, John P., R. R. 1.................................................Norman Park
Keigans, Sam........................................................................Moultrie
Kelly, James O.....................................................................Moultrie
Kent, James (colored), R. R. 1...........................................Harlem
Kent, Grover C., R. R. 1.....................................................Berlin
Kincaid, Oscar W................................................................Moultrie
Kline, Harry R......................................................................Moultrie
Land, George W...................................................................Doerun
Land, Walter H., 221 1st St..................................................Moultrie
Laramore, Rosser A., 500 N. Main St..................................Moultrie
Lasane, John (colored).....................................................Norman Park
Law, Gordon (colored), R. R. 1..........................................Autreyville
Lawson, Simuel L. (colored)................................................Crosland
Lee, Thomas W....................................................................Moultrie
Leggett, Robert L., R. R. 2..................................................Moultrie
Lewis, George......................................................................Moultrie
Lewis, John T. (colored), 303 1st Ave. West....................Moultrie
Lewis, Norman L..................................................................Moultrie
Lewis, Willie Green, R. R. 3................................................Moultrie
Liner, Carl E........................................................................Hartsfield
Long, Guy Odell..................................................................Doerun
Long, Jesse C......................................................................Doerun
Lott, James E.......................................................................Moultrie
Lovett, Charlton A............................................................Norman Park
Lovett, Henry M................................................................Norman Park
Lovett, Steve M...................................................................Ellenton
Lowry, William R.................................................................Riverside
Luke, John C......................................................................Hartsfield
Lunford, Jim (colored), R. R. 3, Box 43..............................Doerun
Lynch, Wilbur G..................................................................Berlin
Lynche, Wade......................................................................Crosland

McClain, John (colored) ..................Norman Park
McClung, John ..................Moultrie
McClurg, Henry H., 603 6th St. N. W. ..................Moultrie
McConnell, Lewis D. ..................Norman Park
McCoy, Cleve (colored), Gen. Del. ..................Doerun
McCrary, John (colored) ..................Moultrie
McDonald, Arthur P. ..................Moultrie
McDonald, Joseph E., R. R. 5 ..................Moultrie
McDougald, Arthur, R. R. 3 ..................Moultrie
McElmurray, Clifford A. ..................Moultrie
McElvin, Prophet (colored), 1st Ave. ..................Moultrie
McGalliard, Howard N., R. R. ..................Hartsfield
McGill, Wesley C. ..................Doerun
McGregor, Franklin T. ..................Norman Park
McGuire, Grover G. ..................Moultrie
McIntyre, Willie (colored), 2 Mid East St. ..................Moultrie
McKinnie, Luther M., R. R. ..................Moultrie
McKown, Henry T. ..................Moultrie
McKee, Albert D. ..................Moultrie
McKinney, Howard (colored) ..................Moultrie
McLendon, James M. ..................Hartsfield
McLendon, Johnie W. ..................Hartsfield
McLeon, Calvin E. ..................Moultrie
McLeon, Homer A., R. R. 1 ..................Moultrie
McMillian, Henry ..................Norman Park
McNeil, Tom (colored), 610 Northeast 2nd St. ..................Moultrie
MackNeill, Clarence, Jr. (colored), 724 2nd Ave. N. W. ..................Moultrie
Mann, Ulas (colored), R. R. 4 ..................Doerun
Manning, Ambrose H. ..................Moultrie
Marshall, Fred (colored), R. R. 1 ..................Doerun
Martin, Walter J. ..................Moultrie
Mashburn, David E. ..................Doerun
Mashburn, James F. ..................Doerun
*Mason, George Franklin ..................Moultrie
Mason, Johnnie (colored), 624 North E St. ..................Moultrie

Mather, William C. .................................................................................Moultrie
*Mathews, Arthur Clarence....................................................................Funston
Matthews, William R., Jr. ......................................................................Funston
Maxwell, Edward B. ..............................................................................Moultrie
May, James R., R. R. 1 ..............................................................................Berlin
Meredith, Earl J. ....................................................................................Moultrie
Mercer, Andrew J(ackson) ....................................................................Moultrie
Mercer, John L., R. R. 1 ..................................................................Norman Park
Miles, Green (colored) ..............................................................................Doerun
Miller, Ernest W. ..............................................................................Norman Park
Miller, Jimmie L. (colored) ....................................................................Crosland
Miller, William O. (colored) .....................................................................Doerun
Minchew, Joseph C., R. R. 1 .........................................................................Berlin
Mingo, James (colored) ..................................................................Norman Park
Mitchell, Sam (colored) ...........................................................................Crosland
Monk, James F. ........................................................................................Moultrie
Monk, George A. .....................................................................................Moultrie
Monroe, James R. (colored), R. R. 5, Box 25 ......................................Moultrie
Moody, Grover C., R. R. 1 ..........................................................................Doerun
Moree, William C., Jr. .................................................................................Doerun
Moree, James G., R. R. 1 ............................................................................Doerun
Morgan, Charles G. .....................................................................................Berlin
Morris, Alvah W. ..............................................................................Norman Park
Morris, John G., R. R. 3 ...........................................................................Moultrie
Morris, Raphael L. .................................................................................Moultrie
Morrison, Charlie (colored) ........................................................................Berlin
Morrison, Willie Lee (colored), 619 2nd St. .........................................Moultrie
Moses, Cliff (colored), R. R. ....................................................................Moultrie
Mullis, Asa ........................................................................................Norman Park
Munford, John C., N. Main St. ................................................................Moultrie
Munn, Mitchell (colored), R. R. 14, Box 114 ........................................Moultrie
Murphy, Millard .....................................................................................Moultrie
Murphy, Newton .....................................................................................Moultrie
Napper, Eldridge (colored), R. R. 1, Box 80 ...........................................Doerun
Neff, Mark C. ..........................................................................................Moultrie

WORLD WAR VETERANS 347

Nelson, Dock (colored) ................................................Norman Park
Nesmith, Ashley................................................................Moultrie
Nesmith, Fred, R. R. 3..................................................Moultrie
NeSmith, Miles Hampton................................................Norman Park
Nesmith, John B................................................................Moultrie
Nesmith, Julian G..............................................................Moultrie
NeSmith, Maillie M., R. R. 1........................................Norman Park
Newberry, Sim (colored), R. R. 3, Box 48......................Doerun
Newell, Asbury..................................................................Moultrie
Newton, Arthur A., R. R. 3............................................Moultrie
Newton, John M................................................................Norman Park
Nickens, Walter (colored)..............................................Moultrie
Nicherson, Frank (colored)............................................Moultrie
Nichols, Elbert L...............................................................Moultrie
Nobles, James D.................................................................Crosland
Norman, Buddie................................................................Crosland
Norman, Frank M..............................................................Moultrie
Norman, Miles B................................................................Norman Park
Norman, Richard I...........................................................Crosland
Norris, Christopher W., R. R. 2......................................Moultrie
Odom, Philip H..................................................................Moultrie
Oneal, Putney A.................................................................Doerun
Oneal, Perry A....................................................................Doerun
Ott, Albert C......................................................................Moultrie
Ott, John A.........................................................................Moultrie
Ott, Wyatt K.......................................................................Doerun
Owens, Henry A.................................................................Moultrie
Owens, Seabon (colored)................................................Moultrie
Parker, Robert (colored)..................................................Moultrie
Parker, Thaddeus H., 5025 Main St................................Moultrie
Patillo, Charlie (colored).................................................Doerun
Patterson, John A..............................................................Moultrie
Peak, Wade (colored).......................................................Moultrie
Perkins, Broadus E., R. R. 1............................................Doerun
Perryman, Jack C., R. R. 1..............................................Hartsfield

Peters, William C., R. R. 1...............Autreyville
Phillips, Joseph H...............Doerun
Phillips, Oscar Eugene (colored)...............Doerun
Pippins, Charlie W...............Moultrie
Pitts, Isaac, R. R. 2...............Moultrie
Pitts, Joseph H...............Norman Park
Plymel, Lee, R. R. 5...............Moultrie
Ponder, Ira A...............Moultrie
Porter, Eustis...............Moultrie
Potts, Curran M...............Moultrie
Potts, Dillard M...............Moultrie
Potts, Frank T...............Moultrie
Powell, Charley H...............Moultrie
Powell, Edward R., R. R. 2...............Norman Park
Powell, William B. (colored), R. R. 2...............Norman Park
Powell, William Nesbitt...............Moultrie
Prather, Duluth L...............Harlem
Prather, William E...............Harlem
Price, Johnny (colored)...............Moultrie
Ragan, Arthur M...............Doerun
Ragan, Howell...............Doerun
Ramsey, John (colored), R. R. 2...............Harlem
Raney, Raymond L...............Moultrie
Ray, Charles O...............Moultrie
Reddick, Jacob S., R. R. 5...............Moultrie
Reddick, Semmie A. (colored), 409 1st Ave...............Moultrie
Reid, Eugene...............Moultrie
Reid, Oscar D. (colored)...............Moultrie
Reynolds, Dornie B...............Moultrie
Rhodes, William H., 223 1st St. N. W...............Moultrie
Richard, Charlie C...............Doerun
Richard, Edgar J...............Doerun
Richardson, Henry D. (colored)...............Autreyville
Ricks, John Wesley...............Moultrie
Roddenberry, Robert, Jr., South Main St...............Moultrie

## WORLD WAR VETERANS

Rosson, Sidney (colored)...............Hartsfield
Roberson, Pate (colored)...............Norman Park
Roberson, Walter (colored), R. R. 2...............Moultrie
Roberts, Henry (colored)...............Moultrie
Rodgers, Arthur (colored)...............Doerun
Rogers, Earl...............Moultrie
Roland, Thomas C., R. R. 4...............Moultrie
Rouse, James A(ddison)...............Moultrie
Rowell, John L., 5th St. & 6th Ave...............Moultrie
Russ, Tom W., R. R. 2...............Hartsfield
Rumph, Isaac (colored), 312 Central Ave...............Moultrie
Rushin, Enice (colored)...............Moultrie
Russell, William (colored)...............Doerun
Sadler, Jennings...............Moultrie
Salter, John T...............Doerun
Sanders, Sam (colored)...............Autreyville
Saturday, James R. P...............Moultrie
Scarboro, Henry L...............Moultrie
Schramm, John F...............Funston
Schuyler, Robert B...............Moultrie
Seals, James M...............Miller
Seay, Lawyer (colored)...............Doerun
Sellers, George W., R. R. 1...............Hartsfield
Sellers, John B. (colored)...............Doerun
Sharpe, Jeff J...............Autreyville
Shephers, Albert R...............Moultrie
Sherman, Henry H., R. R. 2...............Hartsfield
Shipp, William W., 2nd St. East...............Moultrie
Shiver, Jesse C...............Crosland
Shiver, John S...............Crosland
Sikes, Alex...............Doerun
Simmons, Darnell (colored)...............Ellenton
Simmons, Elbert L...............Moultrie
Sims, Henry (colored)...............Doerun
Sims, John E...............Doerun

Sims, Joseph L., R. R. 4...................................................Doerun
Sinclair, William B..............................................................Moultrie
Sirmons, Lucius (colored), 219 6th Ave. N. W............Moultrie
Sloan, Charles H., R. R. 2.................................................Moultrie
Sloan, Elbert L....................................................................Hartsfield
Smith, Colling (colored), 324 W. 7th St..........................Moultrie
Smith, Claud W...................................................................Harlem
Smith, Charles L.................................................................Doerun
Smith, Eddie (colored), 706 5th Ave................................Moultrie
Smith, George R..................................................................Moultrie
Smith, Herbert H................................................................Moultrie
Smith, John E......................................................................Norman Park
Smith, James C., R. R. 4...................................................Doerun
Smith, James P(erry)........................................................Hartsfield
Smith, John Henry, R. R. 1...............................................Moultrie
Smith, Johnnie (colored), R. R. 1....................................Hartsfield
Smith, Leland D., 624 2nd Ave. S. E...............................Moultrie
Smith, Lessie L., R. R. 2....................................................Hartsfield
Smith, Loften, R. R. 1........................................................Doerun
Smith, Rebin (colored).....................................................Norman Park
Smith, R(obert) Leonard..................................................Moultrie
Smith, William O................................................................Moultrie
Snipes, Richard W., R. R. 1..............................................Funston
Sorrell, Luther Jackson....................................................Moultrie
Sorrell, Noah J...................................................................Moultrie
Sowell, William A...............................................................Moultrie
Sowell, Cliff.........................................................................Moultrie
Sowell, Enoch N..................................................................Moultrie
Speer, Daisy B., R. R. 2.....................................................Moultrie
Speight, Walter E., 401 4th Ave. S. E..............................Moultrie
Spivey, Paul L.....................................................................Moultrie
Stakes, Gay C., 224 2nd St................................................Moultrie
Stanaland, Littlejohn J., R. R. 4......................................Moultrie
Stanaland, Robert Melton, R. R. 4..................................Moultrie
Stacy, Wilbur M., 402 6th St............................................Moultrie

## WORLD WAR VETERANS 351

Stallings, James C. ..................................................Moultrie
Stallings, Ottise (colored), R. R. 1 ......................Norman Park
Stephens, Melvin (colored), 609 2nd St. .............Moultrie
Stevens, Alma C. H., R. R. 1 ..............................Moultrie
Stewart, Freddie (colored), R. R. 5, Box 9 ..........Moultrie
Stith, Charles S., R. R. 5 ....................................Moultrie
Stone, Walter W. ................................................Doerun
Strawder, Lewis G. ............................................Berlin
Streeter, Julius ...................................................Moultrie
Streeter, Thomas C., Jr. (colored) .......................Moultrie
Strother, William H. ...........................................Moultrie
Strickland, Charles N. .........................................Moultrie
*Strickland, Henry L., R. R. 1 ..............................Moultrie
Strickland, Warren J., R. R. 5 .............................Moultrie
Striplin, Erastus F. .............................................Moultrie
Suber, John F., R. R. 1 .......................................Hartsfield
Sutton, Jesse Hilbourne, R. R. 2 .........................Norman Park
Tabor, Henry (colored) .......................................Moultrie
Tanner, Joe Herman ............................................Norman Park
Tanner, Mark ......................................................Norman Park
Taylor, Homer F. .................................................Autreyville
Taylor, Perry ......................................................Ellenton
Teems, Thomas B. ...............................................Berlin
Thomas, Ed. (colored) ........................................Berlin
Thomas, Gene (colored) .....................................Norman Park
Thomas, George W. (colored), R. R. 4 ................Moultrie
Thomas, John (colored), R. R. 1 .........................Doerun
Thomas, Johnie (colored) ...................................Harlem
Thomas, Willie (colored) ....................................Harlem
Thompson, John G., R. R. 2 ................................Doerun
Thompson, Moses (colored), 5th Ave. ................Moultrie
Thornton, William B. ..........................................Doerun
Tillman, Marion J., R. R. 4 .................................Moultrie
Tillman, Thomas J., R. R. 1 ................................Berlin
Toner, John (colored) .........................................Moultrie

Tompkins, Nathan (colored) ............... Harlem
Toney, John W. ............... Doerun
Truett, Lacy C. ............... Moultrie
Tucker, Ancel P. ............... Doerun
Tucker, Clem ............... Moultrie
Tucker, James C., R. R. 1 ............... Moultrie
Tucker, John A. ............... Moultrie
Tucker, Lucius L. ............... Moultrie
Tucker, Marion C. ............... Moultrie
Tucker, Micajah P. ............... Doerun
Tucker, Otis C., R. R. 2 ............... Hartsfield
Turner, George H. ............... Moultrie
Turner, John N. ............... Doerun
Turner, John (colored), R. R. 1 ............... Berlin
Turner, Walter (colored), 516 3rd Ave. ............... Moultrie
Tyndall, Benjamin F. ............... Autreyville
Tyler, Clarence L. ............... Berlin
Verdery, Herbert E. ............... Harlem
Vick, Aaron, Jr. ............... Hartsfield
Vick, Tom ............... Hartsfield
Vines, Claud E. ............... Norman Park
Wade, Tom (colored) ............... Berlin
Wages, Virgil W. ............... Harlem
Waits, Cicero J. ............... Moultrie
Walden, Hoke S. ............... Harlem
Walker, Albert ............... Moultrie
Walker, Clifford J. ............... Ellenton
Walker, James (colored), R. R. 4, Box 85 ............... Moultrie
Walker, James F., R. R. 3 ............... Moultrie
Walker, Parrish (colored), R. R. 1 ............... Moultrie
Walters, Arthur (colored), R. R. 3 ............... Doerun
Walters, Buford L., R. R. 5 ............... Moultrie
Wamble, Joseph ............... Hartsfield
Ward, Alfred J. ............... Norman Park
Ward, Fred H. ............... Moultrie

## WORLD WAR VETERANS

Washington, Jesse (colored) ..........................................Norman Park
Watkins, Thomas Watson, R. R. 2..........................................Moultrie
Watson, Sam (colored) ..........................................Moultrie
Watts, Charlie (colored), 626 4th Ave..........................................Moultrie
Weltzbacher, Fred L..........................................Crosland
Webb, Harmon M., 211 W. Central Ave..........................................Moultrie
Weeks, John..........................................Ellenton
Weeks, Montgomery, R. R. 1..........................................Norman Park
Welch, Andrew T., R. R. 5..........................................Moultrie
West, William H., Jr., Box 262..........................................Doerun
White, Amous (colored) ..........................................Crosland
White, George (colored) ..........................................Ellenton
White, Nap..........................................Moultrie
White, Osborne E., R. R. 2..........................................Hartsfield
White, Walter (colored), Gen. Del..........................................Moultrie
White, William A., 415 4th Ave. S. E..........................................Moultrie
Whitehead, Charlie (colored), 724 3rd Ave. N. W..........................................Moultrie
Whitfield, Zackie..........................................Funston
Wiggins, Birdine, R. R..........................................Funston
Wilkes, Leo M..........................................Norman Park
Wilkes, Wallace E..........................................Moultrie
Wilkes, Willie W. (died while in desertion)..........................................Autreyville
Williams, Alfonso, 501 3rd St..........................................Moultrie
Williams, Grant (colored), 3rd St. N. W..........................................Moultrie
*Williams, Henry (colored), R. R. 2, Box 86..........................................Harlem
Williams, Homer B..........................................Moultrie
Williams, James A..........................................Hartsfield
Williams, John W., R. R. 2..........................................Moultrie
Williams, Lonnie (colored), R. R. 5..........................................Moultrie
Williams, Maceo M. (colored), 501 3rd St. N. W..........................................Moultrie
Williams, Richard C..........................................Funston
Williams, Robert M., R. R. 1..........................................Moultrie
Williams, Thomas H..........................................Funston
Williams, William P..........................................Liberty
Williams, Walter (colored)..........................................Moultrie

Willis, Daniel H..................................................Norman Park
Winkfield, George (colored), Central Ave...............Moultrie
Wingate, Henry Grady, R. R. 1..............................Berlin
Wisham, Otis M., R. R. 1.......................................Hartsfield
Wood, Glenn L.....................................................Moultrie
Woods, James (colored).......................................Moultrie
Woodson, William (colored).................................Doerun
Wooten, Charlie V...............................................Berlin
Worley, Alexander, R. R. 1...................................Norman Park
Worley, Fred, R. R. 1...........................................Norman Park
Wynn, Claud W., R. R. 4......................................Doerun

## Deceased

Branan, Maury Edward.........................................Norman Park
Castelberry, Isaac R.............................................Moultrie
Chambliss, Charley (colored)................................Moultrie
Crosby, Henry Melvin...........................................Norman Park
Crosby, James E..................................................Moultrie
Davis, Frank, R. R. 2............................................Hartsfield
Evans, Ellis (colored)............................................Harlem
Greer, William Henry, R. R. 4................................Moultrie
Gregory, Claudius C. M........................................Hartsfield
Hutchinson, O'Bee, R. R. 5, Box 116.....................Moultrie
Jenkins, Cyrus C..................................................Doerun
Jones, Dan L. (colored), Gen. Del.........................Ellenton
Jones, Charlie (colored).......................................Moultrie
Keigans, John S...................................................Moultrie
Keigans, William, R. R. 1.....................................Norman Park
Minshew, David, R. R. 1......................................Berlin
Monk, Rufus A. J.................................................Moultrie
Monroe, Vernon (colored)....................................Moultrie
Ricks, William L...................................................Moultrie
Rome (Rowe), Judson T., R. R. 3..........................Moultrie
Sharp, John R., Jr................................................Moultrie
Smithwick, Floyd L., R. R. 1.................................Moultrie

WORLD WAR VETERANS 355

Sterling, Charlie B., R. R. 4..................................................Moultrie
Teabeaut, Thomas S., Norman Hotel...................................Moultrie
Thomas, John B.......................................................................Berlin
Watkins, Louis F. (colored), R. R., Box 63........................Crosland

### Officers

Brannen, Clem C., P. O. Box 454..........................................Moultrie
Bryant, James Malone............................................................Hartsfield
Buchanan, Ira E.....................................................................Moultrie
Clay, Arvah E.........................................................................Moultrie
Cochran, Arthur M..................................................................Doerun
Coffman, Joseph W., 232 5th Ave.........................................Moultrie
Goldbroun, Jacob....................................................................Moultrie
Labarre, Robert V., 905 5th Ave............................................Moultrie
Leverett, Paul DeWitt.............................................................Doerun
Luke, Herbert Spivey..............................................................Hartsfield
Massey, William Walton, Hill Crest......................................Moultrie
McKenzie, Reid Hill................................................................Moultrie
Monk, James Fred..................................................................Moultrie
Moye, Thomas Ralph...............................................................Autreyville
Stokes, Robert Nichols, 607 3rd St. West............................Moultrie
Whittendale, William Hardman............................................Norman Park

### Navy

Alton, John Rayford................................................................Ellenton
Ashmore, James Oscar............................................................Autreyville
Atkins, John Burton................................................................Funston
Bell, Clifford Hammonds........................................................Doerun
Bloodworth, Eugene Franklin, R. R. 1..................................Doerun
Bryant, Simeon Dykes............................................................Hartsfield
Cannon, Robert E. Lee, R. R. 1.............................................Autreyville
Cates, Arthur W.....................................................................Miller
Clark, Robert Allen................................................................Moultrie
Clark, Zachariah Harrison.....................................................Moultrie

Cobb, Jolly John Anthony..................................................Doerun
Daniel, John Wesley............................................................Doerun
Dell, Mirah Lee Hosea........................................................Berlin
Dewbury, John Bell..............................................................Moultrie
Dismuke, Phil Boyd..............................................................Doerun
Dobbins, Walter Eugene....................................................Harlem
Duke, Joseph........................................................................Moultrie
Evans, Tom Watson, 620 E. Central Ave.............................Moultrie
Gautier, William Jones.......................................................Funston
Hadden, Alex Wright, R. R. 2.............................................Harlem
Hamilton, Arthur Lawton...................................................Moultrie
Hamilton, Oscar William, R. R. 1......................................Moultrie
Hancock, Luther Franklin..................................................Doerun
Harper, Ashburn Park.........................................................Moultrie
Harrell, Eustace Horatious.................................................Moultrie
Harrell, Willie Maurice......................................................Doerun
Hasty, James Phillip............................................................Doerun
Haulbrook, Hugh Lawson, R. R. 1....................................Moultrie
Hay, James David................................................................Moultrie
Hiers, Pafford Marion........................................................Moultrie
Hill, Thomas Dee................................................................Moultrie
Horne, John William..........................................................Moultrie
Humphreys, William Floyd...............................................Berlin
Joines, James Macelous, R. R. 2, Box 63..........................Doerun
Kelly, Oscar..........................................................................Moultrie
Lewis, Willie Kermit, R. R. 3.............................................Moultrie
Lloyd, Tolliver Perry..........................................................Harlem
Lyons, William Lenwood, 317 2nd Ave. N. W.................Moultrie
Manning, Archie Jackson, R. R. 1.....................................Berlin
Mason, John Grady, R. R. 1...............................................Moultrie
Mason, Joseph Lawrence, R. R. 1.....................................Moultrie
Mercer, Ernest, R. R. 1.......................................................Norman Park
Murphy, Charlie Samuel, 707 W. Central Ave...............Moultrie
Nelson, Robert Franklin, 518 1st Ave. S. W....................Moultrie
Newton, James Franklin, R. R. 2.......................................Norman Park

## WORLD WAR VETERANS

Norman, William Lacy, R. R. 2............Moultrie
Powell, Clarence Kennie, R. R. 2............Doerun
Powell, John Miller............Moultrie
Scarboro, Dewey David............Moultrie
Scarboro, James McCann............Moultrie
Sinclair, Dewitt, 519 3rd St. S. W.............Moultrie
Sinclair, Erie Oval............Moultrie
Smith, Elbert............Doerun
Smith, George Madison............Berlin
Southerland, Willie Osker, R. R. 2............Doerun
Swilley, Rufus Samuel............Moultrie
Taylor, Thomas Franklin............Moultrie
Tharpe, William Matthew............Moultrie
Trice, Joseph Ferrell............Doerun
Tucker, Frank ............Funston
Tucker, William Railford, R. R. 1............Moultrie
Turner, Hosea, 308 1st St.............Moultrie
Wheeler, Clarence Wesley............Berlin
Whitfield, Edmund Jacob............Moultrie
Wilkerson, Fred Goree, R. R. 2............Harlem
Wilkes, Homer Gladstone............Moultrie
Willingham, Ellington Barton............Harlem
Willingham, Henry Morgan, Box 89............Harlem
Wingate, Wylie Oscar, R. R. 1............Berlin
Williams, Charles Wesley, Jr., R. R. 1............Moultrie
Williams, Harry Asendorf, R. R. 1............Moultrie
Wilson, Frank Edward............Moultrie
Teague, John Pittman, R. R. 11............Moultrie

\*Deserters.

## Final Word of the Historian

THE ESTIMATED VALUE of the agricultural products of Colquitt County for the year 1936 is as follows: Tobacco, $2,000,000; cotton, $1,500,000; cattle and hogs, $3,500,000; melons, $300,000; peanuts, $500,000; corn and other feed and food crops, $2,000,000—a total of $11,000,000. This is well within the facts.

We think the productivity of our cultivated lands can be doubled by scientific fertilizing and cultivation. We are of the opinion that less than half of our arable lands are now under the plow. We believe, therefore that, at the end of another generation the products of our fields and pastures will have reached forty millions of dollars per annum. This section will "mix it up" with Kansas City and Chicago in the matter of meat production. There are only three commercial problems—To clothe the world; to house the world; and to feed the world. Colquitt is by nature qualified to solve two of these problems as well as any section on earth. There is, as we conceive it, no limit to her future commercial development.

Finally, as we think, the thing of fundamental importance about a community is that it be good for the establishment of families and the training of children. In other words, it is written from the beginning, "Man shall not derive life from bread alone, but by every rule of living that proceedeth out of the mouth of God."

And having ascertained from our study of Colquitts pioneers that they pretty well knew God, we commend their example to the present age as well as to the ages to come. We expect our civilization will endure till the "end of the ages;" because God-fearing men and women have laid its foundations on the rock of faith in the promises of the Lord.

# Heads of Families, Lowndes County, Georgia

(U. S. Census in 1830)

Henry Albritton
Wm. C. Alderman
Sarah Adams
James Allen
Matthew Albritton
Jas. Albritton
Wm. G. Akins
Frances Akins
Wm. Albritton
John Bryan
Thos. Brown
Joshia Browning
Lewis Blackshear
Joshua Browning
Samuel Barker
John Blackshear
Elijah Beasley
Jas. Burnette
Danl. Burnette
Jas. Bird
Thos. Brannon
Mosley Burnette
David Blanton
John Bennett
Adin Boyd
Bane L. Boyd
Geo. Boon
Burton Branch
David R. Bryan
Willson Bates
Jas. M. Bates
Fleming Bates
Jno. Bennett
Jas. Bozeman

Coma Burman
Alex. Campbell
Bozel Cornege
Wm. Cotten
Cannon Cason
Wm. Carlisle
Silas Cason
Henry Colson
Sarah Coward
Henry Clifton
Harmon Crum
Jesse Carter
Thos. Crawford
Hugh Chancey
Geo. Carter
Jno. Carter
Wm. Carter
Isaac Carter
Samuel Carter
Wm. B. Coward
Elizabeth Chaney
Ben Cornelius
Reubin Crawford
Gideon Crawford
Jesse Carter, Jr.
Sam. M. Clyatt
Ann Cummings
Enoch Collins
Isaac B. Carlton
Jas. Crawford
Elijah Cutts
Henry Castleberry
Henry Dean
Elijah Deckel

Benj. Devane
Wm. Dampier
Jno. G. Davis
Wm. Dregors
Jno. Dees
Moses Dees
Wm. Dees
Leonard Dees
Wm. Dooling
Nancy Dukes
Jno. Dampier
Dennis Dooling
Jno. Edmundson
Cornelius English
Love English
Jas. English
Amos Emanuel
Jas. Edmundson
David Fender
Wm. Fletcher
Israel Folsom
Thos. Folsom
Jno. Folsom
Zach Fletcher
Penniwell Folsom
Wright Flowers
Randall Folsom
Thos. Futch
Jas. Faulkner
Lawrence Folsom
Elijah Folsom
Jos. Gates
Thos. Giddens
Abner Griffin
Rebecca Godwin
Hardy Godwin
Nancy Griffin
Bryan Glisson
Simon Gay
James Goff
Wm. C. Goff

Jesse Goodman
Nathan Gornto
David Gornto
William Gay
Jobin Giddens
John Gutery
Geo. Glover
Acquilla Green
Lovick Green
James Gill
Thos. Gray
Emanuel Griner
Fisher Gaskins
Jno. Gaskins
James Gunter
William Hendry
Henry Hamons
Lewis Harrell
Jno. Hall
Simon Hall
Nathan Hodges
Henry Hulette
Saml. T. Henderson
Winnie Henderson
Green Hill
Jno. Hill
Benj. Holland
Wm. Hill
Henry H. Hightower
Daniel Humphrey
Wm. Hancock
Cudar Hancock
Jeremiah Hancock
James E. Henry
John Hendry
Jno. Howell
Jno. Hightower
H. John Harper
Durham Hancock
Jaret Johnson
Isaac Johnson

## HEADS OF FAMILIES

Jno. Jordan
Wm. Jones
Jno. Jones, Sr.
Jno. Jones, Jr.
Abner Jones
Clayton Jones
John Johnson
David Johnson
Wash. Joyce
Jas. I. Joyce
Joshua Kemp
Jno. Kinsey
Jonathan Knight
Levi J. Knight
Jno. Knight
Wm. A. Knight
Wm. C. Knight
Thos. Kelley
Sam. Knight
Danl. Kinard
Wm. Kirby
Willis King
Wm. Knight
Nathan Lindsey
Wm. Lofton
Jno. Lankford, Sr.
Jno. Lankford, Jr.
Joshua Lee
Jones Lexington
Seaborn Lastinger
John Lindsay
Robt. Lindsay
David Lovette
Hester Lindsay
Jno. Lawson
Thos. Matthis
Jno. Matthis, Sr.
Jno. Moore
Tyre Matthis
Sarah Moor
Edmond Matthis

Jno. Moore, Jr.
Roderich Morrison
Jerusha Monk
Jas. Matthis
Malon Monk
Richard Maulden
Mary Morrison
Bunyan Merritt
Judith McFail
Jno. S. McLeod
Isaac McMullan
Hannah McIntyre
Isaac McFail
James McMullan
Miley McLeod
Jas. McDowell
Elizabeth McCall
Wm. McMullan
Ben McDaniel
Danl. McCraney
Jno. McCraney, Sr.
Jno. McCraney, Jr.
Duncan McMillan
Malcom McCraney
Robt. McCall
Margarett McDermit
Thos. Newbern
Dread Newbern
James M. Norman
Willis Newman
Wm. Newbern
James M. Patten
Alex Patterson
Robt. N. Parrish
Ansel A. Parrish
Henry Parrish
Wm. Peters
Daniel Polk
Moses Prescott
Jos. Powers
Ashford N. Parker

Saml. Paulk
John S. Pinkston
Peter Platt
David Platt
John Pike
Joshua Platt
Jno. Platt
Asahol Renfroe
Jno. Roberts, Sr.
Nichabod Rollerson
Jno. C. Roberts, Jr.
Francis Rountree
Wm. Rowell
Seaborn Raney
David Rowell
Thos. Ramsey
Wm. P. Roberts
Jas. Rountree
Lewis Roberts
John Rhoden
Jacob Rhoden
Sam. Register
Martin Snow
Simpson Strickland
Ezekiel Selph
Hansell Singleton
Arc. Strickland
Sam Strawder
Jno. Strawder
Arch Smith
Wm. Smith
Thos. Selph
H. W. Sharp
Wm. W. Sanders
Jno. Stewart
Riley Sapp
Wm. Stokely
Alg Sapp
Abner Sirman
Sam. E. Swilley
James D. Shank

Reason Swilley
Henry Stephens
Ivy Simmons
David Stanford
Levi Starling
Wm. Starling
Nathan Smith
Jno. Sutton
Moses Slaughter
Jonathan Sirman
Elias Skipper
John Sellers
John Studstill
A. B. Shehe
Josiah Sellers
Melus Thigpen
John Tillman
Jeremiah Tillman
Joshua Tillman
Emily Turner
John Tomlinson
Wm. Tomlinson
Austin Thompson
Allen Townsend
John Townsend
Wm. Taitor
Jesse Townsend
Jas. Touchtone
Jemima Tucker
Jno. J. Underwood
Henry Tucker
Drew Vickers
Jesse Vickers
James Wade
Wm. Wood
Jno. S. Whitfield
James Walker
Peter Wetherington
Curtis Wetherington
Dennis Wetherington

# Heads of Families, Eighth District, Thomas County, Ga., now Colquitt County

(U. S. Census in 1840)

Wm. Ayres
Hardy H. Akeridge
Thos. Bennett
Mary Bowen
Jno. Burk
James Bryan
Douglas Black
Emanuel Burk
David Burney
Wm. B. Crawford
Elisha Cutts
Wm. P. Cutts
Robt. Crawford
Jesse Carlton
Peter Crosby
Canon Cason
Danl. Davis
Wright Douglas
Catherine Eason
Baxter Floyd
Wright Flowers
Jno. Gregory
Simon Gay
Sarah Gregory
Robt. Hendry
Nathaniel Hand
Henry W. Hancock
Jeremiah Hancock
Lewis Harrell
Henry Haymonds
Phoebe Highsmith
Thos. Jordan

Murphy Lanier
Nathan Land
Henry Murphy
Holmes Mauldin
Colan Mercer
Jas. McLendon
Jas. A. Newman
Artaxerxes B. Norman
James Newton
Sarah Richardson
Wm. Sloan
John Sellers
Daniel Sloan
Henry C. Tucker
John Tillman
Moses Vick
Jas. P. Vick
Jos. Watson
Reubin Wilson
Redick Watson
Shadrack Wells
William Watson
James M. Horne
Thos. Hall
Kindred Hall
Wm. Hancock
Allan Hancock
James Hancock
Ignatius Hall
Jordan Hall
John Hart
James Hall

Samuel H. Hadley
Geo. Hayes
James T. Hayes
Wm. I. Hopson
Thos. J. Hurst
Geo. W. Jones
Humphrey Jemison
Wm. Jackson
Jno. B. Lacy
Henry Mash
Jackson J. Mash
Richard Mitchell
Taylor H. Mitchell
Robt. Mardre
Angus Morrison
Neill McKay
Daniel McIntyre
Daniel McKinnon
Mary McKinnon
Robt. H. Raines
Lucien H. Raines
Randolph Revill
Sylvanus Pumphrey

Robt. Roddenberry
Isaac Shores
Jas. D. Saules
Elisha Strickland
Isham Strickland
Wm. H. Smith
Thos. M. Slow
John Slater
Dan Stringer
Stephen Smith
Olsy Strickland
Fleming B. Tanner
Barbara Thomas
James Taylor
John Took
Andrew Truluck
Richard Taylor
James J. Vickers
Brinson Wheeler
James Wilson
Alpin Worsham
Mitchell Worsham
Samuel C. White

\* \* \* \* \*

The following are the oldest pioneer settlers of the Colquitt territory so far as our investigation shows:

James M. Norman, born March 18, 1792, died at "Coker's Place," on the Moultrie and Albany Road, on September 12, 1864. His wife, Ruth Tillman, was born September 18, 1798; and died March 8, 1884, at residence of her son-in-law, A. J. Strickland, in Colquitt County.

\* \* \* \* \*

John Tillman, brother of Ruth Tillman, was born in 1800, and died at the age of 86, in Colquitt County. His wife, Sarah Mercer Tillman, died at the age of 82, and is buried at Hopewell Missionary Baptist Church, 9 miles out of Moultrie near the Quitman Road.

Henry Crawford Tucker was born in 1803, and died in 1881, in Colquitt County.

* * * * *

Charles H. Johnson was born in England, in 1790; married an Aunt of "Kentucky" Roberts, at Pavo, Ga., and died in Colquitt in 1886. He is buried with his wife in the burial ground on the "Johnson Farm" in Colquitt County. He was married in 1829 to Elizabeth Roberts.

* * * * *

James M. Norman and his wife are buried at "Pleasant Grove" graveyard, two miles out of Moultrie on the Adel Road.

* * * * *

The graves of all these pioneers are on the point of being lost; and should be remarked. The obligation lies first on their descendants; and second on our historical associations.

* * * * *

Jacob F. Reichert, Sheriff of Colquitt in 1856-7 and in 1859-60, was a native of Wurtemburg, Germany. He removed to Monticello, Fla., in 1861, and is buried in four miles of that place.

* * * * *

Steven Johnson, born in North Carolina in 1789, was blind when the Census Marshal for 1860 called at his home. His wife, born in the same state, in 1801, was named curiously enough, "Delilah."

* * * * *

Reference to the rolls of World War veterans will reveal that "Julius Caesar," colored, was sent from Colquitt among her expeditionary forces. We knew his father, "Grant Caesar," personally; and were told by him that "Julius" was "over dere."

www.ingramcontent.com/pod-product-compliance
Lightning Source LLC
Chambersburg PA
CBHW052129010526
44113CB00034B/1100